WHEN MARKETS FAIL

WHEN MARKETS FAIL
Social Policy and Economic Reform

ETHAN B. KAPSTEIN AND BRANKO MILANOVIC

EDITORS

Russell Sage Foundation · New York

The Russell Sage Foundation

The Russell Sage Foundation, one of the oldest of America's general purpose foundations, was established in 1907 by Mrs. Margaret Olivia Sage for "the improvement of social and living conditions in the United States." The Foundation seeks to fulfill this mandate by fostering the development and dissemination of knowledge about the country's political, social, and economic problems. While the Foundation endeavors to assure the accuracy and objectivity of each book it publishes, the conclusions and interpretations in Russell Sage Foundation publications are those of the authors and not of the Foundation, its Trustees, or its staff. Publication by Russell Sage, therefore, does not imply Foundation endorsement.

Library of Congress Cataloging-in-Publication Data

When markets fail : social policy and economic reform / Ethan B. Kapstein and Branko Milanovic, editors.
    p. cm.
  Includes bibliographical references and index.
  ISBN 0-87154-460-1
    1. Social security—Developing countries. 2. Social security—Europe, Central. 3. Social security—Europe, Eastern. I. Kapstein, Ethan B. II. Milanovic, Branko.

HD7252 .W44 2002
362—dc21

2002026989

Text design by Suzanne Nichols

RUSSELL SAGE FOUNDATION
112 East 64th Street, New York, New York 10021
10 9 8 7 6 5 4 3 2 1

Contents

Contributors

Ethan B. Kapstein is Paul Dubrule Professor of Sustainable Development at Insead Business School, Fontainebleau, France, and Stassen Professor of International Peace at the University of Minnesota.

Branko Milanovic is lead economist in the Development Research Group of the World Bank.

Nicholas Barr is professor of public economics at the London School of Economics.

Nancy Birdsall is senior associate at the Carnegie Endowment for International Peace.

Ricardo Fuentes is a graduate student in economics at Pompeu Fabra University in Barcelona, Spain. Previously, he was in the Research Department of the Inter-American Development Bank.

Stephan Haggard is professor at the Graduate School of International Relations and Pacific Affairs, University of California, San Diego.

Iqbal Kaur is a social protection specialist at the World Bank, Middle East and North Africa Region.

Peter H. Lindert is professor of economics and director of the Agricultural History Center at the University of California, Davis.

Miguel Székely is chief of the Office of Regional Development of the Presidency of Mexico. He worked as research economist at the Inter-American Development Bank from 1996 to 2001.

Zafiris Tzannatos was, at the time of writing this book, manager of social protection in the Middle East and North Africa Region of the World Bank. He is currently adviser to the managing director of the World Bank.

Preface

This book has its origins in a workshop that took place at the Rockefeller Foundation in New York in March 1999. At that time, it occurred to us that, while academics were beginning to talk about social policy in developing countries, very little by way of serious research had actually been conducted on the topic. The work that had been done was largely policy oriented, accomplished by public officials and consultants working in and for national governments and international organizations. As a result, much of the existing literature lacked a critical perspective on the issues at stake or an explicit theoretical focus.

Further, we were unaware of any comparative studies that had been done on social policy reform that was ongoing around the world. As a result, we decided it would be useful to bring together a group of authors with expertise in different regions to share their knowledge of the various experiments and experiences that were taking place, mainly with respect to social insurance and assistance but also in areas such as education and health care. This volume is the result of the discussion that we first launched in New York in 1999 and that the authors have continued to engage in until the present day. As a consequence, our first acknowledgment is to our authors, who took time from very busy schedules to write their chapters, generally on time, and who generously shared ideas and comments with us and with one another.

The project was supported by the Russell Sage Foundation and Rockefeller Foundation, and we thank them both not just for funding the work but also for their constant interest in the volume. The president of Russell Sage, Eric Wanner, has been a penetrating critic, and Katherine McFate at Rockefeller brought her considerable expertise and good sense to this effort. They provide models of what foundation officers can do for their grant recipients.

We also wish to thank the World Bank, the University of Minnesota, and Insead for additional financial and administrative support. In particular, Keith Vargo at Minnesota and Helen Varin and Martina Saada at Insead tracked down authors who had to be reached and turned the chapters into a single volume; we are grateful to them.

Ethan B. Kapstein
Branko Milanovic

August 2002

Chapter 1

Introduction

ETHAN B. KAPSTEIN AND BRANKO MILANOVIC

A T A TIME when most Western governments are seeking to reform their welfare states, developing nations around the world are confronting a growing demand for social policy. The challenges facing these countries run the gamut from establishing social insurance and assistance programs where none had previously existed (as in some Asian countries) to addressing the huge increase in poverty and unemployment that has accompanied economic reform (as has occurred in the post-communist transition states). In all cases, social policies must be shaped in the context of severe fiscal restraints and limited administrative capacity, on the one hand, and an increasing need for policies with respect to pensions, unemployment insurance, and poverty assistance, on the other.

The purpose of this book is to take a careful empirical look at how well emerging market economies in Latin America, East Asia, the Middle East and North Africa (MENA), and Central and Eastern Europe are managing that task. We also examine the role of the international community in providing assistance to this ongoing effort. Lessons are drawn from the history of Western experience, where appropriate.

We argue that social policy (and our focus in these pages is primarily on social assistance and insurance, although some of the authors look at education, health, and labor policy as well) has risen on the agenda of many emerging market governments and international organizations in recent years largely as a consequence of economic reform and globalization. These policy shifts, with the new risks and heightened sense of economic volatility they have seemingly brought in their wake, have catalyzed the demand for social insurance schemes like unemployment compensation, pensions, and targeted social assistance for the poor. The rapid economic changes that have accompanied reform programs, and

1

the sudden and severe financial shocks that many countries have experienced in recent years, have caused workers to feel more insecure about their livelihoods and income streams; they have responded by demanding some degree of protection against job displacement, income loss, and unemployment. In the absence of private markets for such protection (and in most developing countries social insurance and assistance have been provided by extended family networks, which may not be able to cope with large systemic shocks), citizens have turned to the state.

But social policy has become relevant not solely because of its potential role in lending a helping hand to a country's most vulnerable citizens. Beyond that, the presence or absence of welfare state programs could have wider repercussions for political and economic stability. As Dani Rodrik has written, social insurance "cushions the blow of liberalization among those most severely affected, it helps maintain the legitimacy of these reforms, and it averts backlashes against the distributional and social consequences of integration into the world economy" (Rodrik 1999, 98). In this conceptualization, social policy becomes a form of political risk insurance.

Yet many developing countries and transition economies confront a variety of special challenges in designing and implementing effective and efficient social policies. The World Bank reminds us, "The state may well be the best agent to provide insurance, but lack the necessary institutional strength, financial resources, or management capacity." Governments must also face difficult political economy issues in structuring these programs, in that "the political support to allocate resources may also be lacking, since it requires getting the rich to support a program that does not benefit them" (World Bank 2001, 150). In sum, the emerging market economies are subject to a particular set of problems in meeting the needs of their unskilled, unemployed, poor, aged, and sick populations.

Despite the enormous literature on economic and political reform in emerging markets, scholars have paid relatively little attention to the role of social insurance and assistance schemes in the sequencing process, paying relatively more attention to policy measures such as macroeconomic stabilization, privatization, or market liberalization and opening (for exceptions, see Graham 1994; Chu and Gupta 1998; Ghai 2000; Institut Français des Relations Internationales 1996). Social policy did not figure prominently in the early iterations of the so-called Washington consensus program of economic reform, in part because of a widespread belief among economists that the "strong medicine" of "good" policy would produce the sort of sustained growth that promoted employment and wealth creation, making many social policies largely unnecessary (Williamson 1994; Rodrik 1996). And in certain regions, especially East Asia, specific cultural values and deep wells of social capital appeared to make the formation of welfare state institutions irrelevant, if not counter-productive.

Two recent events have shattered that optimistic view: the transition of former Soviet bloc economies from communism to a market orientation and the "Asian" financial crisis of 1997 to 1998 that began in Thailand before launching its global spread to Russia and Brazil. The economic transition, which has plunged millions into poverty and even been associated with shortened life spans in several countries, including Russia, has been labeled "a cruel process" by the United Nations (UNDP 1999), while the Asian crisis is said to have produced, in the words of the International Labor Organization's Eddy Lee, "widespread social distress" (Lee 1998), as unemployment and poverty levels reached heights unseen in recent memory. These shocks, along with the almost daily reminders provided by World Bank officials and other global leaders about the persistence of poverty and inequality around the world, have made policymakers more modest about the prospects for sustained growth in emerging market economies. Following the terrorist attacks of September 11, 2001, Western governments have apparently placed renewed emphasis on foreign aid and economic development. In that context the function of social policy within a broader strategy for reform will likely become central to debates in the Middle East and elsewhere.

This book seeks to contribute to these ongoing discussions of how best to structure social policy in the context of emerging market economies. In so doing, the authors of each chapter have examined in detail the policy experiments and experiences of several major regions over the past decade to see whether any "best practices" have yet emerged and whether the developing world seems to be converging toward some common approaches to policy.

This introductory chapter discusses some of the major themes emerging from this collective project. As will soon become apparent, generalizations are difficult to draw from such a diverse set of regional cases—not surprising when one thinks, for example, of the widely differing demographic trends around the world, from declining populations in Eastern Europe to expanding populations in much of the South—but certain common reference points do exist. Pension reform, for example, is on the policy agenda of almost every nation. The simultaneous treatment of social policy by so many countries suggests the possibility of systemic and not just national influences. Specifically, in this chapter we seek to highlight the role of economic openness—and with it the associated spread of liberal economic ideas and ideology—in catalyzing debate over social policy around the world. In short, social policy has now become part and parcel of the neoliberal economic prescription. Still, the specific policy measures to be adopted engender a degree of controversy that is not equally present in discussions of most other aspects of economic reform, and this book provides a lens for viewing these ongoing debates.

The Emergence of Social Policy

Although most developing countries offer at least some type of social insurance to particular groups of citizens (for example, pensions to public sector employees), there is tremendous variation in both the quantity and quality of welfare state services. In many cases, social policy is largely notable by its absence. As the World Bank states, "In practice, there are almost no insurance markets in developing countries because of problems of contract enforcement and asymmetric information. People . . . have to rely largely on self-insurance and informal insurance instead" (World Bank 2001, 143).

What factors might be leading the governments of emerging market economies to play a more decisive role in the design and implementation of social policy? In searching for answers to this question, we may find some clues in the history of welfare state institutions in Western Europe and North America. But that history continues to be debated by scholars, and no durable consensus about the formation of social policy has yet been forged. Some scholars point mainly to economic factors, including industrialization, urbanization, and unionization. Others point to distinctly political factors, including democratization or the rise of socialist parties. Still others look to contingent, historical factors, including the experience of wars and the state's need for a healthy body of worker-soldiers (for literature reviews, see Esping-Andersen 1990; Kapstein 1999). And some, like Peter Lindert, believe that no universal cause suffices or even necessarily predominates; as he writes in his contribution to this volume, democracy, demography, income growth, and the changing self-interests of different franchised groups have determined the share of social spending in the economy. Lindert also highlights the independent role of ideas in shaping policy change, a theme we return to later in this chapter.

Reflecting Lindert's diverse list of factors, each of our authors tends to favor certain explanations over others in tracing contemporary policy developments, reflecting the peculiarities of the countries and regions they have studied. The chapters by Barr on Central and Eastern Europe and by Tzannatos and Kaur on the Middle East and North Africa tend to focus on economics and demographics in explaining the social policies that have emerged. Birdsall and Haggard, in contrast, highlight the role of democracy in promoting East Asian social policies. This reminds us that country- or region-specific influences must certainly loom large in our story. We argue, however, that global forces are now playing an increasingly important role in shaping social policy as well.

A quick look at each of our regional studies points to the limits of any parsimonious account of such a complex phenomenon as the development of social policy. The democracy variable, for example, is problematic in that many of the welfare programs with which we are concerned in this volume reached their heyday not under democratic but rather under communist regimes; still others, for example in many Middle Eastern and North African countries, were developed under monarchic and autocratic rulers. Indeed, communist governments provided their citizens with total welfare: every aspect of an individual's well-being—his or her employment, education, housing, health care, and pension—was provided by the state. And in Western Europe it was not so much the advance of democracy as the threat of socialism and communism that launched the welfare state in Bismarck's Germany and fostered its later refinement and growth in the periods following the two world wars (Kapstein 1999).

Nonetheless, a growing body of political economy literature, some of which is reviewed by Lindert, hypothesizes that democracies are more likely to promote welfare state institutions; Birdsall and Haggard also make this argument in their analysis of the East Asian case. One reason is due to the preferences of the so-called median- or middle-income voter, who may not have the economic means to protect herself against a possible downturn in fortune. In the absence of private insurance markets for unemployment, pensions, health care, and so forth, this voter will seek to develop public sector programs by taxing the rich. A related theory focuses on the role of organized interest groups, such as labor unions, and the political voice they gain in the process of electoral and policy contestation. Both of these approaches lead to the expectation that, as emerging markets democratize, political pressures will arise for the further development of social insurance programs.

As these comments suggest, most political analyses of social policy emphasize the role of *national* actors and institutions. Less attention is paid to international political and economic pressures. This represents an important gap in the literature, and it is one that we address in the final sections of this chapter.

If political forces do not provide an adequate explanation for the emergence and growth of the welfare state, what other factors might be responsible? An alternative is to look mainly at the economic changes associated with modernization. Industrialization and urbanization, for example, may spur the creation and growth of social insurance. As these processes unfold, workers leave behind the family networks that previously maintained them during hard times, and in their absence, the state provides this system of support; in so doing, the government acts on behalf of the modernization process. These economic factors, when combined with growing political contestation, have played an important role in the evolution of the European welfare state; they have been less influential in shaping the East Asian social contract.

Rising incomes may also create greater demand for social insurance. In this model, social policy may be conceptualized as a luxury good that people buy—up to a point—as they become wealthier. Lindert also provides some support for these arguments, noting that the richer the country, the more it tends to spend on social insurance. Further, he observes that public sector social spending is a fairly recent phenomenon, beginning from a relatively feeble base in the nineteenth century and growing particularly rapidly after the end of World War II.

Demographics have also been featured as a driving force behind the welfare state. To be sure, the aging of the population, especially in the North, has played a key role in putting social security on policy agendas almost everywhere in recent years. But Lindert reminds us that during the welfare state's first period of growth, from 1880 to 1930, European populations were also aging (as well as democratizing); thus we find Bismarck launching old-age pensions among his social insurance schemes.

Looking beyond Western Europe, Lindert's examination of economic and demographic factors leads him to argue that the post-communist transition economies face a particularly potent mixture as they debate social policy reform. For one thing, their populations are old by world standards, raising the demand for public pensions. For another, their social programs had already begun to decline in the 1980s before collapsing in the 1990s due to their economic problems and the huge increase in poverty, unemployment, and inequality. This double bind makes pension reform one of the most pressing problems that these countries must grapple with, on top of all the other overwhelming economic and environmental tasks they confront.

In his chapter on Central and Eastern Europe, Barr agrees with this gloomy assessment. The old system of pensions, he argues, "is ill adapted in several ways to the needs of a market economy." Under communism, the retirement age was low, and numerous special schemes existed for workers in sectors such as coal mining or in particularly harsh regions such as northern Siberia. As a result, by the 1990s, pensions were claiming a double-digit share of public spending.

Barr then lays out the various options for lessening the pension burden and reforming the system. He reminds readers that each of these options—for example, privatization of pension schemes—is fraught with political (and economic) consequences and risks creating a backlash against the larger reform process; again, we are reminded that one argument for social safety nets is to mitigate the harsh effects of liberalization. Barr posits not only that pensioners may vote against economic reform in the future (and pensioners are a large and growing share of the voting population) but also that workers who want to ensure their future benefits may balk at any proposed changes that could turn them into "losers" in retirement. Incidentally, Barr also provides us with some very strong reasons as to why privatization of pensions is not necessarily the "answer" for reform in Central and Eastern Europe, given the existing set of demographic and economic problems (not to mention regulatory problems in many of these countries, which he does not emphasize). The problem here is that private pension schemes must be regulated by public bodies, which either do not exist or lack public confidence, given corruption and the absence of a sound judicial system.

Barr further highlights the weakness of administrative capacity in the transition economies for dealing with the profound economic changes encountered after 1989. The rise in poverty and unemployment led to a widespread demand for income transfers, but basic questions about who should receive these transfers and how much should be paid—again, in light of tremendous fiscal stringency—loomed large. As his data show, they were never successfully resolved. Social policy officials simply lacked the appropriate mechanisms for targeting and reaching those who were hardest hit by the transition. The results have been particularly harsh for women and children.

In several important respects, the social policy challenges facing the countries of the Middle East and North Africa are not altogether different from those facing the countries of Central and Eastern Europe. Like the transition economies, these countries entered the 1990s with a large public sector, one that had swelled in large measure due to the oil revenues of earlier decades. Although the public sector was in many, if not most, instances woefully inefficient, it was remarkably successful in delivering a wide variety of social services to its population. By the 1990s, according to Tzannatos and Kaur, the MENA region had "the lowest poverty rates in the developing world." Other indicators were equally impressive: universal education was now "within reach" and "over 90 percent of the population had access to health services," with sharp declines in infant mortality and morbidity rates.

But as the region entered the millennium, these gains appeared tenuous in light of growing political conflict and rising pressures for economic reform (although the sharp increase in oil prices in 2000 may mitigate at least the short-term fiscal pressures in several countries). Indeed, the reforms made to date have been accompanied by profound social dislocation, especially rising unemployment, providing fuel for radical groups. In the past, employment depended heavily on the state sector, and with growing state interest in the revenues associated with privatization, alternative sources of work must be found. Unfortunately, the new jobs have yet to materialize, and the MENA countries have entered the millennium with rising urban unemployment and the threat of radical uprisings.

Beyond the aggregate levels of unemployment evident in many parts of the developing world—and for many years labor economists basically dismissed the presence of unemployment in most emerging market economies, given their largely rural structure—privatization has also brought labor market mismatches into sharp relief. This also has occurred in the transition economies. The set of skills needed to function successfully in the market economy is not necessarily the same as that necessary for surviving in a state-owned enterprise and state-dominated economy, compounding the employment problem. Human capital formation has thus become a key issue for the governments of Middle East and North Africa, although Tzannatos and Kaur doubt that active labor market policies will have much effect on the overall employment rate. The number of jobless will only be reduced as the conditions for sustained economic growth are established.

Like many other parts of the world, the region is also grappling with aging populations and poorly designed pension schemes. Tzannatos and Kaur report that "pension finances are deteriorating" both for demographic reasons and because governments have used surpluses from the pension funds in the past to finance inefficient projects, leaving these funds seriously depleted. The authors emphasize that privatization revenues will not be sufficient to take care of all the gaps and problems in social funding that currently exist.

Tzannatos and Kaur argue that MENA governments must introduce private social insurance schemes and thus competition into the market if they are to meet the population's growing need for services. That naturally implies a changing role for the state, in which its functions will go beyond social service provision to social insurance regulation. Yet, as we have seen with respect to the transition economies, and indeed most other developing countries, establishing regulatory institutions that win public trust is no easy matter. Corruption, a lack of efficient and effective judicial systems, and simple incompetence make it difficult for ordinary citizens to put their faith in the government; as a consequence, economic activity goes underground. In MENA, as elsewhere in the developing world, the informal sector is a significant generator of employment, but not of tax revenue! Perhaps the oil boom of the early twenty-first century, should it continue, will help at least some of the MENA countries to delay making hard choices, but growing pressures on social policy, from an aging population, on the one hand, and joblessness, on the other, will require major changes in the design and delivery of programs.

In both the transition and MENA economies, governments must struggle with the reform of existing social insurance policies, especially public pension schemes (this is not to minimize other social problems, like poverty, but pension reform is the main budgetary burden that must be lifted). The problem in East Asia, in contrast, is one of fashioning social policies more or less from scratch. As Birdsall and Haggard point out, East Asians had little in the way of social insurance when the financial crisis of 1997 and 1998 swept over them. Instead, social insurance was provided either through enterprises or through family and social networks. More broadly, they write, it was provided indirectly through the promise of sustained and widely shared economic growth.

When that promise was shattered, it led to a sweeping reexamination of the social contract. Birdsall and Haggard show how the World Bank, Asian Development Bank, and International Monetary Fund (among others) urged East Asian governments to develop social safety net programs and Western-style welfare state institutions, and they financed scores of studies and projects aimed in that direction. "The result," they write, "was a proliferation of program initiatives."

But the governments balked at this advice, for several reasons. First, most East Asian states lacked the administrative capacity to carry out widespread social programs. Second, the authors report, "A number of Asian policymakers . . . were wary of the new social agenda because of the potential for leakage not only to the nonpoor . . . but also to local politicians and corruption." Finally, officials were concerned that state-led programs might displace traditional family and social networks that had been responsive to crises in the past; indeed, this social capital is widely viewed as one of East Asia's great strengths.

Birdsall and Haggard also emphasize that, on the demand side, East Asian politics were not organized in such a way as to promote welfare state policies. The political parties and interest groups that had won many social programs in the West during the nineteenth and twentieth centuries (for example, socialist parties and unions) were either weak or nonexistent in many of these countries (with South Korea at least a partial exception to this rule, as labor did have some voice in the deliberations over crisis management). The lack of fully developed democratic institutions dampened the voice of those who were most vulnerable during the economic crisis and prevented them from acting in an organized fashion. In short, history, politics, and culture conspired against the creation of an East Asian welfare state.

What does that portend for the future? Birdsall and Haggard return our attention to the role of democracy in shaping social policy. They conclude, "In the end, democratic politics will be fundamental to shaping a more explicit Asian social contract." And they are optimistic that democratic politics in this region will fashion a more or less inclusive social safety net, in which both poor and middle class receive adequate coverage.

Yet in East Asia, too, demography and economics may quickly overshadow the debate that emerged following the financial crisis, which focused on poverty relief and unemployment insurance. In that region as well, aging populations may place such heavy and unsustainable burdens on family networks that health care and pensions will come to dominate social policy as the first order of business. Combined with a democratic politics that encourages aging voters to organize, this may further skew social insurance priorities. Again, given the lack of history of state-provided pension schemes in the region (except for certain privileged groups), it remains to be seen whether a distinctive Asian model will arise.

As this brief review of our regional chapters suggests, pension policy has emerged as a common theme around the world, in emerging no less than in industrial countries. And in most places, policymakers are at least giving some consideration to pension privatization, meaning a shift from state-sponsored pay-as-you-go systems to schemes in which individuals vest their savings with financial intermediaries in the private sector. How did privatization emerge as a "universal" solution to the pension problem? We treat the globalization of this and other ideas about social policy reform in the following section.

The Role of Liberal Ideas and Ideology

When one observes the changes that have occurred over the past two decades in the role of the state and welfare policy in developing and transition countries, one is struck by the prevalence of policy prescriptions similar to the ones routinely made in the developed Western countries. These include a triad of measures, notably *privatization*, especially of the pension system, *means testing* of social assistance, and *decentralization* of social policy to the regional level. Why have these policy approaches been advocated, by the World Bank and other institutions, as the right ones for both developed countries and emerging market economies? In this section we focus on the spread of ideas, in particular with respect to pension reform.

It was Keynes who stimulated the study of ideas in economic policy, writing in the often-quoted closing paragraph of *The General Theory*, "The ideas of economists and political philosophers, both when they are right and when they are wrong, are more powerful than is commonly understood. Indeed, the world is ruled by little else . . . [T]he power of vested interests is vastly exaggerated compared with the gradual encroachment of ideas. Not, indeed, immediately, but after a certain interval . . . soon or late, it is ideas, not vested interests, which are dangerous for good or evil" (Keynes 1964 [1935], 383).

In our case, we recall that the initial onslaught against the "bloated" welfare state—and against some of the state's functions that many came to associate with developments following World War II in Western Europe and, albeit to a lesser degree, the United States (although we should remember Lyndon Johnson's Great Society)—emerged from the rhetoric of Margaret Thatcher in Great Britain. The same wave washed over to the other side of the Atlantic during the administration of Ronald Reagan and then proceeded to affect the rest of the world.

Most notably for our purposes, the emerging neoliberal rhetoric, with its emphasis on minimal government and "good" economic policy, became transformed for development purposes as the Washington consensus, which had a profound influence on international financial institutions like the International Monetary Fund (IMF), the World Bank, and Inter-American Development Bank. However, the Washington consensus gave social policy short shrift, and its only indirect recommendation was that public expenditures be redirected away from defense, general industrial subsidization, and "white elephant" public works programs and toward preventive health care and primary education. When the author of the Washington consensus, John Williamson, revisited his policy list in 1997, he added targeted antipoverty policies to the list of expenditures that need to be expanded (Williamson 1997).

The international financial institutions do not work, of course, in a vacuum; rather they reflect the dominant ideological atmosphere of their member states. Following the eruption of the Latin American debt crisis after 1982 (which, of course, encompassed Poland, among other non–Latin American countries), these institutions had an opportunity to spread the gospel of the minimalist state through the doctrine of structural adjustment. This doctrine became the heart and soul of post-1982 conditionality programs, emphasizing budgetary restraint, fiscal discipline, the privatization of state enterprise, and economic openness; it profoundly influenced economic policies first in the South and, after the end of the cold war, in the East (on the role of international financial institutions in transition economies, see Deacon, Hulse, and Stubbs 1997).

The policy recommendations made by the financial institutions generally followed the cookie-cutter or one-size-fits-all approach. This was particularly the case after the regime changes in Eastern Europe, in large part because the knowledge base of the World Bank and International Monetary Fund with respect to these economies was limited both in space (only Yugoslavia, Hungary, and Poland were members of these organizations) and in scope (for example, the entire work program of formerly socialist economies focused on macroeconomic issues and the productive sectors).[1] Of course, even if their knowledge had gone deeper, their priorities and policies would naturally have reflected the ideological preferences and predilections of the dominant member states.

The social sphere recommendations that followed in the early days of transition were often criticized for being out of touch with these countries' reality and history. For example, one of Hungary's most eminent social scientists, Zsuzsa Ferge, argued that the World Bank was oblivious to Central European history and culture, which, in ethnically homogeneous societies like Hungary's, stressed the need for social solidarity (much the same could be said about the East Asian case). The reform measures being contemplated, with the likely increase in poverty and income inequality, might tear that solidarity asunder. Some Central European countries were upset at being given the same recommendations as Kyrgyzstan and Uzbekistan. A Bulgarian economist writes, "When I read what the IMF, the World Bank, and other international financial institutions say about Bulgaria, I always ask myself a question: is it the same country where I live and which I see with my own eyes of a citizen and a professional? The true Bulgaria is very, very different from the one presented by the IMF and to a lesser degree by the World Bank publications. And this is particularly true for the social dimensions of transformation."[2]

But in addition to the ideological changes that were exported to emerging markets from outside, at least one important influence came from within the group of developing nations. Moreover, that important example would ultimately influence economists and policymakers working inside the very institutions responsible for exporting policy advice. We have in mind the case of Chile in the wake of General Augusto Pinochet's accession to power. The Pinochet regime adopted three approaches to social policy reform that would heavily influence the thinking of international financial institutions and, through them, other emerging markets as well.

First, Chile initially implemented the major social policy change that we have identified in this section—pension privatization. Privatization of the pension system was a watershed event, so much so that the very details of Chilean privatization techniques were copied in other countries or at least influenced their reforms (for example, in Argentina, Kazakhstan, and New Zealand and in a milder version of so-called "notational contributions" in Croatia, Hungary, Italy, Latvia, and Sweden). The chapter by Székely and Fuentes highlights the role of the Chilean pension scheme in influencing developments in Latin America and beyond.

Second, Pinochet's introduction of workfare and public works programs, which at their peak in 1982 employed 13 percent of the labor force, represented, at least for a developing country, a bold innovation, which was later replicated by several other governments, such as that of Argentina (Graham 1991).

Finally, the effort to put into effect improved targeting of social assistance, with the creation of the Ficha poverty index, was later copied in a number of countries, including most recently Armenia and parts of Russia.[3]

What was so unique about Chile? Chile combined three features that are seldom found together and whose combination made the Chilean experience, at least to development economists, an example to follow. Most prominently, Pinochet's Chile was a right-wing dictatorship devoted, or so it seemed, to maximizing the nation's economic welfare. Unlike many, if not most, dictatorships, this one did not appear to be concerned solely with self-enrichment. Second, the leaders were willing to allow the "Chicago boys," the technocrats, almost free reign in economic matters. The technocrats were not forced to tailor their policies in such a way as to help the rulers amass wealth, on the one hand, or to please the crowd, on the other. Economic policy thus managed to steer clear of the shoals of kleptocracy and populism. Unlike economists advising democratic governments, those in Chile were untrammeled by political parties, trade unions, and parliaments; their decisions were not debated in the political arena. Although development economists might not admit it openly, Chile once represented for many of them the closest one could come, this side of the Hades, to a benign dictatorship (at least alongside Senior Minister Lee Kuan Yew of Singapore) dedicated to maximizing the nation's economic well-being.

The third, and possibly the most unusual, feature of the Chilean regime was that some of the country's neoclassical economists were interested in social issues. Miguel Kast and a number of economists from ODEPLAN, the agency set up to define and implement the new welfare policy, launched an admittedly technocratic, but very important, program of social assistance. The agency's economists designed and implemented targeting of welfare benefits, workfare, and school lunches. The emphasis on the targeting of welfare was not new: it was a key feature of the residual welfare state (as in the United States and Switzerland), but the thoroughness of its application was new for the developing world. No one who has seen ODEPLAN's detailed poverty maps of Chile could remain indifferent or fail to be impressed with the seriousness and thoroughness with which "the fight against poverty" (viewed almost as a disease to be eradicated) was undertaken.

In short, what started in Chile in the mid-1970s as a radical experiment evolved over the next decade to become the orthodox prescription that other developing countries were supposed to adopt. The Chilean model was spread around the world not only by self-promotion and the publicity surrounding its success but also by the leading international financial institutions, which found in Chile the star pupil "bad" students might do well to exemplify. We do not deny the progress that Chile has made along any number of economic and social indicators since the liberal reforms went into effect (although the Chilean pension plan does not reach all members of society and thus is far from universal), but we do question the wider applicability of many of these reforms in different socioeconomic and political settings, where the government may possess less in the way of fiscal resources or administrative capacity.

The Role of Globalization

If the example of Chile provided an "internal" stimulus for social policy reform within emerging market economies, systemic factors in the form of increasing economic openness were also at play. Increasing openness to flows of trade, finance, and investment held great promise for developing nations but also posed new risks for existing economic arrangements. How these forces played out for social policy remains a topic for debate. There are, to simplify our discussion, two views on how globalization has influenced welfare state institutions. Both have some theoretical merit, although neither has enough empirical support to claim victory in the paradigmatic conflict.

One prominent position, drawn mainly from public finance theory (and, more specifically, from the Thiebout hypothesis), holds that globalization leads to what is called a race to the bottom, whereby countries with more developed (and costly) systems of social protection are forced, due to international competition, to downscale their social transfers in order not to loose potential foreign investment (see Deacon 1998a). Writing in this vein, Benvenisti (1999, 167) claims, "Globalization provides ever-growing opportunities for small groups of producers, employers, and service providers to shop the globe for more amenable jurisdictions. An international 'race to the bottom,' spawned by the decreasing exit costs of many businesses, threatens to compromise the achievements of the welfare state."

Implicit in this view is the worldwide dominance of capital over labor. Capital is mobile, which gives it political and economic leverage over labor and the state. Governments want to attract investors to their countries and are willing to trade workers' rights (and social protection in general) against the private rents (for politicians and the elite) and national income associated with greater capital flows. The tradeoff between social security and income is, in this view, quite stark, and if market forces were not enough, the IMF and World Bank have supplied further pressures in this direction. Faced with this prisoner's dilemma—in that each state chooses to compete against others for investment rather than cooperate on reaching some common standards—the individual government goes ahead and implements capital-friendly policies both to keep its own capital at home and to attract funds from abroad, no matter the costs.

A contrasting—one might say more historically oriented—view holds that the maintenance of social cohesion is a sine qua non for globalization to proceed (see, for example, Kapstein 1999, 31; Rodrik 1998, 157). Without social cohesion, the electorate (as represented by the so-called median voter) might easily succumb to the temptation of populists and demagogues who espouse protectionist and nationalistic policies directly opposed to international integration. In this view, in order for globalization to be "safe," it has to be based on the bedrock of social consent, as exemplified by safety net and public insurance programs. Far from being inimical, globalization and social protection are inextricably linked.

If we consider how globalization and the welfare state were related in the past—in order to provide possible lessons for the present—a natural place to start is the "first" era of globalization, which lasted from the second half of the nineteenth century until the outbreak of World War I in 1914.[4] In the words of Karl Polanyi (1985 [1944], 138–39), this is the period when "nothing less than a self-regulating market on a world scale could ensure the functioning of [capitalism]. The expansion of the market system in the nineteenth century was synonymous with the simultaneous spreading of international free trade, a competitive labor market, and the gold standard: they belonged together."

This period also coincided with the birth of the modern welfare state. The first, trend-setting, social insurance was introduced in Bismarck's Germany (health and accident insurance in 1883 to 1884; old-age insurance a few years later).[5] This was done in reaction to the growth of the socialist movement in Germany, and Bismarck's decision to ban the Social Democratic party in 1881 was followed by his introduction of social insurance as a way to undercut that party's popular support by offering workers most of the measures it had advocated.

If we view, as we believe one should, the development of the socialist movement in the second part of the nineteenth century mainly as a response to the "problem" of global capitalism, it then becomes apparent that the extension of the welfare state was *caused* largely by the problems associated with globalization and the insecurities it engendered in the context of the international gold standard. The events of 120 years ago resonate with what we observe today or rather with the dilemmas we face today. This historical analogy thus supports the position of those economists who regard the preservation of the social acquis in the developed countries (and even their expansion) as needed to provide the cushion against which globalization can take place.[6]

How is this to be achieved in poorer, emerging market economies? Even in states with nascent democracies, political voice might be strongly skewed toward those with the greatest economic power, undermining the state's welfare function. That group, through its financial, social, and ideational connections with global capital, may form part of a trans-national coalition whose interest lies in scaling down the welfare state in industrial countries and minimizing it in the emerging market context. This coalition may be sufficiently strong and well organized politically to achieve that objective, as the experience of the past twenty years could be interpreted to suggest.

Racing to the Bottom or the Top?

Implicit in the race-to-the-bottom hypothesis is a view that all (or most) economies will end up with the same, fairly stripped down, system of social protection. An alternative may be a convergence toward the middle, between the large West European welfare state, on the one hand, and the very lean East Asian model, on the other. Two empirical facts point toward such a development.

First, the differences between the various Western models of capitalism seem to be diminishing. In 1990, when Esping-Andersen published his famous book *The Three Worlds of Welfare Capitalism*, the differences between the universalist (Scandinavian), corporatist (continental European), and residual or liberal (Anglo-Saxon) worlds of welfare capitalism still seemed relatively sharp. The past decade and a half have witnessed the erosion of some welfare state functions in the Scandinavian countries (introduction of private pensions in Sweden and reform of the state pension system in 1998; reform of sickness and unemployment benefits in 1993)[7] and changes in the corporatist systems (pension reforms in Germany and Italy; sick pay reform in Germany), diluting the corporatist origins of these systems. In a very detailed study of the evolution of European pension systems after World War II, Johnson (1999) documents this growing convergence.

The role of the European Union in stimulating this convergence must be highlighted, both because a single economic space imposes the same requirements on all member countries and because it ensures a better diffusion of information. The importance of differences in national historical trajectories, which shaped the formation of different welfare cultures in early twentieth-century Europe (for example, the role of the Catholic Church, the more or less exalted position of civil servants, differences in the role of trade unions, differences in the strength of socialist and communist movements, and so forth), has much diminished now.

Consider a few examples. The communist movement, which was strong first in Germany, then in Spain, France, and Italy (but never in Northern Europe), is now practically nonexistent in these countries (of course, former communists are in the government in Italy, but they are neither carriers of nor believers in an alternative ideology). The population growth rates, which differed between Catholic and Protestant countries, have declined in both and are now lower in Catholic Italy or Spain than in Protestant Scandinavia. The secular role of the Catholic Church has declined with decreasing numbers of regular churchgoers: one needs simply to contrast the role of the Catholic Church in the early twentieth century in, say, Hungary, Portugal, or Spain with its role today. Even Poland, where the importance of the Catholic Church peaked during the communist period, is now reverting toward the European mean.

Second, while the erosion of the OECD welfare state (see Boltho 1997) was occurring in the West, East Asian countries—following dramatic increases in real income—introduced new social programs: for example, unemployment insurance in South Korea and Taiwan in 1998 and 1999. Thus the distance between their welfare states and those in the West has diminished.

Tables 1.1 and 1.2 give a schematic representation of developments in the welfare state over the past twenty years (the shaded cells in table 1.2 represent changes). We can summarize them as follows: the erosion and convergence between the three worlds of Western welfare state; diminishing differences between the Western OECD welfare state and the East Asian countries; the end of the communist welfare state, with formerly socialist countries splintering into two groups: Central European countries joining the Western OECD model and others (particularly in Central Asia and the Balkans) slipping toward developing-country status; and continued or increasing marginalization of many developing countries, especially in Africa.

How far this convergence will go remains unclear. Today, a billion people still live in absolute poverty, most of them unshielded by any social assistance whatsoever. On the ideational plane, governments may be moving toward some convergent views regarding social policy and the welfare state, as exemplified by United Nations agreements, conferences, and speeches. But these governments remain far from turning their social agendas into reality.

The Role of the International Community

What is to be done for those emerging market economies that seek to provide a modicum of social insurance and assistance in the context of a globalizing economy? As we have argued, pressures on these states come from within and without. From within, it is unlikely that those who hold wealth will welcome the redistribution that the welfare state must bring. From without, it is equally unlikely that the global economy will support high levels of social protection in emerging markets. In short, developing countries face a terrible political and economic bind.

Table 1.1 Welfare State Around 1980

Service Provision	Communist Countries	Western OECD Countries	East Asian Countries	Developing Countries
Universal or near universal provision of pensions	Yes; high replacement rates in Eastern Europe, low in the former Soviet Union	Yes; high replacement rates	For civil servants only	For civil servants only
Universal or near universal provision of family benefits	Yes in Eastern Europe; not in the former Soviet Union	Yes, except in the United States	No	No
Unemployment insurance	Full employment	Yes	No	No
Socialized health	Yes	Yes, except in the United States	Limited	No (in practice)
Socialized education	Yes	Yes	Yes	Yes (limited)
Score	5	5	2	1.5

Source: Authors' compilation.
Note: Family benefits and unemployment insurance in non–Central European, formerly communist countries, formally do not differ from the those in Central Europe. However, their puny amounts, limited coverage, and large arrears make these rights practically irrelevant. For these reasons, Kazakhstan has recently formally abolished unemployment benefits. The same is true for a formally socialized health care, when receiving even a modicum of "free" health care requires that patients bring in their own drugs and food and pay bribes to the doctors. Score was calculated by giving 1 point for each "yes" and 0.5 point for "limited."

Table 1.2   Welfare State Around 2000

Service Provision	Former Communist Countries		Western OECD Countries	East Asian Countries	Developing Countries
	Central Europe	Others			
Universal or near universal provision of pensions	Yes	Very low replacement rates	Yes; high replacement rates	For civil servants only	For civil servants only
Universal or near universal provision of family benefits	Yes	Limited	Yes, except in the United States	No	No
Unemployment insurance	Yes	No	Yes	Limited	No
Socialized health	Yes	No	Yes, except in the United States	Limited	No (in practice)
Socialized education	Yes	Limited	Yes	Yes	Yes (limited)
Score	5	2	5	2.5	1.5

Source: Authors' compilation.
Note: Family benefits and unemployment insurance in non–Central European, formerly communist countries, formally do not differ from the those in Central Europe. However, their puny amounts, limited coverage, and large arrears make these rights practically irrelevant. For these reasons, Kazakhstan has recently formally abolished unemployment benefits. The same is true for a formally socialized health care, when receiving even a modicum of "free" health care requires that patients bring in their own drugs and food and pay bribes to the doctors. Score was calculated by giving 1 point for each "yes" and 0.5 point for "limited."

As a result, we would argue that international financial and technical assistance can and should play a critical role in promoting investment in social policy development in these economies and that this investment must be targeted at the "losers" from economic and technological change—those who are least advantaged. Indeed, these programs should be part and parcel of international economic policies designed to promote greater opening, and the industrial economies certainly could do much more to open their markets to the exports of developing countries.

The adoption of these recommendations would almost certainly require both an increase in aid funding and a redirection of allocated amounts. Although we recognize the immense political challenges facing both of these developments, we believe that a strong case for this strategy can be made. After all, to the extent that the advanced industrial states are truly committed to promoting globalization around the world, this investment should be seen as a modest contribution to that process.

Clearly, the current spending trend for foreign assistance is not promising. Official development assistance by the major industrial countries reached its postwar high of $70 billion in 1991. Since that time, it has tumbled to insignificant proportions, largely because of decreased spending by the United States; while the U.S. economy constitutes 30 percent of the industrial world total, its aid contributions represent less than 17 percent of all official flows traveling between North and South. As a result, the member states gathered in the Development Assistance Committee of the OECD recently judged "the current level of American aid as inadequate" (OECD 1998, 1).

Overall, the advanced industrial democracies now allocate less than 0.25 percent of their gross national product to foreign assistance, or 50 percent less than they provided at the outset of the 1990s. It is hard to think of any other program, domestic or international, that has suffered such reductions. The end of the cold war, on the one hand, and renewed fiscal pressure on the welfare state, on the other, have doomed aid budgets everywhere. The ironic result is that this may make it more difficult for emerging market economies to create or reform their own social insurance programs.

To be sure, going forward, aid must be better targeted with respect to both recipients and feasible projects. Aid should be targeted not only at those countries that are committed to economic reform, but more specifically at governments that are also committed to expanding education and work opportunities for the least advantaged. All too often, as the World Bank admits, educational expenditure in developing countries has "not always reached groups that have traditionally had low levels of education (the poor and girls, for instance)" (World Bank 1998, 45).

More broadly, our discussion leads to the conclusion that the World Bank, International Monetary Fund, World Trade Organization, and major bilateral donors ought to reexamine their economic programs and policies in light of the connections between openness and social policy. The received wisdom provides an optimistic view about the evolution of the global economy, teaching that open markets promote efficiency, which produces growth and, ultimately, the wealth needed to finance social programs.

But for reasons of domestic and international politics and economics, that outcome may not pertain. Domestically, the rich may balk at paying taxes that support social programs. And internationally, capital may flee regimes that seek to impose high social charges. Reconciling these internal and external forces in such a way as to meet the vital needs of the developing world's most vulnerable citizens represents one of today's greatest policy challenges. Promoting informed public debate over how those needs can best be met is the main objective of this book.

Notes

1. In the United States, the intelligence community devoted considerable attention to the Warsaw Pact's defense economy and defense industries.

2. Mr. Ivan Angelov in a personal communication to Branko Milanovic.

3. The Ficha assigned different weights to a variety of characteristics (but not income) in order to come up with a cardinal measure of eligibility for various social assistance programs (such as complementary feeding, preschool care, school lunch program, and health care).

4. This is, of course, the same approach used when trying to assess the effect of globalization on a number of other economic indicators (such as international trade, foreign direct investment, and migration). Several recent papers (Baldwin and Martin 1999; Williamson 1996) do this, but none has looked at the relationship between the 1870 to 1914 globalization and welfare state.

5. In terms of redistributive old-age pensions (that is, pensions that, in addition to employer and employee contributions, would include a contribution paid directly by the state), Germany was preceded by Denmark (see Lindert 1992, 11). The Danish example, however, did not have nearly as much influence as the German. It is also interesting that Bismarck strongly argued for state participation in funding, but the proposal was twice turned down by the Reichstag (see Taylor 1955).

6. For example, Rieger (1998), quoted in Deacon (1998b), supports the case that openness in the United States and expansion of welfare spending go hand in hand (although one needs to be mindful of the possibility that both are driven by other variables, in which case the causality between the two may be spurious).

7. The unemployment benefit replacement rate was reduced from 90 to 80 percent, with the first five days of unemployment uncovered; the sickness benefit replacement rate was reduced from between 80 and 90 percent to between 65 and 80 percent; the retirement age was raised from sixty-five to sixty-six years.

References

Baldwin, Richard, and Philip Martin. 1999. "Two Waves of Globalisation: Superficial Similarities, Fundamental Differences." NBER working paper 6904. Cambridge, Mass.: National Bureau of Economic Research (January).

Benvenisti, Eyal. 1999. "Exit and Voice in the Age of Globalization." *Michigan Law Review* 98(1): 167–213.

Boltho, Andrea. 1997. "Growth, Public Expenditure, and Household Welfare in the Industrialized Countries." In *Child Poverty and Deprivation in the Industrialized Countries, 1945–1995,* edited by Giovanni Andrea Cornia and Sheldon Danziger. Oxford and New York: Oxford University Press and Clarendon Press.

Chu, Ke-young, and Sanjeev Gupta, eds. 1998. *Social Safety Nets: Issues and Recent Experiences.* Washington, D.C.: International Monetary Fund.

Deacon, Bob. 1998a. "Social Policy in Eastern Europe: Is It Social Dumping?" Paper prepared for the World Congress of Sociology. Montreal (July 24–August 1).

———. 1998b. "Towards a Socially Responsible Globalization: International Actors and Discourses." GASPP occasional paper. Globalism and Social Policy Programme, Helsinki, Finland (November).

Deacon, Bob, Michelle Hulse, and Paul Stubbs. 1997. *Global Social Policy: International Organisations and the Future of Welfare.* London: Sage.

Esping-Andersen, Gøsta. 1990. *The Three Worlds of Welfare Capitalism.* Princeton, N.J.: Princeton University Press.

Ghai, Dharam, ed. 2000. *Social Development and Public Policy.* New York: St. Martin's Press.

Graham, Carol. 1991. "From Emergency Employment to Social Investment: Alleviating Poverty in Chile." Occasional paper. Washington, D.C.: Brookings Institution.

———. 1994. *Safety Nets, Politics, and the Poor.* Washington, D.C.: Brookings Institution.

Institut Français des Relations Internationales. 1996. *Ramses 1996.* Paris: Dunod.

Johnson, Paul. 1999. "The Measurement of Social Security Convergence: The Case of European Public Pension Systems since 1950." *Journal of Social Policy* 28(4): 595–618.

Kapstein, Ethan. 1999. *Sharing the Wealth: Workers and the World Economy.* New York and London: W. W. Norton.

Keynes, John Maynard. 1964 [1935]. *The General Theory of Employment, Interest, and Money.* New York: Harcourt, Brace, and Jovanovich.

Lee, Eddy. 1998. *The Asian Financial Crisis: The Challenge for Social Policy.* Geneva: International Labour Office.

Lindert, Peter. 1992. "The Rise of Social Spending, 1880–1990." Working paper. Davis: University of California, Davis, Agricultural History Center (May).

OECD (Organization for Economic Cooperation and Development), Development Assistance Committee. 1998. *Development Cooperation Review of the United States.* Paris: OECD.

Pierson, Paul. 1994. *Dismantling the Welfare State.* New York: Cambridge University Press.

Polanyi, Karl. 1985 [1944]. *The Great Transformation.* Boston: Beacon Press.

Rodrik, Dani. 1996. *Has Globalization Gone Too Far?* Washington, D.C.: Institute for International Economics.

———. 1998. "Globalization, Social Conflict, and Economic Growth." *World Economy* 4(March): 143–58.

———. 1999. *The New Global Economy and Developing Countries: Making Openness Work.* Washington, D.C.: Overseas Development Council.

Sklair, Leslie. 1997. "Social Movements and Global Capitalism: The Transnational Capitalist Class in Action." *Review of International Political Economy* 4(3): 514–38.

Taylor, A. J. P. 1955. *Bismarck: The Man and Statesman.* London: Penguin.

UNDP (United Nations Development Programme). 1999. *Human Development in Transition: 1999.* New York: United Nations.

Williamson, Jeffrey. 1996. "Globalization and Inequality Then and Now: The Late 19th and Late 20th Centuries Compared." NBER working paper 5491. Cambridge, Mass.: National Bureau of Economic Research (March).

Williamson, John. 1994. *The Political Economy of Policy Reform.* Washington, D.C.: Institute for International Economics.

———. 1997. "The Washington Consensus Revisited." In *Economic and Social Development into the XXI Century,* edited by Louis Emmerij. Washington, D.C.: Inter-American Development Bank; Baltimore, Md.: Johns Hopkins University Press.

World Bank. 1998. *Assessing Aid.* Washington, D.C.: World Bank.

———. 2000. *World Development Report 2000.* New York: Oxford University Press.

———. 2001. *World Development Report 2001.* New York: Oxford University Press.

PART I

REGIONAL PERSPECTIVES

Chapter 2

Welfare States in Central and Eastern Europe

NICHOLAS BARR

WELFARE states in many countries face similar problems, including fiscal constraint and a need to reform the state sector. This paper sets these general issues to one side and focuses instead on what is distinctive about the transition from plan to market in Central and Eastern Europe (CEE). It argues that the communist welfare state was well adapted to the old economic order and—precisely for that reason—is systematically and predictably ill suited to a market economy.

The old economic order can be characterized, very broadly, as having a fairly flat income distribution, generous universal benefits, including extensive subsidies, and full employment with job security. Consequently, there was no unemployment, hence no (or virtually no) unemployment benefit; no poverty, at least officially (since everyone had a job or benefits), hence no poverty relief except for groups like the frail elderly; and no sophisticated targeting; since (given the fairly flat income distribution) none was necessary.

Transitions brought falling output, fiscal crisis, a widening income distribution, and the loss of job security, negating all three characteristics of the old order. As a result, three strategic sets of problems arise:

- *Open unemployment:* There has been a sharp increase in open unemployment to above 10 percent in CEE and the Baltic countries and also, later, in Russia.

- *Rising poverty:* Notwithstanding well-known problems of methodology and measurement (see Barr 1998a, ch. 6), the evidence is overwhelming. The number of people living on less than $4 a day in CEE, the Commonwealth of Independent States, and the Baltic countries has increased, rising from 14 million in 1989 to 147 million in 1996 (World Bank 1999, 6). Radical reformers have experienced substantial increases in the poverty headcount, for example from 6 percent of the population to 20 percent in Poland. In less successful reformers, the increase in poverty has been greater (in Russia, poverty has risen to 50 percent), with little likelihood of any short-run improvement (for details, see Milanovic 1998, table 5.1).

- *Badly targeted benefits:* Benefits—notably pensions—designed for a flat income distribution have been badly targeted in the context of a diverging income distribution.

It follows directly that reform is needed in three areas:

- *Addressing unemployment:* Although unemployment is an effect of transition, the existence of some unemployment is an inescapable price to pay for the dynamic efficiency of market allocation. Institutions to support people's incomes during unemployment and to help them find work are therefore essential.

- *Addressing poverty:* As Milanovic (1998) points out, as a proposition in pure logic, falling output coupled with widening income distribution must lead to increased poverty, making well-targeted poverty relief an urgent priority.

- *Reforming pensions:* The issue with unemployment and poverty relief is one of avoiding gaps in coverage; with pensions, in contrast, the targeting problem is one of awarding benefits to too many people, leading to problems of cost.

In each of these areas, the paper outlines the reasons why reform of the inherited system is an inescapable consequence of transition, the strategic shape of the necessary reforms, and some practical ways of implementing reform. A concluding section discusses reform of the welfare state in CEE in the context of global changes.

Helping Labor Markets to Adjust

Policymakers face a series of interrelated problems, all directly related to transition. The first of these is rising open unemployment, which has afflicted all the successful reformers. Open employment is cyclical, caused by falling output and hence by falling demand for labor. It also is structural, arising from labor with the wrong skills or in the wrong place. The burden of unemployment has fallen particularly hard on some groups.

Women were laid off in larger numbers than men in the early transition. Long-term unemployment increased rapidly, as did youth unemployment; and geographical mismatches between jobs and workers produced large and persistent regional variations.

Second, an acute shortage of resources for dealing with the problem is a major constraint, not least because of a collapse in tax revenues.

Third, the shortage of administrative capacity is acute in the face of intractable administrative problems. Part of the problem is that there was no preexisting system on which to build. The old system had employment exchanges, but their function was entirely different: to find *workers* in an era of labor shortage rather than to find *jobs* in the face of rising unemployment. There is a second set of difficulties. In the West, unemployment benefits are designed on the assumption (unrealistic, but tenable) that there is a binary divide between employment and unemployment. In the transition countries, particularly in less-advanced countries, the problem is complicated by the size of the gray economy and the scope for small-scale agriculture. As a result, the distinction between employment and unemployment has become blurred, making it difficult to define unemployment and even more difficult to find measurable indicators that can be implemented cost-effectively to determine whether a particular applicant is, or is not, eligible for benefits (for a discussion of these problems in Russia, see Barr 1993; for a more recent discussion, see Jackman 1998).

Fourth, there are major incentive problems. Because the inherited wage distribution was compressed, the poverty line, unemployment benefit, and the minimum wage in the early transition were very close to each other. The difference between the minimum wage and the average wage also was smaller than is typical in the West, a problem compounded by declining real wages. Although the wage distribution has decompressed significantly in the advanced reformers, acute problems related to the design of benefits persist in countries where wages are low and wage differentials remain relatively small.

Fifth, impediments to occupational and geographical labor mobility include inadequate housing markets and the fact that many social benefits are organized by enterprises.

Finally, the mix of skills is poorly suited to a modern market economy, with major implications for education and training (for fuller discussion, see Barr 2001).

Policies During the Early Transition

Does higher unemployment help reform? The inherited distortions and sharp decline in output made labor shedding from the state sector both necessary and desirable during the early transition (for fuller discussion of strategic policy directions, see Jackman and Rutkowski 1994; Jackman 1998; Boeri, Burda, and Köllő 1998). A central question, however, is whether higher rates of unemployment speed reform. The answer depends on one's point of view (for discussion, see Jackman 1998). In one view, a rapid shakeout of labor creates a pool of unemployed workers on which the growing private sector can draw. The resulting policy strategy is to subsidize unemployment. An alternative view is that, although some unemployment is necessary, private firms prefer to recruit people currently employed in the state sector. High open unemployment, in this view, is not a prerequisite for restructuring. The resulting policy strategy is to subsidize employment.

In part, the argument depends on the nature of unemployment. Employment in industrial countries is largely a binary phenomenon (that is, a person is either employed or unemployed, either employed or retired), whereas in developing economies the problem tends to be that of underemployment. Thus unemployment, to an important degree, is a social construct rooted in the institutional structure of the labor market (Atkinson 1995, ch. 11, emphasizes labor market institutions; on retirement, see Hannah 1986).

Two patterns of labor market adjustment to some extent parallel these two constructs (for fuller discussion of these patterns, see Jackman 1998; Milanovic 1998, 29–30). In most of CEE, the brunt of adjustment has fallen on employment. In several of the countries of the former Soviet Union, in contrast, the brunt of adjustment has fallen on wages rather than employment. Workers often retain their attachment to their enterprises, even with little or no pay, and thus continue to enjoy some enterprise benefits. Disequilibrium has manifested itself through underemployment.

The design of unemployment benefits has to address two problems: rising unemployment and an acute scarcity of both fiscal and administrative resources. In that context, flat-rate benefits offer particular advantages in the early stages of economic transition. They are cheap, since nobody receives benefits above the minimum. They are easier to administer than earnings-related benefits. A third, more arguable, advantage is that flat-rate benefits, by offering most workers a lower replacement rate than earnings-related benefits, create improved incentives to find work.[1] Thus the short-run strategy for unemployment benefits has been to abandon the objectives of insurance and consumption smoothing, concentrating solely on poverty relief. In short, benefits are limited to risk coping (Holzmann and Jorgensen 1999).

While benefits cushion the short-term impact of economic restructuring, active labor market policies address a second aspect of reform by helping people to find earning opportunities through employment or self-employment. Such policies are of three sorts: job information, training measures, and job creation (see Boeri, Burda, and Köllő 1998, ch. 4 for fuller discussion, including the economic rationale for these programs). In the short run, the most that can be done in most transition economies is to introduce simple, cost-effective job-information and job-matching systems, but even these initiatives face significant implementation constraints.

The lack of effective housing markets is a major impediment to labor mobility. Although the issue cannot be solved in the short term, starting reform *is* an early task. A second impediment is the fact that many social benefits are tied to the enterprise. This made sense in an era of full employment, jobs for life, and soft budget constraints. Enterprises administered most short-term benefits, and they paid contributions en bloc on behalf of their workers. As a result, the social insurance and pension authorities knew neither about individual contributors (unnecessary when everyone had a full record of contributions) nor about individual recipients (unnecessary for universal benefits). Thus a system that was rational under the old economic order is dysfunctional in a world where not everyone has a job, where labor mobility is high, and where competitive pressures, especially international competitive pressures, make enterprises sensitive to the compliance costs of benefit administration.

Thus a major direction for reform must be to move most benefits out of the enterprise—for example, transferring most administration of contributions and benefits to the social insurance and pension authorities. This has proved difficult, however: on the one hand, many local administrations are not prepared to accept this burden, while, on the other, many enterprises prefer to continue receiving the state subsidies that flow from support of the firm's social assets.

Thus, although the nature and direction of long-run change are clear, its speed is not. If the strategy, as in the advanced reforming countries (mainly Poland and the Baltic states), is to privatize, restructure, and allow open unemployment, firms must be liberated of their social obligations. If, as in Russia, many workers retain their formal attachment to large state enterprises, the case for decoupling is perhaps less urgent.

Policies for the Medium Term

Policy in the early transition has had to concentrate on poverty relief (that is, concentrating resources on protecting the minimum benefit). But as economic conditions permit, there are advantages to strengthening the relation between contributions and benefits, thus moving toward a system in which contributory benefits provide insurance and consumption smoothing, with poverty relief increasingly based on tax-funded benefits such as social assistance and family allowance. In World Bank parlance

(Holzmann and Jorgensen 1999), this brings risk mitigation back into the social policy picture, as in the Organization for Economic Cooperation and Development (OECD) countries.

As fiscal and administrative constraints relax in the transition economies—as they have in several Baltic states—more sophisticated labor market policies will become an option. However, although there is general agreement about the importance of mechanisms to help match unemployed people with prospective employers, the cost-effectiveness of training and public employment schemes is controversial (see assessments by OECD 1997; Godfrey and Richards 1997; Boeri, Burda, and Köllő 1998). There are two reasons why they do not appear to have made much difference, even in the advanced reformers. First, expenditure on such programs has been low, typically because the rapid growth of unemployment means that benefit spending crowds out active labor market policies. Second, on limited evidence, programs have not been particularly effective, as they fail to address market demand for particular skills.

Summary Assessment

Troubling issues of labor market adjustment to the transition remain. First, the measures discussed in this section have not prevented the emergence of long-term unemployment, particularly in CEE. Western evidence shows that the longer a person remains unemployed, the lower is his or her probability of escaping from unemployment.

A second, more radical, question is whether the strategy of introducing Western-style unemployment benefits—that is, subsidizing unemployment rather than employment—has been the right one. Jackman's (1998, 152) assessment of labor market policy in the transition leads to a disturbing conclusion:

> There would be some point to such a policy if unemployment played a productive role in economic restructuring, but we have seen that the opposite is the case. Unemployment is not the route by which workers move from the declining state sector to the private sector. Unemployed workers are less attractive recruits for private firms than workers in state firms, and a policy leading to higher unemployment may thus have restrained rather than encouraged the growth of the private sector.

Strengthening Poverty Relief

Policymakers face three sets of problems in helping the poor during transition:

- The number of poor people is rising. Poverty has increased sharply in all former-communist countries. Single-person pensioner households and large families have been particularly afflicted.

- The shortage of resources is acute as a consequence of falling output and the resulting fiscal crisis.

- The shortage of administrative capacity is severe in the face of intractable administrative problems. Targeting, particularly via an income test, is administratively demanding at the best of times. Perhaps even more than with unemployment, matters are complicated by the extent of activity in the gray economy. It is therefore difficult to measure income accurately or cost-effectively, reducing the usefulness of income testing as a mechanism for targeting.

Policies During the Early Transition

During the early transition, there is a clear and uncontroversial need for a wide-ranging system of poverty relief capable of administering income support to large numbers of able-bodied people. (For fuller discussion of strategic policy directions, see Sipos 1994; Milanovic 1998.) Depending on fiscal capacity, countries have a choice between two strategies seeking, respectively,

- To eliminate poverty by bringing everyone up to poverty line, or
- To ameliorate poverty by concentrating on the poorest of the poor.

The problem for policymakers is to find ways to implement poverty relief with few resources and little administrative capacity, where income testing is difficult or impossible.

One way forward is to award benefits on the basis of indicators of poverty that can be measured more easily than income—for example, unemployment, ill health, old age, and large numbers of children in the family. (On the analytics of targeting, see Barr 1998a, 237–40; the classic article is by Akerlof 1978.) Indicator targeting has significant advantages over income testing. Where indicators are highly correlated with poverty, targeting is accurate. Where the indicator is beyond the control of the individual, adverse incentive effects are weaker. Further, where the indicator is easily observable, it is less demanding administratively.

This suggests a strategy in which targeting is based on variables such as age (for example, extra assistance to the very elderly), family size, employment status, and health. Although it has major advantages, the approach is not flawless. Indicators are never perfectly correlated with poverty, and, as a result, there are gaps in coverage and leakages of benefit to people who are not poor.

A different approach—as a complement to or substitute for indicator targeting—is through local discretion plus block grants. Localities may be better informed than central government about who is genuinely poor and thus better able to target on a discretionary basis. The World Bank, in particular, has tried to emphasize a decentralized approach to poverty relief.

Under decentralized schemes, benefits can be in the form of cash, in kind, or both. However, when the central government underwrites the costs of local poverty relief, localities have no incentive to contain costs. Thus local discretion should be combined with block grants from the center to localities. The resulting package has the advantage of containing costs and minimizing administrative demands, while being reasonably well targeted.[2] Less optimistically, discretion can have an arbitrary element and thus open the way to horizontal inequity (identical poor families in different localities are treated differently), to corruption, or to discrimination (for example, against the Roma). The approach may be a feasible short-run stopgap but is no panacea.

In sum, a successful strategy for coming to grips with poverty in the early transition would have been based on the following elements:

- focusing benefits on the poorest of the poor;
- using indicator targeting where possible;
- making use of informal mechanisms (at a minimum, legislation needs to facilitate the operation of nongovernmental organizations rather than, as under communism, discourage it); and
- keeping the system as simple as possible, given the constraints on administrative capacity.

Unfortunately, only a few countries have responded appropriately, due to errors associated with transition overload and the political reality that the poor have only a small voice in the transition process. This point reminds us of Peter Lindert's generalization about the role of voice in social transfers in the West.

Policies for the Medium Term

As fiscal and institutional capacity advances, more ambitious antipoverty targets become possible, at least in theory. In the early transition, it is fiscally impossible to bring everybody up to a realistic poverty line (that is, to eliminate poverty), so that concentrating on the poorest of the poor is the only option. Over time, it becomes possible to aim at closing an increasing fraction of the poverty gap. Second, more effective enforcement activity becomes possible on both the tax and benefit sides. Third, as a result, judicious use of income testing becomes more realistic. Finally, as the rule of law builds up and administrative capacity strengthens, a move from discretion toward a rules-based system of poverty relief becomes realistic.

Summary Assessment

An archetypal Western-style scheme of social assistance pays benefits designed to bring people up to a published poverty line on the basis of an income or wealth test. All the transition countries have reformed or introduced systems of social assistance, but, as analyzed by Milanovic (1998), with important differences:

1. Having low income is necessary to qualify for benefits, but in all countries, recipients must also fulfill other criteria, for example, the presence in the household of someone who is old or handicapped.

2. The strategy for poverty relief places heavy reliance on indicator targeting, for example, old-age and disability pensions, family allowance, milk and food for schoolchildren, and additional assistance for regions with disproportionate numbers of poor people.

3. Assistance is often in kind.

4. Benefits are designed to alleviate poverty, not to eliminate it; benefits are not intended to make up the whole of the difference between a family's income and the poverty line.

5. Administration is often local, and benefits may depend on the local availability of resources—that is, there is a local budget constraint.[3]

These deviations from Western-style benefit systems respect the constraints facing transition countries. They minimize the requirement to measure income exactly (the second element), attempt to respect fiscal constraints (the first and fourth elements and to some extent the fifth), and minimize administrative demands (the third and fifth elements) and thus can be argued, at least strategically, to be moves in the right direction.

Table 2.1 draws on Milanovic's (1999) study of social assistance in five countries, based on household surveys, to characterize the different systems for disbursing benefits:

- Concentrated systems, in Milanovic's terminology, disburse generous benefits to relatively few households. Coverage is narrow, but deep. Poland pays social assistance to only 3.7 percent of households (line 1) but, partly for that reason, pays

Table 2.1   The Effectiveness of Poverty Relief in Select Countries

Indicator	Poland 1993	Estonia 1995	Hungary 1993	Russia 1993	Bulgaria 1995
Coverage (percentage of households receiving social assistance)	3.7	2.7	24.4	13	2.55
Average benefit per recipient household (U.S. dollars per month)	54	33	17	5	10
Benefit as a percentage of expenditure of recipient households	22.1	14.8	4.7	3.5	4.1
Targeting efficiency (percentage of social assistance expenditure going to the lowest decile)	20.5	34.7	27.2	8.2	22.3
Effectiveness in relieving poverty (spending on social assistance as a percentage of the poverty gap of the lowest decile)	9.4	7	28.8	3.3	1.3

Source: Milanovic (1999, tables 11 and 12).

the most generous average benefit of $54 a month, making up 22 percent of a recipient household's total spending. Estonia has adopted a similar approach.

- Dispersed systems pay relatively small benefits to relatively large numbers of households, that is, coverage is broad, but thin. Hungary, with nearly one-quarter of households receiving benefits, has by far the greatest coverage, followed by Russia, with 13 percent. In both countries, however, benefits cover less than 5 percent of recipients' expenditure.

- Irrelevant systems pay small benefits to few people and hence do little to relieve poverty. Bulgaria is a case in point.

How effective are these expenditures in relieving poverty? The fourth line of table 2.1 gives a measure of targeting efficiency, defined as the percentage of total social assistance expenditure going to the poorest 10 percent of households. Targeting is far from perfect: even in Estonia, the country with the tightest targeting, only about one-third of social assistance spending goes to the lowest decile of households. Targeting in Russia is staggeringly bad—the poorest 10 percent of the population receives considerably *less* than 10 percent of social assistance spending.

Targeting is a measure of *who* benefits; the last line of the table measures *how much* they benefit, showing the extent to which spending on social assistance reduces the poverty gap for the lowest 10 percent of households.[4] In Hungary, with relatively generous benefits for a large fraction of households, benefits relieve nearly 30 percent of the shortfall below the poverty line of the incomes of the poorest decile. In Poland social assistance relieves close to 10 percent. In Bulgaria, in contrast, it relieves barely more than 1 percent of the poverty gap of the poorest 10 percent of households.

A major implication of these figures is how much poverty remains unrelieved, even in the advanced reformers.

Reforming Pensions

With unemployment benefits and poverty relief, the central targeting problem is to avoid gaps in coverage. With pensions, the targeting issue is different: to avoid fiscally unaffordable leakage of benefits (for fuller discussion of pension reform, see Barr 1994; 2000).

The old system of pensions, although perhaps well adapted to the old economic order, is ill adapted in several ways to the needs of a market economy.

The first problem is related to access to benefits. In the early transition, retirement age is low, an outcome regarded as one of the victories of socialism. In addition, many workers receive a pension below that age, for example, the concessions to miners, military personnel, and civil servants and, in some countries, ballerinas, teachers, and the like; access to disability pensions is also generous. The number of pensioners is increased further by generous early-retirement provisions in the early transition. According to the World Bank (1996, 78),

> as a result [of low pensionable age], the typical woman in the Czech Republic enjoys five more years of retirement than her American counterpart and seven years more than her German counterpart. For men the difference is closer to one year. The comparison for Hungary, Poland, and Russia is broadly similar.

For more detail, see Barr (1999, table 11.1).

A second problem is the unsustainable cost. Pension spending is high in almost all the transition countries. The worst case is Poland, where public pension spending in 1997 was 15 percent of gross domestic product (GDP). The comparable figure was 14 percent in Slovenia, above 10 percent in Croatia, Latvia, and Macedonia, and around 9 percent in the Czech Republic and Hungary. The primary cause of this high spending is not generous pensions, but the large number of pensioners resulting from the low retirement age. Table 2.2 illustrates the scale of the problem. Column 1 shows the age dependency ratio (that is, the fraction of the population of pensionable age), and column 2 shows the system dependency ratio (that is, the fraction of the population receiving a pension). If nobody below pensionable age received a pension, the ratio of column 2 to column 1 would be 100 percent. In reality, there are always some recipients below pensionable age—for example, disability pensioners—so there is always some "leakage." In Croatia, Latvia, and Lithuania, the leakage was around 20 percent in 1996. In Poland, in contrast, the leakage was 75 percent, and in Slovenia it was 86 percent. Thus in Poland and Slovenia, close to half of all pensioners were below the official pensionable age in 1996.

A third problem is that pensions are generally low—the result of a head-on collision between ease of access and fiscal constraints. The result is like trying to spread a small piece of butter over an enormous slice of bread: giving too little to too many at too high a fiscal cost.

Finally, privileged groups receive generous pensions. The various concessions to particular groups like miners have already been mentioned. Although pensions always have a political dimension, such concessions are the outcome of nontransparent politics.

Table 2.2   Age Dependency Ratio and System Dependency Ratio in Select Countries, 1996

Country	Age Dependency Ratio (1)	System Dependency Ratio (2)	Ratio of (2) to (1) (Percentage)
Croatia	32.3[a]	39	121
Estonia	35	46	131
Hungary	36	41	114
Latvia	35	42	120
Lithuania	32	39	122
Poland	28[a]	49[a]	175
Russia	30.5	46[a]	151
Slovenia	29[a]	54[a]	186

Source: Author's compilation based on European Bank for Reconstruction and Development data.
[a] 1995 data.

Strategic Policy Directions During the Early Transition

The inherited system of pensions was organized on a pay-as-you-go (PAYG) basis—that is, pensions were paid out of current contributions and taxes. One strand of reform concerns the introduction of private, funded arrangements, in which pensions are paid from an accumulated fund built over a period of years out of the contributions of its members.

Increasing output is by far the most complete solution, not least through its effect on fiscal capacity (for fuller discussion of the underlying analytics, see Barr 1998a, ch. 9). However, in all but a handful of advanced reformers, output remains below its 1989 level. Thus achieving higher output is more a medium-term solution.

Reducing the number of pensioners is the second approach. Raising the retirement age has been discussed, and Poland, Hungary, Croatia, and the Czech Republic have legislated a higher retirement age. However, the average age of retirement has not yet risen. Indeed, the average age at which a pension is first paid has declined in most countries (World Bank 1996, 78). Although the facts are clear, policy is a difficult balance between competing objectives. The reason for raising the pensionable age is to reduce public spending. There are two arguments for caution. First, moving too precipitately risks the political sustainability of the reforms. Second, the demotivating and debilitating effects of long-run unemployment, especially for the young, are well known.

Another way of reducing the number of pensioners is by withdrawing the right to combine work and pension. Again, there is a conflict of objectives. On the one hand, current policy is costly. This suggests that there should be a retirement test (for example, withdrawing the pension, partly or wholly, from anyone who earns more than a fairly small amount). The counterargument is that early retirement makes it easier to make older workers redundant and thus assists restructuring. This suggests that, during the early transition, rather than impose a *retirement* test, it is worth considering a change-of-job test, whereby individuals who retire but find another job are allowed to keep at least part of their pension. This approach is easier in theory than in practice. Soviet enterprises were adept at organizing fictitious job changes.

Reducing the average pension is the remaining policy direction. Up to a point, pensioners have been relatively protected in comparison with other groups in the population. Milanovic finds that "poverty rates for people of retirement age . . . are only about one half of the country average in Hungary and Poland, and even less in the Czech Republic and Slovakia" (Milanovic 1998, 102–3). This finding should not be misinterpreted. The fact that pensioners are *relatively* protected does not mean that they are *fully* protected in absolute terms. Real pensions have declined: in many countries the pension is not indexed, so that over time people are pulled down to the minimum pension (which is indexed), approximating a system of flat-rate pensions. In addition, evidence suggests that single-person pensioner households—disproportionately very old women—are prominent among the poor.

In the short run, the ability to contain pension spending may be very limited. Perhaps this is the right outcome, not only on grounds of practicability and political feasibility but also on grounds of intergenerational equity. A case can be made for special treatment of the current older generation. According to World Bank (1996, 80), "In much of CEE and the [Commonwealth of Independent States] inflation destroyed the financial savings of the elderly. Unlike the young, they will not have the opportunity to recoup their losses in the market economy. A case can therefore be made on equity grounds for special treatment."

Strategic Policy Directions in the Medium Term

Output growth has resumed in most of the reforming countries, and the number of countries whose income exceeds that prior to transition will increase, correspondingly easing pension finance.

The first strategy is to increase the age of retirement. The only politically feasible (and, arguably, the only fair) way to do so is to phase in the change over time.

The second strategy is to strengthen the relation between contributions and pensions. There are at least three reasons for strengthening the relationship once economic conditions permit: to promote equity, since the early retirement provisions for privileged groups discriminate against other groups in the workforce; to minimize distortions to individual retirement decisions; and to reduce the strong incentive to evade contributions that exists if workers do not see a clear relationship between contributions and benefits.

Although there is a strong case for strengthening the relationship between contributions and benefits, the extent to which the relationship is *strictly* actuarial is a policy option—that is, individual benefits do not have to be related exactly to contributions, but benefits should be related *at the margin* to individual contributions, and contributors and beneficiaries should perceive this to be so. The argument is important. Suppose that benefits are strictly actuarial. If worker A's lifetime earnings are twice those of worker B, A will get a pension of (say) 200, and B will get one of 100. An alternative approach is to include some redistribution, so that A's pension at age sixty-five is (say) 175, and B's is 125, but to ensure that the adjustment for early retirement is fully actuarial. Thus if A retires at sixty-two, his pension is not 175; it is reduced actuarially to reflect the fact that he will be retired for three years longer. This arrangement ensures that, at the margin, people face an actuarially determined budget constraint and hence no artificial incentives to early retirement. This is possible even if the pension overall contains some redistribution.

The third strategy is to phase in private pensions. This topic is discussed in more detail later in this section.

Reforming State Pensions

There have been much discussion and significant action on pension reform throughout CEE. From a welter of detail, two strategic trends emerge: a move toward more actuarial state pensions and a move toward private, funded, second- and third-tier pensions. Both aspects are discussed more fully by Rutkowski (2001).

Pension reform in several transition countries has been influenced by recent reform in Sweden, where legislation passed in June 1998 introduced what is known as a "notional defined-contribution" state pension (Sweden, Federation of Social Insurance Offices 1998).[5] Poland's reform introduced a first-tier pension based on a similar conception (for more detailed discussion, see Góra and Rutkowski 1998). The key features of the Polish scheme are as follows:

- It is a universal, mandatory, publicly managed PAYG scheme financed by social insurance contributions.

- Although this year's contributions are paid out in this year's benefits, the social insurance authorities open a notional (or virtual) individual account that keeps track of contributions, just as for a "real" fund. Specifically, each worker's cumulative account attracts a notional interest rate reflecting average income growth.

- Benefits are defined contribution, in the sense that a person's pension is actuarially related to her lifetime contribution. Specifically, her pension depends only on the extent of her notional capital accumulation, her age at retirement, and the average life expectancy of the relevant cohort.

- During a contributor's working life, her notional fund is indexed in line with the growth of the real wage bill (and hence in line with trends in productivity and employment); in retirement, pensions are indexed to a pensioner price index.

- The minimum retirement age is sixty-two for men and women; other than that, the decision to retire is a matter of individual choice, the pension being actuarially adjusted.

Latvia has introduced a similar scheme. Hungary, in contrast, has adopted less far-reaching reforms to its state pension (see Gerencsér 1997; International Social Security Association 1998, 16–17). Under reforms in 1998, the state pension was amended by increasing the retirement age to sixty-two for men and women, strengthening the link between contributions and benefits, increasing the qualifying period for full pension, subjecting benefits to taxation, and making indexation less generous. In Croatia, the retirement age is being raised over time to sixty-five for men and sixty for women, and the pension formula is being made less generous by basing pensions on a person's full career rather than on his or her best ten years and by changing the basis of indexation. Pension reform in other CEE countries, for example the Czech Republic, has been more modest, mostly aimed at improving the sustainability of the PAYG scheme.

The idea of notional defined-contribution pensions is for social insurance pensions to mimic an annuity, in that the pension a person receives bears an explicit relationship to contributions, is based on lifetime contributions, and is adjusted for life expectancy and economic developments. Individuals can respond by adjusting their age of retirement. The introduction of life expectancy is an important innovation.

There are important arguments in favor of these arrangements. First, they simultaneously give people choice *and* face them with efficient incentives. For example, they assist choice about retirement by allowing people to choose their preferred tradeoff between *duration* of retirement and *living standards* in retirement but face them with the actuarial cost of those decisions. In addition, the closer is the connection between contributions and benefits, the greater is the extent to which contributions are perceived as contributions rather than taxation; to that extent, notional defined-contribution schemes reduce the tax wedge. In contrast, as Gruber and Wise (1998) show, badly designed state schemes contain incentives that can have strong adverse effects. There are a number of disadvantages, not least the fact that such schemes do not redistribute from rich to poor, which conflicts with some people's definition of equity.

These arguments point to something that is insufficiently understood—there is much flexibility *within* PAYG schemes. Many of the problems of state social insurance systems are not inherent in the social insurance mechanism; they are soluble. Thus the reforms in Poland and Latvia represent considerable progress. Most particularly, making the retirement age endogenous, albeit the obvious solution, is a major advance.

Introducing Private Pensions

Virtually all countries have discussed the introduction of private, funded pensions, and a significant number have begun drawing up legislation, including Estonia, Hungary, Latvia, Lithuania, Poland, and Slovenia among the CEE and Baltic countries and Russia, Ukraine, and Kazakhstan among the countries of the former Soviet Union. In Poland, Hungary, Croatia, and Latvia, the initial phase of reform has already been enacted.

The Polish reforms take an integrated approach. Alongside the first tier is a mandatory, privately managed, defined-contribution second tier. The two tiers are closely linked: they use the same contribution base and retirement age, both are defined contribution, and both are mandatory for people born after 1969.

The second-tier pensions are managed by competing funds. Regulation of those funds includes constraints on the composition of their investments and major requirements about disclosure of information. The freedom of individuals to change funds is heavily circumscribed. These arrangements are supplemented by a third tier of voluntary contributions, with incentives to encourage employees and employers to set up voluntary group pension schemes.

Hungary, too, has introduced a second-tier pension through individual funded accounts. Such funds may be established by employers, professional associations, the Pensions Insurance Administration, voluntary pension funds, or local governments. Each pension fund must be approved by the newly established Pension Fund Supervision Office. In contrast with Poland, individuals are free to move between funds provided they pay the costs of such a move (see Gerencsér 1997).

Croatia also has legislated to bring in second-tier pensions, which became mandatory for people under forty as of July 2000. The scheme is financed by diverting a fraction of pension contributions to individual accounts. A number of other countries, notably Estonia and Latvia, are actively considering a mandatory, private, funded second-tier pension.

Kazakhstan is an outlier: in advocating a move to a Chilean-type system, in which mandatory, privately managed, competitive, funded pensions replace the state scheme, the government is contemplating reform that would be radical for any country and a fortiori for a Central Asian country.

How should these developments be assessed? In an overview paper like this, detailed, country-by-country assessment is neither possible nor desirable. Elsewhere (Barr 2001), I have put forward four key arguments that provide the necessary background for assessing actual and proposed reforms: private pensions have important prerequisites; the range of choice over pension design is large; risk is unavoidable in any scheme, whether public or private, funded or pay-as-you-go; and the links between funding and growth are complex and controversial.

The discussion that follows is, for the most part, limited to the first two topics, which are central to assessment of pension reform. A conclusion considers the overall strategy of a move toward private pensions.

Prerequisites   In discussing pension reform, it is useful to distinguish prerequisites that apply to *all* reforms, over which policymakers have little choice, and features over which policymakers have to make explicit choices.

A number of apparently obvious points about financial assets and markets are usefully emphasized. First, private pensions require that government and citizens are reasonably well informed about the operation of financial markets. In some less-advanced reforming countries, there is still a belief, even at high levels of government, that if a fund is "private" and the money is "invested," a high real rate of return is inevitable. Second, and equally obvious, funded schemes require financial assets for pension funds to hold and financial markets to channel savings into their most productive use. Two apparent solutions are blind alleys. If pension funds hold only government bonds, the resulting schemes are PAYG, with no budgetary gain, no channeling of resources into productive investment, and considerable extra administrative cost. Another option is to get round the lack of domestic financial markets by buying financial assets in the West. This approach, however, entirely forgoes the growth-inducing potential of private pensions.

Private sector capacity is essential, given the heavy administrative demands of private pensions. Inadequate capacity runs the risk that excessive administrative costs will erode the investment return to pensioners, at its worst putting at risk the viability of private funds. Since there is a fixed cost to running an individual pension account, the issue is of particular concern for small pensions.

Effective government is essential whichever approach to pensions is adopted (see Barr 1996 for fuller discussion). Bad government harms PAYG schemes through fiscally irresponsible promises. Bad government also can harm funded schemes. As Thompson (1998, 22) puts it,

> It is also too early to know how effectively the new systems based on the defined contribution model will be insulated from irresponsible behavior. Politicians are not the only people who are prone to promise more than they can deliver. The defined contribution model requires sophisticated oversight and regulation to ensure that one set of problems resulting from public sector political dynamics is not simply traded for a different set of problems derived from the dynamics of private sector operations.

Nor is this a problem only for countries with less well-developed governments, as the British pension reform scandal amply illustrates (for fuller discussion, see U.K. Pension Law Review Committee 1993; U.K. Treasury Select Committee 1998).

In contrast, effective government assists both state and private schemes:

- Governments throughout the OECD are putting into place cost-containing measures in the face of demographic prospects (see U.K. Department of Social Security 1993). Recent reform in Sweden and earlier reform in the United Kingdom are prime examples.

- For private schemes, effective government is necessary to ensure macroeconomic stability vital to protect pension accumulations, which are sensitive to unanticipated inflation and to ensure effective regulatory capacity in financial markets for reasons of consumer protection in areas too complex for consumers to protect themselves.

The key lesson from countries like Chile, which has adopted radical pension reform, is that successful reform rests on two legs: private sector capacity *and* government capacity. There is an essential role for the state in pensions, even if one distrusts politicians.

Political sustainability is a fourth prerequisite. Pension reform, particularly large-scale reform such as the introduction of funded pensions, is not an event but a process. Pension reform needs continuing commitment from government, both for technical reasons and to encourage continuing political support. Reform regarded as a single, once-and-for-all event runs the risk of neglect, discredit, and eventual reversal (on the politics of pension reform in Hungary, see Nelson 1998).

Transparency is important both for political reasons, to ensure the legitimacy and hence political sustainability of reform, and for economic reasons, as a necessary ingredient if pensions are to fulfill their efficiency function of steering savings into their most productive investment use (for fuller discussion of the importance of fiscal transparency, see International Monetary Fund 1998). With state pensions, transparency is needed regarding their cost to the taxpayer and the relation between contributions and benefits. With private pensions, there should be transparency about the costs of tax relief and annual statements detailing a person's pension accumulation, predicted pension, and administrative charges. Chile sets a good example for more advanced countries by requiring information to be issued to pensioners in a standard way, thus ensuring direct comparability between the claims of competing funds.[6]

Table 2.3 summarizes the essential prerequisites and serves as a checklist for policymakers contemplating pension reform and as a guide to commentators assessing actual or proposed reforms. In meeting these prerequisites, advanced reformers like Poland and Hungary have the capacity for the sort of sophisticated reforms they are proposing.[7] It was precisely because of the demonstrable failure to meet several of the pre-

Table 2.3   Prerequisites for Pension Reform

Prerequisite	Essential for State Scheme	Essential for Private Schemes
Public sector prerequisites		
Budgetary sustainability of state scheme	✓	
Political sustainability of pension reform package	✓	✓
Capacity to maintain macro-economic stability	✓	✓
Effective regulatory capacity		✓
Private sector prerequisites		
Financial assets		✓
Financial markets		✓
Adequate private sector administrative capacity		✓

Source: Author's compilation.

requisites that in 1998 the World Bank—courageously but completely correctly—withdrew its support for proposals to bring in mandatory second-tier pensions in Russia. Reference to the same criteria calls seriously into question the strategic direction of reform in Kazakhstan.

The Range of Choice   Pension design is controversial. A central debate is whether there is a single, dominant strategy. My answer is that there is not and that policymakers face a large range of choices (for fuller discussion, see World Bank 1996, 81–83). The following questions far from exhaust the list: Should the first-tier pension be a minimum guarantee or larger? Should the first tier be more redistributive or less redistributive? Should a second-tier pension be funded or PAYG? Should it be managed by the state (Canada) or by the private sector (Australia, Latin America)? Should membership of a second tier be voluntary (Czech Republic) or compulsory (Chile)? Should opting out of state arrangements be allowed (United Kingdom) or not (United States)? How broadly should risks be shared: should the individual face all the risk (individual, defined-contribution schemes), or should risk be shared with employers (employer defined-benefit schemes) or shared with the taxpayer (where private schemes receive some sort of state guarantee)? To what extent does the state assist with indexing pensions—an important issue since pensions based on an annuity are vulnerable to unanticipated inflation?

The purpose of listing these questions (and there are many others) is to illustrate the potential range of choice facing policymakers. Answers will depend not only on economic variables but also on a country's culture and history. In the transition countries, given the range of choice and the extent of misinformation, well-informed public debate is particularly critical to ensure that any reforms, once enacted, take root.

How Useful Is the Move Toward Private Pensions?   This is not the place for an overall assessment of the role of private pensions.[8] The point I want to make is more narrow, namely to warn against relying on private pensions to solve problems they cannot solve. Pension systems in the countries of CEE face acute fiscal pressures and, separately, demographic pressures, both of which have motivated much of the discussion of private pensions. However, private pensions qua private pensions solve neither problem. In the short run, the only solution to excessive public pension spending is to make state pensions less generous. In the medium term, the only solution is to increase output. Funding does nothing to address the first; and, as discussed in Barr (2000), the impact of funding on output growth is complex and controversial and is, in any case, only one of a considerable menu of policies that contribute to growth.

The conclusion I would like to suggest is twofold:

- A rush to private pensions in the face of fiscal and demographic pressures is misplaced, since funding per se addresses neither problem directly.

- The sequencing of pension reform is more subtle than some literature suggests. At a minimum, there should be no such move unless the prerequisites can be met.

The Welfare State in a Changing World

This section puts forward six interlinked propositions. Together they argue that the "crisis" of the welfare state should not be overstated, indeed that the welfare state, properly constructed, is desirable in equity terms, essential in efficiency terms, and, in the post-communist countries, necessary to maintain continuing political support for reform.

Proposition 1: The Welfare State Has Benefits as Well as Costs

There has been much recent discussion about the fiscal sustainability of the welfare state. In many OECD countries, public spending on the welfare state absorbs 25 percent of GDP and in some countries more. Economics has important things to say about designing systems so as to avoid excessive spending, that is, spending whose costs (through disincentive effects) in terms of reduced economic growth outweigh its benefits. There are two lines of counterargument. First (proposition 3), the arguments that the welfare state is fiscally unsustainable should not be oversimplified. Second, economists of all people should need no reminder of the flaws in an argument that considers costs but ignores benefits.

Expenditure on the welfare state is not just "unproductive spending"; rather it has major benefits. In equity terms, the welfare state serves at a minimum to provide poverty relief. For many voters and policymakers, it also has a broader role: to reduce relative poverty, to reduce income inequality, to reduce other dimensions of inequality (for example, by gender or ethnic origin), and—at its broadest—to address social exclusion.

In addition to its equity purposes, the welfare state has an important efficiency role in the face of major market failures (the central argument in Barr 1992). It offers insurance against risks, including unemployment, inflation, and important medical risks, which private markets either would not insure at all or would insure badly in the sense of providing an inefficiently low level of cover. For these reasons, a welfare state of some sort would continue to be necessary even if all distributional problems had been solved—for example, even if the world consisted only of educated, healthy, articulate middle-class people.

If the welfare state had only costs (what might be called—perhaps unfairly—the Ministry of Finance view), the objective for policymakers would be to minimize those costs. Given its benefits, the objective is to optimize spending rather than minimize it. To illustrate the argument, consider what most citizens want. A plausible answer is that they want growth (rising living standards) and security. The challenge to the welfare state is simultaneously to promote security by offering mechanisms for consumption smoothing, insurance, and poverty relief and to assist growth. The welfare state can do so positively. For example, an effective system of unemployment compensation assists labor mobility; it also does so in a passive sense, through fiscally sustainable expenditure levels, thus not interfering with growth deriving from other sources.

The issue for policymakers is one of balance. Suppose that in state-of-the-world A (unreconstructed capitalism), there is little security, but rapid growth; if many people (even the better off) are prepared to vote for slightly lower growth in exchange for greater security, welfare is improved by introducing mechanisms that increase security. This is a stylized representation of the development of the welfare state in the OECD for most of the twentieth century.[9] In state-of-the-world B (communism), there is considerable material security, but growth rates are negligible or even negative. People are therefore prepared (as in the former-communist countries) to vote for arrangements that offer higher living standards but at a cost of reduced security. In short, too little security is welfare-reducing; so is too much.

Proposition 2: Structure Should Not Be Confused with Scale

The distinction between structure and scale is critical. There are two questions:

- What is the appropriate *structure* of the state's activity (that is, the public-private mix)? Which activities should be publicly funded or publicly produced, and which should become largely or wholly private? This issue is essentially technical: market allocation is preferable where markets work well; public activity may be warranted in the presence of major market failures.

- What should be their *scale* (that is, what should be the level of public spending on the welfare state)? This is largely a matter of budgetary balance.

It is important to keep the two issues logically distinct. Structure is a microeconomic matter: the central question is whether or not market failures are sufficiently large and government sufficiently effective for intervention to be welfare improving. Scale, in contrast, is largely a macroeconomic matter, although it also has a significant political economy dimension.

Thus a fiscal crisis is *not* an argument for privatization (which should be decided on the basis of whether the state or the private sector is more efficient), but an argument for reducing the scale of the activity.

Proposition 3: Fiscal Pressures Should Not Be Over-Simplified

The argument that the welfare state is unsustainable and therefore should be rolled back is criticized by Atkinson (1999) as being too simple. One of his main conclusions is that richer theory leads to a more complex range of outcomes than the simple unsustainability–roll-back argument suggests (Atkinson 1999, 8):

> The emphasis by economists on the negative economic effects of the welfare state can be attributed to the theoretical framework adopted, . . . which remains rooted in a model of perfectly competitive and perfectly clearing markets. *[This] theoretical framework incorporates none of the contingencies for which the welfare state exists* . . . The whole purpose of welfare state provision is missing from the theoretical model. (emphasis added)

Atkinson's point, which harks back to proposition 1, is that a model based on perfect information and market clearing systematically rules out the market failures that the welfare state is intended to address. The choice of such a model focuses entirely on the cost side and implicitly rules out some of the welfare state's main benefits. This is *not* an argument that fiscal constraints should be ignored, but an argument that policy needs to be based on richer theory that incorporates market failures.

Proposition 4: Global Pressures Should Not Be Exaggerated

The core of the globalization argument is that, because of technological change, much economic activity has become "dematerialized," that is, takes the form of computer-transmitted information. As a result, national boundaries become porous, making competition global and reducing the freedom of any country to conduct an independent economic policy. The argument is important. Many activities are genuinely becoming more global, as exemplified by growing commercial activity over the Internet. But the implications for the welfare state are not necessarily apocalyptic.

The world is not wholly global. Although global competition is powerful, it is not all-powerful. Not all goods are tradable. Nor are all factors mobile: labor mobility is reduced by choice (people generally maximize utility rather than profit; they prefer to stay with their language, culture, and family); mobility is also reduced by constraints such as immigration controls. For these and other reasons, Burtless (1996) concludes that the globalization of the U.S. economy explains less than one-fifth of the large increase in inequality in the United States since 1970.

The Western countries can and will adapt. The distinction between structure and scale has already been stressed. Free capital movement might mean that countries with low social spending can exert competitive pressures on OECD countries. That, however, is not an argument for dismantling the welfare state, still less for radical structural change such as privatization. If it is believed that welfare state spending is incompatible with fiscal constraints, the answer is to make it less generous (for example, the Swedish pension reforms), not to seek spurious solutions through privatization. For this reason governments throughout the OECD are taking measures to restrain welfare state spending (U.K. Department of Social Security 1993).

The newly industrialized countries may also adapt. A third reason why globalization is not the death knell for the welfare state is that in all the industrial countries, social spending has been a superior good: as incomes have risen, electorates have voted to increase the share of such spending in GDP. In some countries, the process may have gone too far, but that does not mean that the premise is flawed. Unless the countries of East Asia are very different, rising incomes and weakening family ties will lead to demands for rising social expenditures.

A plausible outcome of global competition is some convergence between the OECD and Asian countries. Competition will continue at the margin to exert downward pressure on wages and social benefits in the OECD; rising incomes will lead to increased social spending in the newly industrializing countries.

Proposition 5: Country Differences Matter

Objectives may differ, albeit only in terms of emphasis; more important, the constraints countries face differ enormously.

Objectives may differ. Consider the balance between individualism and social solidarity. As a very broad illustration, it can be argued that the Americas (North and South) tend to put more weight on individualism (including voluntary charity). This is explicit in much U.S. political discourse, and it is implicit in the pension reforms adopted by Chile in the 1980s. Many European countries, in contrast, give more weight to social solidarity (a term hardly used in U.S. debate). As a result, welfare-state-type institutions in Europe tend to be more fully articulated, and welfare state spending tends to be proportionately higher than in America. From a European perspective, the United States is in many ways an outlier on social policy. It is not *the* model, but *a* model.

Constraints differ across at least four dimensions:

- *Economic:* Countries where income is lower and fiscal constraints consequently tighter can afford only parsimonious benefits.

- *Institutional:* Countries with limited institutional capacity can implement only administratively simple structures.

- *Social:* Social spending is lower in countries where enterprises play a larger role or where the Confucian tradition allows continued reliance on the extended family.

- *Political:* Social spending is lower in countries with less political support for redistributive policies.

In comparison with the countries of Central and Eastern Europe, the East Asian economies have a more-or-less single, overriding objective: economic growth and a political consensus that, by implication, gives a fairly low weight to equity objectives and to social solidarity. They tend to have authoritarian regimes. Notwithstanding post-communist reform, they face fewer constraints than the countries of Central and Eastern Europe: China apart, they have well-developed market systems, a sophisticated banking system (albeit one in need of reform), and well-developed capital markets; and they need no *overall* restructuring. The last, together with their high level of spending on education, means that they have a more appropriate mix of skills than countries with a legacy of communist education. Finally, the extended family remains a significant, albeit declining, part of their social structure. The message is *not* that post-communist countries have nothing to learn from those of East Asia, but that East Asian institutions cannot simply be transferred to countries with less clear-cut objectives and very different constraints.

The same set of arguments explains how institutions may converge over time. Rising real incomes in the East Asian countries are already leading to demands for higher public social spending, for example, recently enacted systems of unemployment benefit in South Korea, Thailand, Singapore, and Taiwan. Operating in the same direction, increased urbanization and the declining force of Confucianism will create pressures to increase welfare state spending (as an example of weakening family ties, recent legislation in Singapore empowers parents to sue children who fail to support them adequately in old age). In Europe, conversely, international competitive pressures (together with an aging population) might well exert downward pressure on the generosity of benefits.

These pressures are real, but not overriding. Differences will remain both in objectives and in constraints and, as proposition 4 suggests, these differences will not be eliminated by international pressures. Choices remain, as the range of choice over pension reform makes clear. Country differences matter and will continue to matter. One size does not fit all.

Concluding Proposition: The Crisis in the Welfare State Should Not Be Overstated

In some countries, given demographic trends, past promises may be too generous to be compatible with fiscal constraints. Countries have responded by making promises less generous, the reform of the Swedish pension system being an important example. A more sophisticated set of arguments making the same point can be found in Atkinson (1999).

Esping-Andersen (1996) argues that political and other institutions are enormously important for managing potential conflict between efficiency and distributional objectives. He argues that during the 1950s and 1960s, and in some countries longer, it was possible to pursue distributional objectives with little efficiency cost because there was a consensus of acquiescence to wage restraint in return for full employment (see also Atkinson and Mogensen 1993; Blank 1994). That consensus, it can be argued, underpinned the early success of Keynesian policies, providing a positive-sum solution to the tradeoff between growth and equity. According to this view, institutions have become more fragmented. Because of changes in social norms (Lindbeck 1997) and a weakening of some institutions, the tradeoff between growth and equity is now less favorable than formerly (for theoretical discussion of how social customs can influence economic outcomes, see Akerlof 1980).

Although the issue is of critical importance, it does not counsel despair. Parts of the system clearly require change—generous tax-funded pensions, for example, are more feasible the fewer the number of pensioners. In this area, as elsewhere, the welfare state is adapting:

- There is emphasis in many countries on improving the incentive structure of the benefit system.

- The generosity of some benefits is being reduced, both for economic and, in some countries, political reasons.

- Other reforms, such as raising the age of retirement, are part of the menu of options.

The welfare state will continue to adapt. Demographic and global change will continue to create pressure to contain total spending: in consequence, pensions and health care will continue to face resource constraints, creating upward pressure on the age of retirement. Not least because of labor market trends, inequality will be a continuing problem. There will be pressures for social insurance to become more actuarial: such moves, if well designed, could facilitate labor market flexibility and enable women, in the face of more fluid family structures, to have their own pension entitlement. There will be mounting pressure for new insurance instruments (public, private, or mixed) to cover contingencies, such as long-term care in old age. New lending instruments will emerge: for example, income-contingent loans will increasingly pay for part of the costs of postcompulsory education and training (see, for example, Barr 1998b).

In all these points, the word "adapting" is key. The welfare state faces problems; as a result, its institutions adapt; this does not mean that there is a crisis. The proper debate is about the form and extent of adaptation.

Notes

1. The replacement rate is the ratio of income from benefits to net income from work, that is, with a 40 percent replacement rate, an unemployed person receives benefits equal to 40 percent of his or her previous wage.

2. Variations on the underlying principle are possible. It has been suggested in one transition country, for example, that block grants from central government cover 80 percent of estimated local needs coupled with a 50 percent matching grant up to 120 percent of local needs. This approach contains

third-party incentives, while simultaneously giving localities an incentive to use some local resources.

3. One argument for local administration is lack of administrative capacity at the center. However, there are other reasons—for example, flexibility and responsiveness to local needs. Thus a number of Western European countries also administer at least some poverty relief locally.

4. The poverty gap is the total shortfall of people's income from the poverty line, as a fraction of either the poverty line or total income. The first index measures the depth of poverty; the second measures the relative cost of relieving it.

5. With private pensions, under a *defined-contribution* scheme, a person's pension is an annuity whose size is determined *only* by the size of her lifetime pension accumulation. Thus the individual bears the risk of varying rates of return to pension assets. Under a *defined-benefit* scheme, usually run at a firm or industry level, the firm pays an annuity based on the employee's wage in his or her final year (or final few years) of work and on length of service (a typical formula is one-eightieth of final salary per year of service). Thus the risk of varying rates of return to pension assets falls on the employer (and also on the taxpayer).

6. Hidden charges for private pensions are a besetting problem in the United Kingdom and one on which policy action is urgently needed. As a simple example of what is needed, all credit card companies in Western countries are required to use the same definition of the interest rate they charge customers in their promotional literature, making it easy for people to see which company is offering the best rate.

7. Visiting Poland, in January 1990, I was faced with a radical pension privatization proposal at a time when the monthly inflation rate was 80 percent and when, since there were no financial markets, there was no financial market regulation, violating two essential prerequisites. Things are very different now.

8. For contrasting views, see World Bank (1994) and Feldstein (1996), which are in favor of private pensions, and Beatty and McGillivray (1995) and Aaron and Reischauer (1998), which are more skeptical. For an assessment of reforms in Chile in the 1980s, see Diamond (1996).

9. The tradeoff between growth and security was more acute at some times than at others. Not least because of a political consensus to accept slightly lower wage increases in return for full employment, the tradeoff between growth and security in much of Western Europe in the twenty-five years after the end of World War II was particularly benign.

References

Aaron, Henry J., and Robert D. Reischauer. 1998. "The Case for Preserving Social Security: How Should It Be Done?" In *Countdown to Reform: The Great Social Security Debate*. New York: Century Foundation.

Akerlof, George A. 1978. "The Economics of 'Tagging' as Applied to the Optimal Income Tax, Welfare Programs, and Manpower Planning." *American Economic Review* 68(1): 8–19.

———. 1980. "A Theory of Social Custom of Which Unemployment May Be One Consequence." *Quarterly Journal of Economics* 94(June): 749–75.

Atkinson, Anthony B. 1995. *Incomes and the Welfare State: Essays on Britain and Europe.* Cambridge: Cambridge University Press.

———. 1999. *The Economic Consequences of Rolling Back the Welfare State.* Cambridge, Mass.: MIT Press.

Atkinson, Anthony B., and Gunnar V. Mogensen. 1993. *Welfare and Work Incentives: A North European Perspective.* Oxford: Clarendon Press.

Barr, Nicholas. 1992. "Economic Theory and the Welfare State: A Survey and Interpretation." *Journal of Economic Literature* 30(2): 741–803.

———. 1993. "Income Transfers in Russia: Problems and Some Policy Directions." *Economics of Transition* 1(3): 317–44.

———. 1994. "Income Transfers: Social Insurance." In *Labor Markets and Social Policy in Central and Eastern Europe: The Transition and Beyond,* edited by Nicholas Barr. New York: Oxford University Press for the World Bank (also available in Hungarian, Romanian, and Russian).

———. 1996. "Comment on 'Government Provision and Regulation of Economic Support in Old Age,' by Peter Diamond, Michael Bruno, and Boris Pleskovic (eds.)." In *Annual World Bank Conference on Development Economics 1995.* Washington, D.C.: World Bank.

———. 1998a. *The Economics of the Welfare State,* 3d ed. Oxford: Oxford University Press; Stanford, Calif.: Stanford University Press.

———. 1998b. "Higher Education in Australia and Britain: What Lessons?" *Australian Economic Review* 31(2): 179–88.

———. 1999. "Pension Reform in Central and Eastern Europe: The Good, the Bad, and the Unsustainable." In *Regulation Strategies and Economic Policies: Essays in Honour of Bernard Corry and Maurice Peston,* vol. 3, edited by Sami Daniel, Philip Arestis, and John Grahl. Cheltenham, U.K.: Edward Elgar.

———. 2000. "Reforming Pensions: Myths, Truths, and Policy Choices." Working paper WP/00/139. Washington, D.C.: International Monetary Fund.

———. 2001. "Reforming Welfare States in Post-Communist Countries." In *Transition and Growth in Postcommunist Countries: The Ten-year Experience,* edited by Lucjan T. Orlowski. Cheltenham, U.K.: Edward Elgar.

Beatty, Roger, and Warren McGillivray. 1995. "A Risky Strategy: Reflections on the World Bank Report *Averting the Old Age Crisis.*" *International Social Security Review* 48(3–4): 5–22.

Blank, Rebecca, ed. 1994. *Social Protection versus Economic Flexibility.* Chicago: University of Chicago Press.

Boeri, Tito, Michael Burda, and János Köllő. 1998. *Mediating the Transition: Labor Markets in Central and Eastern Europe.* Forum Report of the Economic Policy Initiative 4. London: Centre for Economic Policy Research; New York: Institute for EastWest Studies.

Burtless, Gary. 1996. "Widening U.S. Income Inequality and the Growth in World Trade." *Tokyo Club Papers* no. 9: 129–59.

Diamond, Peter A. 1996. "Social Security Reform in Chile: An Economist's Perspective." In *Social Security: What Role for the Future?* edited by Peter Diamond, David Lindeman, and Howard Young. Washington, D.C.: National Academic of Social Insurance.

Esping-Andersen, Gøspa. 1996. "After the Golden Age? Welfare State Dilemmas in a Global Economy." In *Welfare States in Transition: National Adaptations in Global Economies,* edited by Gøspa Esping-Andersen. London: Sage.

Feldstein, Martin S. 1996. "The Missing Piece in Policy Analysis: Social Security Reform." *American Economic Review* 86(2): 1–14.

Gerencsér, Laszlo. 1997. *Information on the Pension Reform in Hungary.* Budapest: Central Administration of the National Pension Insurance Fund.

Godfrey, Martin, and Peter Richards, eds. 1997. *Employment Policies and Programmes in Central and Eastern Europe.* Geneva: International Labor Organization.

Góra, Marek, and Michal Rutkowski. 1998. "The Quest for Pension Reform: Poland's Security through Diversity." Social protection discussion paper 9815. Washington, D.C.: World Bank.

Gruber, Jonathan, and David Wise. 1998. "Social Security and Declining Labor-Force Participation." *American Economic Review: Paper and Proceedings* 88(2): 158–63.

Hannah, Leslie. 1986. *Inventing Retirement.* Cambridge: Cambridge University Press.

Holzmann, Robert, and Steen Jorgensen. 1999. *Social Protection as Social Risk Management: Conceptual Underpinnings for the Social Protection Sector Strategy Paper.* Social protection discussion paper 9904. Washington, D.C.: World Bank.

International Monetary Fund. 1998. *Code of Good Practices on Fiscal Transparency: Declaration on Principles.* Washington, D.C.: International Monetary Fund.

International Social Security Association. 1998. *Trends in Social Security 1998,* vol. 2. Geneva: International Social Security Association.

Jackman, Richard. 1998. "Unemployment and Restructuring." In *Emerging from Communism: Lessons from Russia, China and Eastern Europe,* edited by Peter Boone, Stanislaw Gomulka, and Richard Layard. Cambridge, Mass.: MIT Press.

Jackman, Richard, and Michal Rutkowski. 1994. "Labor Markets: Wages and Employment." In *Labor Markets and Social Policy in Central and Eastern Europe: The Transition and Beyond,* edited by Nicholas Barr. New York and Oxford: Oxford University Press for the World Bank (also available in Hungarian, Romanian, and Russian).

Lindbeck, Assar. 1997. "Incentives and Social Norms in Household Behavior." *American Economic Review* 87(2): 370–77.

Milanovic, Branko. 1998. *Income, Inequality, and Poverty during the Transition from Planned to Market Economy.* Washington, D.C.: World Bank.

———. 1999. "The Role of Social Assistance in Addressing Poverty." Unpublished paper. World Bank, Washington, D.C.

Nelson, Joan. 1998. "The Politics of Pensions and Health Care Delivery Reforms in Hungary and Poland." Paper presented to the Focus Group on Fiscal Reforms, Collegium Budapest. Budapest (March 27–28).

OECD (Organization for Economic Cooperation and Development). 1997. *Lessons from Labor Market Policies in the Transition Economies.* Paris: OECD.

Rutkowski, Michal. 2001. "Restoring Hope, Rewarding Work: Pension Reforms in Post-Communist Economies." In *Transition and Growth in Postcommunist Countries: The Ten-year Experience,* edited by Lucjan T. Orlowski. Cheltenham, U.K.: Edward Elgar.

Sipos, Sándor. 1994. "Income Transfers: Family Support and Poverty Relief." In *Labor Markets and Social Policy in Central and Eastern Europe: The Transition and Beyond,* edited by Nicholas Barr. New York and Oxford: Oxford University Press for the World Bank (also available in Hungarian, Romanian, and Russian).

Sweden, Federation of Social Insurance Offices. 1998. "Sweden." In *The Future of Social Security.* Stockholm: Federation of Social Insurance Offices. For updates, see also: *www.pension.gov.se.*

Thompson, Lawrence. 1998. *Older and Wiser: The Economics of Public Pensions.* Washington, D.C.: Urban Institute.

U.K. Department of Social Security. 1993. *Containing the Costs of Social Security: The International Context.* London: Her Majesty's Stationery Office.

U.K. Pension Law Review Committee. 1993. *Pension Law Reform, Report of the Pension Law Review Committee.* Vol. 1: *Report,* and Vol. 2: *Research.* London: Her Majesty's Stationery Office.

U.K. Treasury Select Committee. 1998. *The Mis-selling of Personal Pensions,* 9th report. Vol. 1: *Report and Proceedings of the Committee.* HC712-1. London: Her Majesty's Stationery Office.

World Bank. 1994. *Averting the Old Age Crisis.* New York: Oxford University Press.

———. 1996. *World Development Report 1996: From Plan to Market.* New York: Oxford University Press.

———. 1999. *World Development Indicators.* Washington, D.C.: World Bank.

Chapter 3

After the Crisis:
The Social Contract and the
Middle Class in East Asia

NANCY BIRDSALL AND STEPHAN HAGGARD

T HE ASIAN financial crisis that began in Thailand in July 1997 put in bold relief two big differences between the Asian and the Western economies. One has been hotly contested; the second has been virtually ignored.

The first is the difference signaled by the label "crony capitalism"—the notion that the Asian model of conservative state-managed capitalism was too reliant on close ties among government, business, and banks, lacking in transparency, and thus prone to moral hazard and vulnerable to crisis. Of course, this model cannot be held altogether culpable; it had produced high growth in the past, and the crisis must be attributed at least in part to regional contagion and financial panic. Nonetheless, the crisis did reveal important structural weaknesses, and financial corporate restructuring are now viewed as central to the region's long-term growth.

The second big difference between Asian and Western economies is the nature of the social contract. The Western contract is an agreement between the citizens and the government that has arisen out of a sometimes-contentious democratic process. Varying across countries in its extent, the social contract provides for policies and programs to protect citizens from the vicissitudes of an impersonal market economy. The social safety net provides insurance both against personal circumstances, such as old age, infirmity, or bad luck in the job market, and against nationwide economic downturns, when many people suffer wage and job losses. In Western economies, the contract has evolved over time and has been shaped and insured by certain underlying rights, including membership in political groups, the right to collective bargaining in the workplace, and the vote.

In the fast-growing "miracle" economies of East Asia, when the crisis hit, there was little, if any, formal social safety net and only a weak semblance of the political arrangements that might sustain and monitor the states' management of collectively agreed safety net programs. Governments offered limited social insurance and denied citizens effective political voice. The social contract was implicit; governments guaranteed growth that would be rapid and broadly shared via widespread employment opportunities and virtually constant wage gains. The crisis showed that growth was not inexorable and that many people were vulnerable to economic bad times. Yet in the aftermath of the crisis, there is something between indifference and neglect with respect to developing a more explicit social contract.

Thus the state in East Asia, though it has been heavily involved in economic matters, remains reluctant to expand the social safety net. In light of the crisis, this is odd. For one thing, the international community, including the International Monetary Fund (IMF) and the World Bank, has been as vocal and as supportive financially of safety net programs as of corporate and financial restructuring. Indeed the World Bank, in particular, tried hard to use the crisis to catalyze movement toward a less "Asian" and more "Western" style of social contract. In addition, as we show in this chapter, the poor were not the only group hit by the crisis; a larger group was also affected—an emergent urban middle class that we call the strivers—who might be expected to command more political presence and to be pressing now for a more explicit social contract.

As it turns out, the social consequences have lost their political salience, both internationally and domestically. But there are costs to the current neglect. The obvious one is that, without a more explicit safety net reflecting healthy political agreements on the costs and tradeoffs, the next shock will find the poor and the emergent middle class again vulnerable. Combined with other sources of tension, these circumstances could generate the political and social explosions that seemed all too likely in 1998 and 1999. The more corrosive one is that the political demands of the new urban strivers—so far not channeled—will produce some sort of backlash. Populist fiscal indiscipline does not seem a likely risk in East Asia. But a reversion to insider politics, delayed corporate and financial restructuring, increasing recourse to inefficient market policies, and even the erosion of democratic politics are risks.

What went wrong? Why, despite the crisis and a slew of sensible programs meant to address its social consequences, has there been so little progress on an indigenous and sustainable social contract in Asia? And what might be done to get onto a sensible path?

The chapter proceeds as follows: First, we note that, before the crisis, years of rapid and widely shared growth had created limited pressures for an explicit and broad social safety net. Second, we discuss the effects of the crisis on various groups and the efforts of governments to minimize its social costs. Third, taking into account history and political realities, we conclude by offering some principles for a new, Asian version of a social contract more likely to be politically acceptable and sustainable.

History and Politics Shape Social Programs

Prior to the financial crisis, countries in East and Southeast Asia, with a few exceptions, had no publicly financed formal social safety net. Instead, they relied on a three-part package to insure against risk: broadly shared growth, high and effective public spending on education and health, and a strong informal safety net consisting of family support and private transfers.

Growth was not only high but also broadly shared. Broadly shared growth was the outcome of rapid employment growth, increasing participation in the formal labor force (especially of women before marriage), and rising real wages. Fiscal and monetary discipline generated macro-economic stability, reasonable access to credit (sometimes subsidized) contributed to high levels of investment, and competitive exchange rates contributed to rapid growth of labor-intensive manufactured exports. Land reform (in Korea and Taiwan), substantial public investments in rural infrastructure and agricultural technologies, and the absence of the implicit and explicit taxes on agriculture typical in other developing regions ensured healthy income growth in rural areas (World Bank 1993).

In the three decades before the crisis, as gross domestic product (GDP) rose, public spending on human development also rose rapidly. Although social expenditures were generally concentrated on programs that benefited the poor, such as primary and secondary education and basic curative and preventive health care, there was no explicit emphasis on targeting the poor. The approach was instead *universal* or "encompassing" (Nelson 1999), with an emphasis not on social protection but on human capital *investment*. Education policy was particularly important. The combination of a greater supply of basic education with greater demand for educated workers associated with the strategy of export-led growth created a virtuous cycle: rapid growth and good returns to education made it rational for households and individuals to invest in education (Birdsall, Ross, and Sabot 1995). The result was a dramatic increase in average levels of schooling and, equally impressive, a rapid decline in the inequality of schooling.[1] Public and private investment in education, particularly primary education, also had the effect of lowering inequality by minimizing the wage premia for scarce educated labor captured in other regions.

Meanwhile, an informal safety net was based on high levels of household savings, strong traditions of family support and private transfers (for example, from urban workers to rural households and between generations), and, in Korea's large firms, the apparent assurance of lifetime employment. With high growth, households falling on hard times could rely on family and community support. Economywide crises in which family savings would be insufficient and fellow family members could not easily help were infrequent and short lived.

New Pressures in the 1990s

Strains in this approach were becoming obvious already a decade ago. Slow but inexorable increases in the proportion of the aged population—in Northeast Asia that proportion will grow from 7.2 percent of the population in 1995 to 17.6 percent in 2025—and large expected increases in urbanization rates throughout the region in the next twenty-five years are beginning to undermine the informal family- and community-based safety net. More obvious in the 1990s, the foundation of rapid and shared growth—the export model—was fraying. Hong Kong, Korea, Singapore, and Taiwan were becoming relatively high-wage countries surrounded by lower-wage competitors entering the export game. There was a sharp decline in the previously rapid growth rate of exports in Korea, Malaysia, and Thailand in the second half of the 1990s and a mild decline in Indonesia (Ranis and Stewart 1998, table 1); the fact that these declines were associated with exchange rate problems as China entered the market does not obviate the general point of increasing risks to the long history of steadily rising employment and wage levels. Similarly, more open capital accounts, whatever their merits or demerits, were generating obvious vulnerabilities.

Another source of strain came from evidence of rising income and wealth inequality, a new phenomenon for most countries of the region. The portrait of East Asia as a region of shared or equitable growth was not based on substantial *reductions* in inequality; in the 1970s and 1980s Indonesia, Korea, Malaysia, and the Philippines saw modest reductions in inequality, but by international standards the level of inequality in Malaysia, the Philippines, and Thailand was high. Rather, the record was based on the region's success in achieving rapid growth without the *increases* in inequality hypothesized by Kuznets. Even before the crisis, increases in inequality were becoming marked in Thailand and Hong

Kong as well as China and were visible in Indonesia and Malaysia (table 3.1 and figure 3.1).[2] In Korea, the Gini coefficient of inequality of urban wage income rose substantially between 1993 and 1996 from 26.3 to 28.2, a big increase, although from a very low level.[3] With the crisis, even where inequality of income had not increased, the potential for conflict over the distribution of income and assets was high. Pre-crisis booms in stock and property markets in the 1990s had generated large and visible gains for the very top of the income distribution, while the subsequent collapse revealed that some of these gains were the result of insider dealing, crony-ism, and corruption. The steep losses imposed on urban workers and their households and the efforts of corporate owners and managers to secure bailouts were another likely source of resentment.

The limited safety net and highly implicit social contract also have a shortcoming. Even though the most prosperous countries of the region continue to have regional pockets of poverty analogous to those in Appalachia in the United States, East Asia has made dramatic gains in reducing poverty. Using the international standard of $1 a day per capita at 1985 prices, poverty in Hong Kong, Korea, Malaysia, Singapore, Taiwan, and Thailand had been virtually eliminated by 1995.[4] However, in 1995, 11.4 percent of Indonesians (21.9 million people) and 25.5 percent of Filipinos (17.6 million people) still lived in poverty; and in Korea and Thailand, using those countries' own official poverty lines, 15 percent of their populations lived in poverty.[5] Moreover, for the middle-income countries (excluding Indonesia), it is likely that whatever poverty remains is much more difficult to eliminate by growth alone.

The Politics of the Missing Social Contract

So for at least three decades, beginning about 1960, rapid and broadly shared growth trumped the notion of a social contract defined to include a safety net. In 1960 many households were poor or not far above the poverty line. But the exit from agriculture, increased mobility, and rapidly rising incomes generated strong expectations of future improvements in welfare, expectations that were generally realized.

Perhaps more important, lack of pressure for a social contract also reflected the political strength of the business community in these coun-tries, on which the governments relied to deliver growth. Export-oriented growth strategies made business particularly sensitive to both taxes and labor costs and thus spawned private sectors that, although friendly to social investment in education, which enhanced labor productivity, typi-cally were hostile to a broader social agenda. The truncated nature of the political spectrum, limitations on interest groups, and outright repression attenuated any nascent political demand for state-run social safety nets.

Table 3.1 Gini Coefficients in High- and Low-Inequality East Asian Countries, 1978 to 1998[a]

	High-Inequality Countries					Low-Inequality Countries				
Year	Malaysia	Hong Kong	Philippines	Thailand	Year	China	Indonesia	Rep. of Korea	Singapore	Taiwan (China)
1978					1978		38.6		37.0	28.4
1979	51.0	37.3			1979					27.7
1980					1980	32.0	35.6	38.6	40.7	28.0
1981		45.2		43.1	1981		33.7			28.2
1982					1982	28.8		35.7		28.5
1983					1983	27.2			42.0	28.5
1984	48.0				1984	25.7	32.4			28.8
1985			46.1		1985	31.4		34.5		29.2
1986		42.0		47.4	1986	33.3				29.3
1987					1987	34.3	32.0			29.7
1988			45.7	47.4	1988	34.9		33.6	41.0	30.0
1989	48.4				1989	36.0			39.0	30.4

(Table continues on p. 64.)

Table 3.1 *Continued*

	High-Inequality Countries					Low-Inequality Countries				
Year	Malaysia	Hong Kong	Philippines	Thailand	Year	China	Indonesia	Rep. of Korea	Singapore	Taiwan (China)
1990				48.8	1990	34.6	33.1			30.1
1991		45.0	45.0		1991	36.2				30.5
1992				51.5	1992	37.8				30.8
1993					1993		31.7	31.0		30.8
1994					1994					
1995	48.5				1995	41.5				
1996					1996		36.5			
					1997			29.5		
								27.1[b]		
					1998			30.1[b]		
Average	49.1	42.4	45.6	47.6	Average	33.4	34.2	32.5	39.9	29.3

Source: Deininger and Squire (1996); for Korea, Nicholas Prescott on World Bank data (1999); Korea National Statistical Office (1998).
[a] Ginis are based on household distributions of income per capita, except for Indonesia, where Ginis are based on household distribution of expenditure per capita.
[b] The 1997 and 1998 data for Korea are calculated observing urban household income for wages and salary earners only. Korea experienced an increase in inequality from 1997 to 1998: according to quarterly data on urban household monthly income, the top 20 percent/bottom 20 percent inequality ratio was 4.8 in the first quarter of 1997 and evolved in the following quarters to 4.4, 4.5, 4.3, reaching 5.5 in each one of the first three quarters of 1998.

Figure 3.1   Gini Coefficients in High- and Low-Inequality East Asian Countries, 1978 to 1998

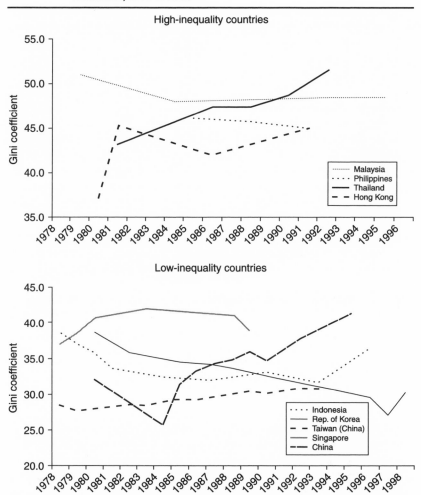

Source: Deininger and Squire (1996); for Korea, Nicholas Prescott on World Bank data

During periodic political or economic crises, such as the ethnic riots in Malaysia in 1970 or the oil shocks of the 1970s, some governments responded to social pressures by instituting new programs. But they did so as Bismarck had over a century before: preemptively and on terms set by the government and conservative political forces. The result was formal mechanisms that limited direct state expenditure, relied on schemes funded by business and labor, and, with the exception of Malaysia's ethnic affirmative action policies, shunned redistributive objectives.

Although a number of commentaries have emphasized the "shared" nature of East Asia's growth and the existence of an implicit social compact (Campos and Root 1996), such agreements were not achieved through democratic political processes (Haggard 1990). Rather, they were the outcome of authoritarian paternalism. Prior to the democratic transitions of the 1980s and 1990s, all of the developing countries in the region were authoritarian or at best semi-democratic. Social democratic political parties were weak and restricted. Labor movements were weak, repressed, or both, and interest groups and nongovernmental organizations or civil society groups had only the narrowest space in which to operate.

The effect of authoritarian politics on industrial relations was also important. By allowing labor markets to clear relatively freely, East Asian economies avoided the labor market dualism visible in Latin America and Africa, with positive implications not only for efficiency but also for equity. However, they achieved this result by direct and indirect government controls over the labor movement (Birdsall and Sabot, forthcoming). Governments could not push wages below market-clearing levels, but they could guarantee that labor had little say either in the wage-setting process or in the rules governing the shop floor. In some cases, government paternalism did introduce some rigidities. For example, in Korea, the system of industrial relations established under Park Chung Hee made it difficult for firms to fire employees. But high growth meant that the constraints associated with such policies were rarely binding.

It is true that, prior to the crisis, the politics supporting a limited or absent social contract were also changing—but not necessarily in a manner conducive to new initiatives. In Korea, the Philippines, Taiwan, and Thailand, democratic transitions had created incentives for politicians to address social issues in some form and encouraged mobilization of new social groups. But the political changes in those countries had a quite conservative cast. In Korea, the first transitional election was won by an ally of the outgoing dictator. In Taiwan, a dominant political party—the Kuomingtang (KMT)—retained office until 2000. In Thailand, gradual democratization in the 1980s occurred under military auspices and was interrupted by a coup and brief military interregnum. The "revolution" in the Philippines was led by elements of the armed forces and supported by (among others) the church and Manila's middle class.

These political changes reflected and reinforced incentives for politicians to address social issues in some form and encouraged mobilization of new social groups. Even the dominant party and authoritarian systems of Indonesia and Malaysia were not immune from pressures. In Indonesia, social protest and violence did not end with Suharto's resignation; they escalated. In Malaysia, Mahathir's incumbency has been challenged by a reformasi movement that includes elements of the urban intelligentsia and middle classes as well as Islamic parties and groups. In a sense, broad political changes prior to the crisis were spawning a new level of political participation among a wide array of social groups, including the new urban strivers. Yet the crisis, although it clearly affected these very groups, also revealed their political impotence.

The Response to the Crisis: International Concern Encounters Business-Friendly Politics

The economic effects of the crisis on a broad swath of people in three of the hardest hit countries—Indonesia, Korea, and Thailand—were visible and widespread. The actual response of governments was limited and focused largely on temporary interventions, and many "emergency" programs were not implemented easily or quickly. With the partial exception of Korea, the foundation for more institutionalized social insurance was not established. Despite enthusiasm and financial support from international funders, the lack of a political constituency—representing the vulnerable strivers, let alone the poor—meant that administrative and bureaucratic obstacles and the legacy of conservative, business-friendly political arrangements dictating limited government involvement in social transfers could not be overcome.

Who Got Hit?

The combination of capital flight and devaluations with which the crisis began and the initial policy response of tight monetary and fiscal policy brought layoffs, declining demand for new entrants into the labor market, declining real wages, and a resultant squeeze on the informal sector. Table 3.2 shows the effect of the crisis on unemployment, real wages, and consumption. These, along with heavy reliance on high interest rates to defend failing currencies, hit workers as well as small business owners very hard.[6] Countries also undertook controversial fiscal adjustments. Asian countries did not have severe fiscal problems, and some even had surpluses. But the IMF initially pushed for fiscal cuts as necessary to the overall current account adjustment, to provide "space" for financing the private sector and in anticipation of the large costs of financial sector restructuring programs. The resulting fiscal stance compounded the initial severe contraction in demand and the accompanying declines in employment and income.

The rural poor and urban households dependent on work in the low-productivity informal sector were particularly vulnerable to the result-

Table 3.2   Growth and Unemployment in East Asia, 1996 to 1998

Country and Year	Percentage Change in Real GDP[a]	Unemployment Rate[a]	Percentage Change in Average Wage	Percentage Change in Per Capita Consumption
Hong Kong				
1996	4.6	2.8		
1997	5.3	2.2	1.7[b]	
1998	−5.0	5.0	−0.1[b]	
Indonesia				
1996	8.0	4.9		
1997	4.6	5.4		−34.0[d]
1998	−15.0	15.0	−34.0[c]	−33.0 (urban)[e]
				−13.0 (rural)[e]
Korea				
1996	7.1	2.0		
1997	5.5	2.7	2.4[f]	4.2[g]
1998	−7.0	7.0	−8.1 (1st Q)[f]	−10.7[g]
			−8.6 (2nd Q)[f]	
			−14.2 (3rd Q)[f]	
Malaysia				
1996	8.6			
1997	7.8	2.2[h]		
1998	−6.4	3.8[h]		
Philippines				
1996	5.7			
1997	5.1	7.8[d]		
1998	−0.6	9.4[d]		
Singapore				
1996	6.9	3.0		
1997	7.8	2.4		
1998	0.0	4.4	1.0[h]	
Thailand				
1996	5.5	2.0		
1997	−0.4	4.0		
1998	−8.0	6.0	−6.0[i]	

Source: IMF (1998).
[a]1998 GDP and unemployment figures are forecasts.
[b]Hong Kong Census and Statistics Department (1999).
[c]Formal sector wages. Manuelyan-Atinc (1999, ch. 6).
[d]Knowles, Pernia, and Racelis (1999).
[e]Thomas et al. (1999).
[f]Private, nonagricultural only. Moon, Lee, and Yoo (1999, 14).
[g]Korea, National Statistical Office (1999).
[h]Second quarter 1998 to second quarter 1999. Statistics Singapore (1999).
[i]February 1997 to February 1998 (8.3 percent in urban areas; 4.7 percent in rural areas).

ing economywide recessions. But a second group, more broadly defined and including many households with formal sector workers, was also hit. The least well-off segment of this second group is difficult to distinguish from the currently poor. Indeed, there is growing evidence that in many countries many households move in and out of poverty from year to year. Thus in East Asia many households above the poverty line in the late 1990s faced a reasonable probability of falling into poverty even in the absence of a major economic shock.[7]

We have labeled this admittedly ill-defined group of vulnerable households the urban strivers. They are likely to include many households whose heads have low-wage but steady jobs or thriving small businesses, but relatively limited education and few accumulated physical assets. Across countries, the group is best defined in terms of their absolute income and education rather than their relative income or education status within each country. We provide a comparison of absolute income by quintiles of the population for the three main crisis countries plus Malaysia in figure 3.2. In absolute terms, the average income per capita of the richest 20 percent or quintile of households in Indonesia, at about $7,000, is slightly below the average of the middle quintile in Korea. (This average for Indonesia's richest 20 percent includes but obscures the very high income and wealth of the perhaps 1 percent of households that constitute the now-notorious insider class.) In Indonesia 80 percent of households and in Thailand more than 60 percent of households have income per capita below $5,000. Households at and somewhat below this income level of $5,000 are likely to be in the new class of urban strivers.[8] This group is in the top 40 percent of the distribution in Indonesia, closer to the middle in Thailand, and closer to the bottom in Korea, although still mostly above Korea's poverty line.[9] Similarly, with respect to education (figure 3.3), individuals with no more than six years of schooling are among the 40 percent with the most education in Indonesia, while they are in the middle of the distribution in Thailand and near the bottom in Korea.

In Indonesia, with 11 percent of the population in poverty, the social-risk of the crisis seemed greatest.[10] Government estimates in June 1998 put the number of people living in poverty at 40 percent of the population, and the international media ran stories predicting widespread malnutrition and even starvation. But the initial fears of dramatic increases in poverty were unwarranted. Although most of Indonesia's poor live in rural areas, the effects of the crisis were concentrated in the urban economy. Construction and industry were especially hard hit. Household per capita expenditures fell an alarming 34 percent in urban areas compared to 17 percent in rural areas.[11] Daily wages fell 20 percent for urban men

Figure 3.2   Average Absolute Household Income per Capita (1997 Purchasing Power Parity Dollars), by Quintile in Select Countries

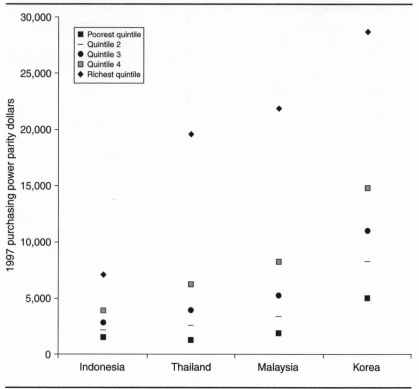

Source: Authors' calculations from World Bank (1999); Deininger and Squire (1996).

compared to 6 percent for rural men. The number of self-employed expanded rapidly, as did employment in agriculture; the informal and rural sectors played the role of shock absorbers.

Household expenditure data show only modest declines in *median* expenditures (5.0 percent for urban households and 1.6 percent for rural ones); this suggests that expenditures of the better off fell most sharply. And, in fact, real per capita expenditures of the top 20 percent of households (in terms of per capita expenditures) fell much more dramatically than expenditures of the bottom 40 percent (–23 percent versus about –10 percent), although the fall in expenditures at the very bottom of the income distribution contributed to the increase in the poverty rate. Similarly, the less well educated fared better than the educated.

Figure 3.3   Average Years of Schooling per Adult (More than Twenty-Five
              Years of Age), by Quintile, in Select Countries, 1990

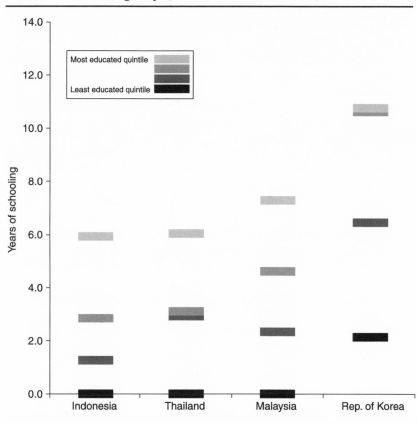

Source: Calculated using Barro and Lee estimates of completed adult schooling by level
(Barro and Lee 1996), Duryea formula (Duryea 1998).

Education and health data point to the same conclusion—relatively
better-off households in urban areas were the hardest hit. Enrollment
in junior secondary school in 1998 compared to 1997 fell more in urban
than in rural areas. Use of both public and private health care fell most
among middle-income households. In agriculture, those parts of Java
with closer links to the formal economy—and therefore higher
incomes to begin with—were the hardest hit. Other islands, including
large parts of Maluku, Sulawesi, and Sumatra, were either minimally
affected or actually gained because of the effect of the depreciation on
export crop earnings.

These findings suggest why the effects of the crisis on poverty and other key social indicators, like school dropout rates, were somewhat dampened even before we take into account the government's response: many of those most seriously affected by the crisis were among the *relatively* well off to begin with.

In Thailand as in Indonesia, the urban formal sector was hit hard. Unemployment doubled from 1997 to May 1998, with the greatest losses in urban construction (–32 percent). Small and medium firms were responsible for the bulk of unemployment, while employment in the service sector grew somewhat, indicating the role of the informal sector in absorbing the unemployed.

As in Indonesia, wage declines between 1997 and 1998 were greater in urban areas (–8.3 percent) than in rural areas (–4.7 percent). Men working in urban construction and women working in urban manufacturing saw larger-than-average losses (–24 percent in construction). In contrast, agricultural households fared somewhat better than the average household if we compare 1996 and 1998, and the one-quarter of farming households that were net producers of food actually profited from initial price increases for their crops. Overall, increases in poverty were relatively contained, and inequality worsened only marginally.

The economic welfare of the *average* Thai household actually improved between the first half of 1996 and the first half of 1998. Indeed, consistent with this, school dropout rates continued to decline nationwide for all age groups, with the exception of the lower secondary level in and around Bangkok.[12] At the same time, the welfare of the *median* household in Thailand (at an income level below the average and closer to our $5,000 marker) declined, implying new insecurity for households in the middle of the income distribution.

In Korea—the richest, most urbanized, and most industrialized of the most seriously affected economies—similar groups were at risk as in Indonesia and Thailand. Although closer to the bottom of the income distribution, they were also urban and in absolute terms at the marker income of about $5,000. Overall unemployment in Korea rose sharply during the crisis, from 2 percent in October 1997 to almost 9 percent in February 1998, near its peak. The loss of employment was concentrated in manufacturing and particularly construction (–21.3 percent); as in the other Asian countries, agriculture and fishing picked up some of the slack. Contrary to the argument that the Korean labor market showed major rigidities, rising unemployment was accompanied by sharply falling real wages, which declined more than 12 percent from mid-1997 until end-1998.

Urban employment losses were concentrated among the less well-paid poorer temporary and day laborers in small and medium firms, while workers in large firms saw only slight declines. Those with less than secondary education bore the brunt of employment losses (Moon, Lee, and Yoo 1999, table 3.9). The number of employed professional, managerial, technical, and administrative workers actually rose. Thus in Korea the fall in income was most serious for the bottom 20 percent of households (–23.7 percent versus –2.5 for the top 20 percent). For the poorest of the poor—those with incomes less than 80 percent of the poverty line—the numbers in poverty rose even more rapidly.

In sum, in all three countries the effects of the financial crisis were by no means limited to the traditional poor in rural areas and in the urban informal sector. The newly vulnerable group included workers in the formal urban sector, particularly in construction and to a lesser extent manufacturing, workers and owners of small and medium enterprises, and many who, although with less than secondary education, had completed primary education and had risen above the poverty line. The crisis, in short, affected precisely those emergent, transitional, and weakly organized "striving classes" to whom high growth had historically granted social mobility. The social consequences of the crisis were partly mitigated because this group was able to draw on personal savings, rely on intrafamily transfers, shift to informal employment, work longer hours, migrate, and reallocate expenditures to protect investments, including investments in human capital. In this sense, the outcome could be seen as vindicating the region's reliance on informal mechanisms and a relatively limited role for government. However, it also could be interpreted as revealing the limited political clout of this group and their consequent economic exposure, if not to dire poverty, at least to sudden and severe income and welfare losses.

The Response: Recalcitrant Governments and Ambitious Outsiders

The immediate social response to the crisis, including strikes, demonstrations, and in a few cases riots, generated official interest in minimizing social tensions. Governments also felt some external pressure, as a stream of international visitors produced reports on the social consequences of the crisis. The World Bank, the Asian Development Bank, a host of United Nations agencies, and even the IMF issued reports on the potential social costs of the crisis. Governments needed substantial external financial support to stem panic and manage their budgets. Thus interests were joined. The governments and the multilateral institutions agreed that overall financial support should be linked to government efforts to develop and provide a better social safety net.

The result was a proliferation of program initiatives, summarized in table 3.3 for the most seriously affected countries. In some areas, such as

Table 3.3 Social Safety Net Programs in East Asia During the Crisis

Country	Food Security	Cash Transfers	Social Funds	Health and Education	Workfare Programs	Unemployment Assistance, Insurance and Severance Pay	Active Labor Market Policies
Rep. of Korea		Temporary noncontributory means-tested livelihood protection program (new); social pension for the elderly (new)			Public workfare scheme (new)	Unemployment insurance program (expanded)	Active labor market programs in vocational training, wage subsidies, and job placement (expanded)
Malaysia							Training for unemployed (expanded)
Thailand		Social pensions for the elderly and cash transfers to needy families (expanded)	Community-based programs (new)	Low-income health care for the poor and voluntary health insurance for the near-poor (programs expanded); scholarships and educational loan program	Public workfare scheme (new)	Severance payments (increased); new Employee Welfare Fund set up to partially finance unpaid	Training for skills development for unemployed (expanded); self-employment loans

Country				
Philippines		(expanded); allowing fees to be paid in installments; fee waivers; and provisions for free uniforms to students; school lunch program (expanded)	severance claims for workers from bankrupt firms	Computerized job assistance network launched and some expansion of training
Indonesia	Program of targeted cheap rice (OPK) distribution (new)	Community-based programs	Back-to-School program launched (to provide scholarships for the poorest students and school grants for schools in the poorest communities); subsidies to maintain prices of essential drugs	Existing padat karya programs expanded and subsequently redesigned

Source: Manuelyan-Atinc (1999, ch. 6).

maintaining levels of health and education expenditure in the short run or launching emergency public works employment programs, outside intervention supported governments' own inclinations to meet immediate and visible needs; support for education and jobs was also consistent with past success emphasizing the productivity benefits of social spending. However, in varying degrees across countries and programs, ideas for undertaking specific antipoverty efforts and for broadening the policy response beyond temporary measures ran into institutional and political difficulties.

The problems facing the East Asian governments were in the first instance administrative. In all cases, and particularly in Indonesia, the large size of the informal and self-employed sectors posed daunting administrative problems for reaching the poor and even more so for constructing a broader system of social insurance. Lines of bureaucratic responsibility were not clear, and the agencies with responsibilities for social issues lacked reliable information on the income status of households. Bureaucracies not only lacked the capacity to respond in a timely fashion but also were poorly positioned to act as political advocates for those affected. As a result, delays in responding to the social dimensions of the crisis were a common feature of all cases.

A deeper problem was that a number of Asian policymakers, as well as political opposition and nongovernmental organizations, were wary of the new social agenda because of the potential for leakage not only to the nonpoor (always a legitimate technical concern with social welfare subsidies) but also to local politicians and corruption. These concerns were present in Thailand and were particularly acute in Indonesia, where controversy about corruption in antipoverty programs engulfed initial World Bank efforts.

A third problem was that many of the programs encouraged by the international community were focused on the needs of the structurally poor (see table 3.4). This reasonably implied substantial emphasis on *targeting* programs to avoid technical leakage and minimize fiscal costs.[13] However, the targeting approach with its implied emphasis on transfers was not particularly relevant to the experience of countries whose social programs had emphasized broad-based education and the creation of employment opportunities. In the Asian context, targeting, which can create social stigma for beneficiaries, ran the risk of undermining the social solidarity undergirding the informal safety net and may have discouraged the use of programs by the new poor and near poor who were seriously affected by the crisis. And, of course, a highly targeted approach missed many individuals above the poverty line who were hit hard by the crisis.

Table 3.4   Response to Crisis: The Social Contract

Country	Government Response	International Community Response	Political and Institutional Constraints
The three IMF-supported countries	See table 3.3	Revision of initially stringent fiscal targets (International Monetary Fund)	Weak or absent "social demo-cratic" political parties, repre-senting urban working class and poor
		Balance of payment support conditional on maintaining public spending on health and education (Inter-national Bank for Reconstruction and Development, Asian Development Bank)	Labor unions weak (Indonesia) or not represen-tative of most workers (Thai-land, Korea)
		Emphasis on targeting the poor (all donors)	Weak local gov-ernment and poor informa-tion in central government social bureau-cracies
Indonesia	See table 3.3	Encouragement of switch from general rice subsidy to tar-geted cheap rice dis-tribution	Fear of corruption Political resistance to redirecting spending to poor provinces
		Heavy emphasis on redesign of programs to minimize corrup-tion	Weak transitional government (1998 to 1999)
		Delay of social loan dis-bursements due to broader political risks (World Bank 1999)	
Thailand	See table 3.3	Emphasis on community-based ini-tiatives and strength-ening of civil society	Central govern-ment resists European-style welfare state

(Table continues on p. 78.)

Table 3.4   *Continued*

Country	Government Response	International Community Response	Political and Institutional Constraints
			Strong state enterprise: unions resist wage flexibility and employment policies
		Balance of payment support conditional on maintaining public spending on health and education (International Bank for Reconstruction and Development, Asian Development Bank)	Labor unions weak (Indonesia) or not representative of most workers (Thailand, Korea)
Rep. of Korea	See table 3.3	Encouragement of expanded coverage and enlarged eligibility for existing (tiny) unemployment insurance programs	Labor unions in organized sector resist layoffs

Source: Authors' compilation.

Equally important, efforts to institutionalize explicit forms of social insurance faced fundamental political barriers. Governments in Korea, Malaysia, and Thailand expressed concern about taking on the spending and transfer programs of the Western welfare state. Social insurance commitments are relatively modest in the countries in question. Malaysia's Employees' Provident Fund (EPF) is the most comprehensive but covers just under half of all employees and involves no direct government commitments. This skepticism combined legitimate doubts about the European model with a traditionalist rhetoric that emphasized reliance on family and community and past success in harnessing work, discipline, and responsibility at the individual level. The idea of new social welfare programs that included entitlements to government transfers faced strong resistance from conservative forces, which argued that they were costly to business and undermined the roots of past economic success (Goodman, White, and Kwon 1998).

Governments faced some economically motivated demonstrations and strikes in the wake of the crisis. But with the partial exception of Korea, none of the political systems had strong parties that represented the interests of those most seriously affected in an ongoing and institutionalized way. Many of those hit are difficult to organize anyway—for example, the small business sector—in the absence of highly pluralistic and well-developed democratic processes. European-style social democratic parties are altogether absent in the region, and links between parties and civil society are generally weak. Where opposition parties sought to exploit social issues, they often did so by appealing to other identities, such as Islam in Indonesia, ethnicity in Malaysia or region in Thailand (the Northeast) and Korea (the Cholla provinces).

Finally, the organized groups that are historically most associated with the advance of the social agenda—namely labor—were either controlled by the government (as in Malaysia), weak (in Indonesia), or concentrated in sectors where they did not necessarily speak for the interests of those most seriously affected by the crisis (for example, state-owned enterprises in Thailand). Korea, again, is a partial exception. Thus in the absence of any organized, politically relevant pressure to expand the social contract, official skepticism prevailed.

Indonesia

The crisis was most severe in Indonesia. Prior to the fall of Soeharto, the government's social policy response was confined to ensuring adequate supplies of basic foodstuffs. A subsidy flowed to all consumers regardless of income level (and had the perverse effect of encouraging rice exports exactly as the government was fearing shortage).

Once Habibie assumed the presidency and the political situation was at least temporarily stabilized (and the IMF had agreed to loosen fiscal targets), the government responded to the donor community's insistence on a more coherent response. It instituted a targeted program of rice distribution to poor families that was reaching nearly 10 million families by early 1999. Although the program no doubt reached many poor in rural areas, the benefits to the poor and newly poor in urban areas were limited. Only 5 percent of recipients were urban (World Bank, Thailand office, 1999a). Long-standing pressures from politically well-placed rural districts and the weak organization of labor and, as always, the urban poor limited the expansion of the program to households in the cities.

Even the efforts to maintain education and health spending and to generate public employment, with strong support from external agencies, experienced problems in implementation. Government expenditures on social safety net programs for the first nine months of fiscal 1998/

1999 were only 37 percent of the annual budgeted amount (World Bank 1999a, 6). Donors pressed the government to reallocate education spending to the poorest groups, and a stay-in-school program providing block grants to the poorest schools and fellowships (direct transfers) to the poorest students was popular and successful, perhaps because it was consistent with maintaining the historic broad-based approach to education. But the financing for this program ended up reducing financing for secondary schools and encouraged a high level of dropouts during the crisis.

Implementation of programs was inhibited by fears of corruption. In a political setting characterized by a weak transitional government, impending elections, and the proliferation of political challengers from both inside and outside the government, the risk that funds would be diverted to political and electoral uses or outright corruption was high. Indeed, the World Bank was stung in mid-1998 by the "revelation" that some Bank-supported programs were subject to political leakage. A loan document outlining a comprehensive social safety net program approved in mid-1999 refers to "implementation delays, fund leakage, budget allocation issues, and inadequate or inappropriate design" (World Bank 1999a, ii), euphemisms for corruption and the political use of funds.

The risk of misuse of funds was compounded by the effort to increase social spending rapidly and the emergence of strong populist pressures in the system. A $600 million World Bank social safety net loan devised a complex governance structure that attempted to improve accountability, in part by engaging nongovernmental organizations directly in monitoring disbursements in the hope of "less misuse of funds . . . better targeting and design, and less delay" (World Bank 1999a, iii). Even with these controls, the World Bank temporarily suspended some loan disbursements prior to the elections of June 1999 to avoid charges by the opposition that they were indirectly supporting the government (*Asian Wall Street Journal,* April 13, 1999).

Some crisis programs worked relatively effectively given administrative constraints: for example, the emergency "cheap rice" program and the stay-in-school program. But employment generation programs pushed by the international funders—labor-intensive public works programs, demand-driven community funds, and credit schemes to small and medium enterprises—ran into trouble because the beneficiaries had no political base. Provincial leaders from better-off areas resisted efforts to redirect spending to poorer areas, and employment creation programs failed to get off the ground. Moreover, despite well-intentioned efforts by the World Bank and other funders and donors to institutionalize efforts, little had been done with respect to a longer-term agenda by the end of 1999.

Thailand

In Thailand as well, the crisis failed to generate longer-term changes in the design of the social contract. The response to the crisis was slow and cautious, as the government was reluctant to undertake new social insurance commitments. When the crisis hit, Thailand had a social security system that provided benefits to workers in the private sector and to self-employed professionals. But the program covered only 6 million workers, and its benefits were limited to sickness, childbirth, death, and disability; it did not provide unemployment benefits (Kittiprapas and Intaravitak 1998). The strongest safety net for urban workers was severance pay. Under pressure from labor, the government extended the length of severance payments from six to ten months and launched a special program to provide free health care to laid-off workers and their families as well as job placement services. But these were special crisis-linked benefits not to be institutionalized and, of course, were limited to workers in the formal sector.

The Chuan government (which took office in late 1997 after the crisis hit) was openly resistant to expanding the social security program, including a prior government commitment to the development of the pension system (*The Nation*, August 5, 1998). The government argued these commitments had high fiscal costs but involved transfers that raised issues of moral hazard and entitlement. In the words of one government official, "The reason behind giving them such a tiny amount of money is to create an incentive for them to look for jobs; otherwise they may want to live on social security for the rest of their lives and take advantage of others" (*The Nation*, June 7, 1998).

This reluctance can be traced in part to fiscal constraints but also to important features of Thai politics. Despite the significance of greater Bangkok in the Thai economy, the country remains largely rural. As a result, the urban-based parties need to accommodate rural interests, as they did, for example, in devising a rural debt forgiveness scheme and microlending programs that fell outside the ambit of multilateral financing. At the same time, the nature of organized labor interests reflected relatively privileged segments of the working class, such as workers in the state-owned enterprise sector. As a result, the government has resisted calls from both donors and domestic political opponents for a formal safety net. Rather, the Chuan administration has favored temporary measures, more attention to education and training, which have lagged in Thailand, and various forms of local self-help.

As part of its crisis-induced external financing package, the government signed social loans with the Asian Development Bank in 1998 and, after considerable negotiation, with the World Bank in 1999. Given the weakness of existing machinery for managing the social safety net and the reluctance of government to move into new social insurance programs, the loans generally supported or expanded existing programs, particularly in education and health (World Bank, Thailand Office 1999a). The health program expanded funding for the poor, and the education component increased funding for a student loan program to keep children in school. The loan also supported existing government programs designed to provide jobs to the poor.

The most innovative dimension of the World Bank loan was its emphasis on decentralization and local community development through the creation of a Social Investment Fund (SIF), whose objectives were broadly in line with the new constitution's emphasis on devolving power to lower levels of government.[14] The SIF provided grant support for small-scale subprojects proposed by local governments, nongovernmental organizations, or community groups, as well as on lending support to larger, revenue-generating projects in select municipalities.

But the opportunity provided by the social funds for patronage, particularly given the coalition nature of the cabinet, made both the government and the multilateral banks cautious in approving projects. Less than 10 percent of all project money had been allocated by April 1999 (*Bangkok Post*, April 3, 1999). Despite the constitutional changes, the development of effective local government remained a long-term project that faced resistance from within the central government bureaucracy.

Malaysia

Malaysia did not negotiate large financial packages with the World Bank and donors during the crisis and, as shown in table 3.3, was much less active in initiating safety net programs. Comments of Prime Minister Mahathir summarize well the resistance to certain forms of social insurance visible elsewhere in the region, including Thailand and Korea. Referring to social safety nets in the form of unemployment benefits, Mahathir argued,

> This method will only wreck the economy. When the unemployed is [sic] paid an allowance, then many will choose not to work. The Government will need to allocate money for dole which can only be done through raising taxes on the employed ... Of course the production costs for goods will increase, so will the cost of living. So each time dole is raised, taxes follow suit and the cost for manufacturing goods will only reduce our competitiveness in the world market. (*New Straits Times*, June 11, 1999: 2)

Malaysia does have an Employees' Provident Fund, which insures against disability and old age. But in line with the Asian welfare model, the fund is financed entirely by mandated contributions from employers and workers, and direct transfers are minimal. Only one poor household in ten receives a government transfer, and transfers account for only about 1 percent of the poor's gross income (Manuelyan-Atinc 1999, 4).

Korea

In some contrast to Indonesia and Thailand, Korea had two more obvious signs of an incipient social contract before the crisis: active labor unions and a government-managed system of unemployment insurance that, though modest, was more institutionalized than elsewhere. In Korea more than in Indonesia and Thailand, the crisis seemed to catalyze new initiatives, in part because of pressures from organized labor and an administrative head start. But even in Korea, the bottom line was still only limited steps toward a modern and sustainable social contract.

As with the state-owned enterprise workers in Thailand, the Korean government faced a particular dilemma: on the one hand, unemployment in Korea was the most serious of the three countries, with fewer opportunities for the rural and informal sectors to absorb displaced workers from the small and medium enterprise sector. On the other hand, the high degree of concentration had resulted in fairly strong and militant unions, which, although representing only 12 to 13 percent of wage and salary workers, were dominant in large firms and public enterprises. This meant that, while small firms faced little resistance to layoffs and could adjust to redundancy illegally, large firms had to resort to early retirement, voluntary leave, and wage restraints.[15] Such measures were not likely to encourage the corporate restructuring envisioned by the government. Moreover, these labor market rigidities could act as a deterrent to foreign investment in sectors such as banking.

To secure labor agreement to greater layoffs, President Kim Dae Jung, elected in late 1997, resorted to a mechanism not used in Korea with any success before: the tripartite commission. In return for agreement to permit layoffs, the government established a 5 trillion won unemployment fund, agreed to give public servants the right to form a labor consultative body and teachers the right to unionize, and reversed a long-standing prohibition on labor involvement in political activities. The tripartite agreement eventually broke down; labor walked out in early 1999 following repeated government interventions to encourage downsizing and to break strikes during 1998. However, an important precedent had been set—of labor bargaining for a better safety net to offset greater risks of layoffs.

Meanwhile, in adjustment loans negotiated with the World Bank and the Asian Development Bank, the government entered into a series of commitments to expand eligibility and coverage of its unemployment insurance (initially covering only workers in firms of thirty or more employees) to small firms. The government also agreed to increase budget outlays (budgeted in 1998 at a mere 1.3 percent of GDP) for social assistance and unemployment programs, although only should the numbers of those below the poverty line increase. Under further pressure, including from the World Bank, the government raised the budget allocation for these programs closer to 2 percent in 1999. Reflecting concern with incentive effects and the risks of "welfare disease," benefits under these programs are low: 70 percent of the minimum wage, which is itself just 25 percent of average earnings (Moon, Lee, and Yoo 1999, 43).

Actual implementation, moreover, fell short. As of June 1998, among the 1.5 million unemployed, only 7 percent had received unemployment benefits. The extension of benefits to day laborers, formally set in October 1998, had not been implemented a year later due to lack of administrative capacity (Park 1999, 205). Public assistance, confined to those without family members able to assist, is less than 9 percent of average earnings, probably not enough to cover basic expenses.

In sum, the most seriously affected countries on which we have focused experienced a wide variety of circumstances during the crisis, from dealing with immediate food shortages to managing organized labor. But in all four, the response to the social dimension of the crisis was limited. The social risks were not ignored; governments responded to the threat of social unrest and were pushed along by the multilateral banks and the IMF, on whose resources they were greatly reliant. But with the possible exception of Korea, the crisis did not generate a broader debate on the wider social contract.

Lessons of the Crisis for a New Social Contract

A new social contract should address the problem of poverty that, in the miracle years, was so effectively managed through high growth. At the same time, it should also deal with the new insecurities arising for the working and middle classes as a result of more open economies in a global marketplace.

The Safety Net: Social Insurance and
Social Assistance

In every country, social safety net programs need support from the politically relevant working and middle classes and therefore must have two characteristics. They have to address risks that are real for this group, including individual risks such as permanent disability and old age that prevent working, and the systemic (or covariant) risks of an economy-wide recession leading to widespread layoffs and potential loss of homes, small businesses, and other assets. At the same time, they have to avoid burdening those groups with taxes for programs that end up reducing incentives to work, thus supporting the so-called "lazy and undeserving." For these reasons, success in establishing a safety net in the West came first, with collective agreement on *social insurance* programs—universal and incentive-compatible programs such as contribution-based unemployment insurance and protection from inability to work due to infirmity or old age.

These programs can be compared with the other half of a complete safety net today in most Western economies—that is, so-called *social assistance* programs that are aimed more explicitly at the nonworking poor, such as nutritional supplementation for poor children and cash entitlements and health programs for single mothers and their children. Although the current vision of the social safety net and the one embraced by and encouraged for all developing countries by the World Bank includes these programs for the persistently or structurally poor, in the West antipoverty programs were developed only later and generally as a by-product of broad universal programs. In the United States, for example, Lyndon B. Johnson's War on Poverty came only three decades after Franklin Delano Roosevelt's New Deal.

The economic and moral logic of protection for the poor is unassailable. But in the aftermath of the crisis in East Asia, there are two problems with the "poverty" or social assistance half of the conventional Western safety net. The first is political. Even in mature democracies, the poor are unlikely to command political voice consistent with their numbers. In addition to the reality that money talks in politics, the poor have less time and less command over information and influence. Adding to the political unpopularity of poverty programs are the problems of moral hazard—that programs designed for the poor will induce the very behavior that leads to poverty—and of leakage—that programs meant for the truly poor will benefit the nonpoor (always a legitimate technical concern with social welfare subsidies) or, worse, will become a source of patronage and corruption. The idea of "targeting" social expenditures very carefully to the truly poor, by defining strict eligibility criteria or minimal benefits only attractive to those in great need, is in part a reaction to the political difficulty of financing permanent poverty or "welfare" programs for the structurally poor. Targeting minimizes the financial burden on middle-class taxpayers and is meant to minimize moral hazard. But it implies a limited number of beneficiaries who, by definition, are not politically powerful.

It requires avoiding leakage, which is technically difficult and raises administrative costs. And it means that a certain stigma may be associated with poverty programs, making some potential beneficiaries reluctant to claim benefits and contributing further to their political unpopularity.

The second problem, made more visible by the crisis, is that targeted programs designed to assist the persistently poor fail to protect the larger swath of the population, including the strivers, that is not currently poor but is *vulnerable* to poverty. The numbers cited for Indonesia indicate that an informal safety net that provides family help in the event of a particularistic or individual shock (illness, sudden job loss) will be full of holes in the event of an economywide downturn. Yet maintaining this vulnerable group's assets and indirectly their stake in the market economy may be critical to achieving renewed economic growth and a stronger democracy.

The Post-Crisis Logic of Unemployment and Other "Social Insurance"

Thus the crisis has highlighted the logic of establishing more formal systems of social insurance in the middle-income countries of East Asia—programs that would protect the vulnerable, including both those who are currently "poor" in income terms and the often-larger group of those who risk becoming poor without the safety net that insurance against predefined shocks would provide. A permanent system of unemployment insurance is likely to be particularly salient to the striving class. The most comprehensive system consists of universal (rather than targeted) unemployment benefits, financed by some form of earmarked contributions made by employers and employees[16] and paid out over a certain period based on contributions, age, and so on or paid in the form of a lump sum payment (a severance payment) that is ideally portable from one employer to another. Where a large segment of the labor force is in the informal sector, the equivalent "insurance" can be provided through labor-intensive public works programs financed by general revenue. During the crisis, such public works programs were initiated in all of the Asian countries, although on an ad hoc basis. Such programs could be a permanent feature of the social contract, legislated to kick in and shut down more or less automatically in response to the business cycle.

There are at least three economic advantages to social insurance. First, unemployment insurance plays a macroeconomic role as a countercyclical Keynesian stabilizer, stimulating an economy that is structurally sound but at risk of a deflationary episode. In Latin America, one could imagine risks to fiscal and macroeconomic stability of insurance programs that are too generous and are automatically triggered. But East

Asia provides little risk of such an eventuality given its history of fiscal rectitude. At the microeconomic level, unemployment insurance helps to protect the assets (such as small businesses and incomplete investments in children's schooling) that are hard to recover once lost, allowing urban strivers to take on the risks of investment and innovation that are important for broad-based growth. Social insurance also has the potential to complement rather than substitute for and thus discourage the informal safety net. This occurs to the extent that beneficiaries tend to be providers for others before and after the contingency that triggers their benefits and, with insurance, can maintain some support for others even at the time of a shock.

Second, unemployment and other social insurance (particularly old-age insurance) can be a means of deepening capital markets and encouraging much-needed financial reforms. Social insurance schemes based on individual contributions create long-term financing (one outcome of the pension system in Chile) and provide alternative sources of financing to commercial banks; aggressive and incautious bank-led finance, often to related parties, was one source of the crisis. The reform of social insurance can also democratize the capital markets by encouraging participation by small investors, in turn giving them a political stake in a market-oriented economy.

Third, unemployment insurance can encourage job mobility—an advantage to economies undergoing needed structural change—and reduce resistance to temporary layoffs, often a more efficient step for firms than reducing wages or firing workers.

The economic conditions for launching initiatives in this area are in some ways more propitious in Asia than in other developing countries. Household savings are already high in the region, and formal insurance schemes would simply channel some portion of these savings through new institutional mechanisms. Most middle-income Asian countries have good records with respect to the conduct of fiscal policy, so both internal and external markets are likely to tolerate the fiscal effects of rule-based spending with clear sunset provisions.[17] There are also political advantages to focusing on social insurance. We have emphasized the potential appeal of more encompassing or universal programs, especially after the experience of the crisis, and the appeal of contribution-based systems grounded in the work ethic, particularly in economies so successful with broad-based job-intensive growth. In addition, once insurance systems are established, their administrative costs are low compared with those of targeted social assistance programs, and they are much less vulnerable to misuse for political patronage and to corruption in general.

However, the politics of even these insurance programs are by no means clear-cut. In East Asia, progress in social insurance, let alone in a more explicit and complete social contract, must be made in the context of a new democratic politics in which political pressures for the status quo are surprisingly strong and top-down politics continue to operate in important ways. The political channels through which the strivers, especially urban informal sector workers and small entrepreneurs, can express their views remain limited, in part because democratic politics are relatively new.

What, then, are the political bargains that would support progress, initially with social insurance and eventually with a broader Asian social contract, while avoiding a number of important political risks that might arise?

First, as is obvious, there will be differences among the post-crisis countries. For both political and administrative reasons, contribution-based insurance is likely to emerge earlier in the more developed countries—Korea, Singapore, possibly Malaysia—in which a substantial portion of the workforce is in the formal sector, as the example of Korea already suggests. Indonesia, the Philippines, and Thailand are likely to follow only later. In this second group of countries, emphasis should be placed on improving the design and administration of public works and on institutionalizing them to ensure that they are triggered automatically in response to crises.

In the first group of countries, conservative biases and the absence of either strong encompassing unions or social democratic parties suggest that such schemes should avoid emphasizing redistributive objectives and instead focus on an ethic of individual responsibility. For insurance schemes, this would imply an emphasis on prior contributions and, in the case of other forms of insurance such as pensions and health, the maintenance of individual accounts. This approach is more likely to be supported by a powerful and conservative business sector. The financing design can appeal to an ethic of individual responsibility, while also reducing social risk, through mandatory but flexible programs that give individuals defined rights to borrow against their insurance accounts not only during spells of unemployment but also for housing, children's education, and small business investments (Stiglitz 1999).

In public works programs, emphasis on the ethic of individual responsibility implies setting wages below the prevailing market in order to avoid the work disincentives that have plagued European unemployment insurance programs. More generally, unemployment programs financed by general revenues can be made more politically palatable, as well as efficient, if the macroeconomic conditions under which they kick in are transparent and automatic.

Gaining political support for such programs will still require overcoming financing concerns. Smaller businesses are most likely to complain about the cost of employer contributions, and the support of larger export-oriented firms facing stiff cost pressures is by no means guaranteed. Moreover, it is far from clear that the strivers themselves will necessarily support such programs. The debate over social policy in Korea showed that organized labor in larger firms may prefer measures that ensure job security over forms of insurance that make layoffs and downsizing more acceptable. Where the informal sector is large, as in Indonesia, potential beneficiaries are poorly organized and certainly will resist making contributions.

The Korean experience suggests that the optimal political sequence for initiating insurance schemes should begin with workers in larger firms. This approach is vulnerable to the criticism that it addresses the needs of the best organized first. But if successful, the program will generate its own demand for expansion to other categories of workers, including smaller firms and even the self-employed. Western experience also suggests that the largest firms may have sufficient interest in worker loyalty to accept such programs (and may see them as a less costly alternative to private plans).[18]

Gaining political support for such programs also depends critically on their governance structures. Governance structures must guarantee effective oversight of funds and prevent theft and diversion. This can be done by ensuring the political independence of fund managers or their regulators, while simultaneously insisting on high degrees of transparency and opportunities for citizen oversight through participation on boards or panels. A few countries have developed mechanisms that remove government from direct management responsibility of social insurance schemes (Chile in the case of pensions). This seems appealing where there is a history of cronyism and corruption. However, even with management in private hands, the government needs to play a strong and independent regulatory role to avoid capture by powerful financial interests.[19] The problem of government involvement in public works programs is more immediate. In Indonesia, the padat karya programs were welcomed by incumbents and bureaucrats, but hotly contested by opposition groups, which saw them as little more than traditional patronage.

Labor Relations

The formulation of social insurance programs is heavily dependent on a second component of a broader social contract: a new approach to labor relations. As we have argued, the traditional social bargain in East Asia rested on an authoritarian approach to labor relations in which unions simply were repressed or more typically were brought under various forms of government control (Deyo 1989). Democratization made such arrangements anachronistic, and in all of the newly democratic countries, old unions sought to remake themselves, and new competing federations and unions entered the political fray.

A wide array of factors will influence the nature of the new union structure and its relationship with government. These include industrial structure and the size of the informal economy, political factors such as the nature of the authoritarian status quo, the party system, and the partisan identity of incumbents, and current economic conditions.[20] Despite these variations, some simple principles can guide a new political deal for labor in the region and thus indirectly advance the cause of the new social contract. The first task is to get government out of the union business and to recognize the right of workers to form unions, engage in collective bargaining, and strike. In return, the government should insist on its right to guarantee that unions themselves are organized and run in a democratic and transparent fashion and to mediate disputes that cannot be settled between management and labor directly.

Once this broad framework is in place, it is difficult to predict what political role labor will play. Various patterns are possible. For example, in Korea the existence of a government-controlled federation, a relatively concentrated industrial structure, and a high share of manufacturing in total output resulted in two competing federations following the transition to democratic rule in the late 1980s. Competition between them, a conservative incumbent government, and an economic boom generated a brief populist phase in which strike activity rose and union wage demands far outstripped productivity growth. In Indonesia, by contrast, the agricultural and informal sectors are large, and the sheer size of the country and the fragmented party structure generated a plethora of new federations and unions in 1998 and 1999. Strike activity also increased dramatically, but the crisis meant that unions wielded limited influence over wage setting.[21]

Despite this diversity, we can identify some possibilities for policy change. Where union organization is relatively concentrated, governments may draw labor into broader tripartite discussions. In Korea, Kim Dae Jung's government was able to trade new political rights and innovations in unemployment insurance for greater managerial flexibility with respect to layoffs. Government policy also can encourage union involvement in the organization and provision of training and in the design of industrywide skill certification programs, which encourage labor mobility by recognizing workers' acquisition of new skills. Indeed, such certification programs can be part of a larger bargain in which workers acquire enhanced mobility across employers, and employers acquire greater flexibility in hiring and firing. Singapore's experience shows that governments can, in principle, run efficient schemes geared to private sector needs, in part by creating strong channels for private sector input. But the requisite public sector efficiency is an exception, and in most settings it is more practical to strengthen the past strategy of providing incentives for private sector training and involve labor more actively in the design and certification of programs.

The prospects for policy change will depend on the political position of labor, which played a pivotal role in the development of the Western European welfare state. In the end, however, expectations about labor's political role should be modest. In some countries and sectors—for example, large firms in Korea and state-owned enterprises in Thailand—labor unions are relatively strong. For a number of reasons, however, labor's overall influence in East Asia has been small, in part because of the newness of democratic rule and in part because of structural factors such as the size of the small firm and informal sectors and the emphasis on export-oriented manufacturing. A new system of industrial relations is as likely an outcome as an input to a new social pact.

Because labor is relatively weak, the nature of political parties and other civil society groups is critically important. Political parties are able to aggregate—and reconcile—the interests of poorly represented, diverse, and sometimes conflicting groups, from the new middle class to workers in small firms and the urban informal sector, and thus can stand as a counterweight to powerful conservative and pro-business forces. Yet these parties also need to be pushed by a denser organization of independent civil society groups. Such groups provide information and signals to politicians and represent both geographical and functional constituencies that have been ignored in the past. In some cases, they also can play a direct role in monitoring and implementing new social initiatives.[22]

Other Aspects of a New Social Contract

The unusually rapid improvement in the amount and distribution of education in most countries of East Asia was not the result of specific efforts to target the poor. On the contrary, education policy emphasized universal access to education; only Thailand stands out for its relatively poor performance in raising secondary school enrollment rates in line with per capita income growth. East Asia's good record in education was based on universal access, ensured via heavy public spending on primary and secondary education. In contrast to the pattern in Africa and Latin America, public spending on university education remained relatively low (Birdsall, Ross, and Sabot 1997).

An obvious ingredient of a post-crisis social contract is a guarantee that public spending on primary and secondary education will not be cut in the event of future economic downturns. There is evidence that education (and health) were initially cut in the early attempts to reduce public spending and meet IMF fiscal targets. If fully implemented, spending cuts would fall especially hard on inputs such as books and supplies that could be reduced more quickly than personnel costs, creating substantial inefficiencies and hitting hardest the households most reliant on good schools.

In addition, the reductions in enrollment rates at the junior secondary level in Indonesia, including in urban areas, are a worrying reminder that parents have to be active participants in schooling investments and that children's enrollment is still vulnerable to temporary losses of income. Given this, the stay-in-school subsidy program initiated in Indonesia was a particularly noteworthy crisis-induced innovation, well worth assessing and institutionalizing for application in any future downturns.

In education, however, the biggest challenges will come at the tertiary level. Political pressures for increased public spending on university education will inevitably mount as the emergent middle class seeks upward mobility for its children. The demands of a number of technology-intensive sectors will require that the middle-income countries of Asia, while maintaining incentives for private research and development, also ratchet up public investment in basic and applied research. The larger firms are likely to support public-private partnerships with universities.

The key principle for a post-crisis social contract on higher education should thus be the need to channel public spending on universities primarily to research and other public goods, while avoiding the across-the-board support that can contribute to overbuilt and inefficient public university systems. Misguided spending on tertiary education can be highly costly, particularly in poorer countries, draining human and administrative as well as financial resources from other levels of education and ultimately making public spending on education highly regressive. Adequate access for students to university training can then be based on the deepening of capital markets that is critical to healthier financial systems and on government-led management of student loan and scholarship programs for the sons and daughters of poorer members of the striving class.

A final element of the social contract, one that is likely to garner widespread social support under democratic conditions, is the greater decentralization of social programs. The arguments in favor of decentralization of service provision—as well as the risks—have been examined in detail elsewhere and need not be fully rehearsed here. Greater decentralization is a critical part of the new social contract because education and health services that are publicly financed will only continue to be efficient and effective where providers, whether public or private but with public financing, are accountable to immediate consumers. Across a range of other social services, from water to identification of the poor, local governments are likely to have superior information than higher levels of government and to be more responsive to local tastes. The political dilemma of any effort to decentralize services is that it requires political decentralization to be fully effective. A number of Asian countries remain highly centralized and unitary in their political structure, and politicians and bureaucrats at the center resist ceding power to lower levels of government. Yet to fully realize the social benefits of decentralization requires not only the ceding of greater functions to lower levels of government but also the institution of electoral accountability, local revenue-raising capacity, and the involvement of local community groups and nongovernmental organizations in the process of decisionmaking and implementation. These changes clearly are not just administrative; rather, they replicate at the local level the national process of democratization, including the formation of responsible and accountable governments, the formation of local party organizations that can recruit leaders and politicians, and the institutionalization of accountable and transparent government. These are clearly long-term tasks, but they are likely to be advanced by the development of local civil society groups, for which the barriers to entry into the political game are clearly lower at the local level.

The Risks of Democracy

We have made the point that democratic politics are relatively new, reducing the channels by which the poorly organized vulnerable strivers can express their views as an economic group. In fact, immature or incomplete democracies create some risks in the area of social policy.

The first risk is that democratic politics will place demands on government that politicians will attempt to meet at the cost of fiscal and macroeconomic stability, what might be called the Latin American disease. There is little evidence for such an eventuality. In no East Asian case has political reform been accompanied by an unsustainable expansion of government. The reasons for this are multiple, including the conservative nature of the democratic transitions and the absence of the yawning social deficits and inequalities that generate populist politics. Rather, the risk is almost exactly the opposite: changing tax and expenditure patterns that are increasingly regressive in their structure, as the example of university funding suggests. A sound social contract would have at its core either near-neutrality in the incidence of government or biases in favor of the structurally poor rather than the middle classes or rich; by and large countries in the region achieved this enviable feat in the early years of their growth (World Bank 1993).

However, in the aftermath of the financial crisis, the situation is less pretty. The opening of capital markets in the 1990s led to collusion between the corporate and banking sectors in which the rich used the banks to accumulate debt-financed wealth. A substantial portion of the resulting liabilities in the form of nonperforming loans has now been assumed directly or indirectly by government. This socialized debt will ultimately be paid off by the taxpayers, as the increasing share of debt servicing in government expenditures already demonstrates. In short, the risk to a new social contract comes not from populist demands but from the threat that the cleanup of the financial crisis involves fiscal commitments that will squeeze out social expenditures and thus erode the categories of public spending that were most progressive. This threat is particularly real in Indonesia, where the burden of the crisis is heaviest.[23]

A second and related risk is that democratization will allow newly freed interest groups, particularly labor and the "popular sector," to launch an assault on market-oriented policies. This is the much-touted fear of "backlash" that has become common currency in both academic (Rodrik 1997) and popular (Friedman 1999) discussions. Examples of such backlash might be new business-labor alliances for greater protection, resistance to privatization, or the crafting of various labor entitlements that reduce labor market flexibility and exacerbate dualism and inequality. The Brazilian Constitution of 1988 is perhaps the most egregious example of the latter, devoting no less than eight pages to the length of the work week, vacation pay, severance pay obligations, and other policies whose costs ultimately fall on both capital and unorganized workers.

Yet, again, the risks seem very much the opposite. Outside of some isolated areas, labor seems relatively weak in the region, and if there is a threat of future populism or backlash, it is likely to come not from politicians' response to a strong, well-organized labor movement but from political frustration on the part of the weak that manifests itself in strikes, demonstrations, and even social violence. The strategy of incorporation that is an underlying theme of our emphasis on social insurance, industrial relations, and education is designed precisely to forestall such an eventuality.

A third and more troublesome risk stems from corruption. This risk takes a bewildering variety of forms, from the expropriation of individual retirement accounts by unscrupulous financial agents (as in Albania) to the political use of fiscal resources either to benefit cronies or to advance electoral aims. Such risks are real, but they also were apparent under authoritarian rule and arguably were even more egregious. Lacking other sources of legitimacy, authoritarian rulers typically resorted to payoffs to secure political loyalty. Moreover, the closed and nontransparent nature of government provided ample, and in some cases virtually unlimited, opportunities for malfeasance.

Thus the antidote to this risk lies at least to some extent in democracy itself. Democratic politics does generate electoral pressures for corruption, particularly because of the importance of campaign financing in seeking office. And all governments are vulnerable to the misappropriation of public funds, no more or less in the area of social policy than in other areas such as spending on infrastructure and defense. But democracy has the advantage of providing opposition groups with incentives to ferret out such abuses in the process of political competition. Moreover, democratic governance allows for various forms of participation by outside parties that, while running the risk of capture and undue influence, also provide opportunities for oversight and monitoring.

A final risk is that the new democratic politics and the new social contract we have outlined will do little to protect the very poor. For their own reasons, authoritarian governments in the region had incentives to pursue policies from which the poor benefited, even if that was not their initial design. Under democratic rule, however, the poor are seldom well represented politically, and their interests may be pushed aside in the interests of business, the middle class, or even the somewhat better-off strivers on whom we have placed so much emphasis.

Again, our suspicion is that these fears are misguided, and although it is not a foregone conclusion, the prospects for social protection of the poor seem more, rather than less, secure under democratic rule. First, where the poor have benefited from programs of social protection, it is often because the middle class endorses program designs that provide help to all who face some risk of falling into poverty under well-defined circumstances. Indeed, the poor may gain more from a small portion of a large program than from a large portion of a targeted but underfunded program (Nelson 1999). Second, we cannot rule out the fact that political entrepreneurs do have incentives to appeal to the poor wherever they can be counted on to vote; the strong showing of Megawati in the Indonesian elections was based in no small measure on her implicit appeals to the urban disadvantaged.[24] Finally, social solidarity and moral impulses are relevant. Historically, once citizens act collectively through government to provide social protection in some form, the moral imperative of including the poor is likely to receive at least some attention. In politics, relying only on the play of interests is too narrow a focus; some understanding also is needed of reciprocal obligations that have deeper cultural roots.

We began by noting that the social contract is necessarily the outcome of a sometimes-contentious democratic process. Indeed, the social response to the crisis showed the stamp of a new democratic politics at a number of points: in the efforts of Kim Dae Jung to bring labor into the policy dialogue in Korea; in the role of urban and middle-class civil society groups in the emergency social programs in Thailand; in the refor-masi movements in Malaysia and Indonesia. We conclude by noting that, over the next decade, the deepening of democratic processes and the evolution of a social contract can ideally reinforce each other in East Asia, in turn also providing social and political support for the economic restructuring that is central to the region's long-term growth. The social contract, including specific safety net programs and the underlying rights that shape and insure it—rights to membership in political groups, to collective bargaining in the workplace, and to the vote—are in the end the outcome of political bargains that are bound to be forged locally. Asia has a long tradition of adapting and remolding ideas from outside. During the crisis, international pressure and the financial incentives of the World Bank and other lenders provided the context for initiating various poverty and social insurance programs. But in the long run, we must look to democratic politics to see which ideas took root and in what forms they will blossom in different settings. In the end, democratic politics will be fundamental to shaping a more explicit Asian social contract.

An earlier version of this essay was published as a monograph of the Carnegie Endowment for International Peace, under the auspices of the Carnegie Economic Reform Network. The authors are grateful for the support of that program, and to the Institute for International Economics.

Notes

1. Birdsall and Londoño (1998) compare East Asia and Latin America. The coefficient of variation of schooling in East Asia declined from over 1.6 to above 0.9 between 1960 and 1990.

2. Moreover, although in the 1980s and 1990s East Asia as a whole was much more equal than Sub-Saharan Africa and Latin America, it was no more equal than the Middle East and North Africa and less equal than South Asia or the advanced industrial states (Ahuja et al. 1997, table 3.1).

3. Based on the data made available by Nicholas Prescott of the World Bank; probably calculated from the household income and expenditure survey reported monthly by the Korean National Statistical Office, which covers household and urban wage and salary workers.

4. Ahuja et al. (1997, table 2.1, 6) shows the percentage of the population in poverty in Malaysia and Thailand to be below 1 percent in 1995.

5. Gupta et al. (1998, table 1). The poverty line per person (dollars per month) was $227 in Korea (apparently 1990s dollars). There continues to be some controversy about how the poverty line is set in Indonesia; a comparative

assessment of the poverty lines that Indonesia and the Philippines used in the 1980s suggests that the incidence of poverty in Indonesia was understated compared to that in the Philippines at that time (Asra et al. 1997).

6. High interest rates in normal circumstances restrict access to credit more for small than for large borrowers. In Korea, for example, the number of bankruptcies doubled between November and December 1997 and remained above the pre-crisis level until August 1998. Unemployment data confirm that workers in small firms were most likely to be laid off.

7. Pritchett, Suryahadi, and Sumarto (2000), using survey-based information on the variability of expenditures per capita from year to year and assuming that 20 percent of households are poor, estimate that an additional 30 percent of households in Indonesia face a better-than-even risk of falling into poverty in a three-year period. They report that households in Indonesia with heads with primary education and in urban areas experience greater variability in expenditures than households with heads with less than primary education and in rural areas. Thus, although such households are less likely to be poor in any one year than less-educated rural ones, they are also more "vulnerable" to poverty over several years.

8. The income figures cited here are in purchasing power parity (PPP) terms, which are higher for these countries than conventional estimates of gross national product (GNP) per capita. Estimated per capita GNP for Indonesia in 1995 was $3,880 in PPP terms and $980 in conventional terms; the PPP and conventional estimates for the United States in that year were both $26,980 (World Bank 1997). The PPP estimates take into account differences across countries in local prices of nontradables; those prices tend to be lower than the lower average income in a country.

9. Some household data indicate that among the richest 25 percent of households in Indonesia, almost half the household budget went for food in 1996; this high percentage indicates the relatively low absolute income even of the relatively well off. The proportion of income spent on food by the average household is 70 percent in Indonesia compared to 10 percent in the United States (Poppele, Sumarto, and Pritchett 1999).

10. The principal sources for this section are for Korea, Park (1999), Moon, Lee, and Yoo (1999), and Fields (1999); for Indonesia, Beegle, Frankenberg, and Thomas (1999), Poppele, Sumarto, and Pritchett (1999), and Thomas, Frankenberg, and Beegle (1999); for Thailand, Brooker Group (1999), World Bank, Thailand Office (1999a, 1999b), Pongsapich and Brimble (1999), and Kittiprapas and Intaravitak (1998). For an excellent review covering all countries, see Manuelyan-Atinc (1999).

11. SMERU (1999, 6); Thomas, Frankenberg, and Beegle (1999) correct for differences in inflation, leading to a higher estimate of the decline in rural areas.

12. World Bank, Thailand Office (1999b).

13. The focus on targeting by the international community also reflected political difficulties in the donor countries, especially the United States, with per-

manent "poverty" or "welfare" programs for the structurally poor. (Because such programs are not appealing to the middle class and therefore are politically vulnerable and less securely funded, they tend to be narrowly targeted, with strict eligibility criteria to minimize their costs.)

14. The World Bank has supported the social fund approach extensively in Latin America and Africa; in those regions, the targeted beneficiaries are the most poor.

15. As of July 1998, wages had dropped 12.4 percent in real terms (Park 1999).

16. Even when these contributions are, for all practical purposes, payroll taxes, they are typically understood to provide "insurance" rather than unearned transfers. Even when employers contribute, it is not clear who bears the real costs of the payroll tax. Employers can pass on the costs to consumers in the form of higher prices as long as the demand for their product is not too price-elastic. In open economies, this will be difficult in the tradable sectors. Employees will indirectly bear the costs of employer contributions the more flexible are wages.

17. To the extent the markets remain wary of resulting fiscal deficits, the IMF can play a role in distinguishing between countries depending on their fiscal history and in supporting appropriate countercyclical efforts in settings where fiscal discipline has been the norm.

18. It is Singapore, with a dominance of American, Japanese, and European multinationals, that has the most comprehensive—and costly—form of social insurance in its Central Provident Fund.

19. In the case of Chile, for example, efforts to reduce the high administrative costs of the privately managed funds by, among other steps, reducing the number of eligible managers, were resisted, although eventually overcome.

20. See, for example, Deyo (1989); Frenkel (1993); Frenkel and Harrod (1995).

21. Diwan (1999) shows that, in general, financial crises are associated with declines in the share of labor, which are not made up fully in the aftermath of the crisis.

22. In the short run, the absence of center and center-left parties, which in the West played this role, is a constraint; the question is whether a political force representing the diverse interests of these groups will emerge as a healthy counterpoint to the historically powerful conservative and pro-business forces.

23. Recent estimates of the cost of the financial crisis are as high as 30 percent of annual GDP, far higher than the previous records of about 15 percent in such countries as Mexico and Venezuela (Pangestu, personal communication, 1999).

24. Graham and Kane (1998) show that politically "opportunistic" social expenditures may benefit the poor (and help to build the case for economic reform), but at the risk of inefficiency and misuse.

References

Ahuja, Vinod, Benu Bidani, Francisco Ferreira, and Michael Walton. 1997. *Everyone's Miracle?* Washington, D.C.: World Bank.

Asra, A., I. P. David and R. V. Virola. 1997. Poverty Assessment in the Philippines and Indonesia: A Methodological Comparison. *PIDS Journal of Philippine Development* 24(2), second semester.

Barro, Robert J., and J. W. Lee. 1996. "International Measures of Schooling Years and Schooling Quality," *American Economic Review* 86(2): 218–23.

Beegle, Kathleen, Elizabeth Frankenberg, and Duncan Thomas. 1999. "Measuring Change in Indonesia." Report to the International Bank for Reconstruction and Development. Santa Monica, Calif.: Rand Corporation (May).

Birdsall, Nancy, and Juan Luis Londoño. 1998. "No Tradeoff: Efficient Growth via More Equal Human Capital Accumulation in Latin America." In *Beyond Trade-Offs: Market Reforms and Equitable Growth in Latin America,* edited by Nancy Birdsall, Carol Graham, and Richard Sabot. Washington, D.C.: Brookings Institution and Inter-American Development Bank.

Birdsall, Nancy, David Ross, and Richard Sabot. 1995. "Inequality and Growth Reconsidered: Lessons from East Asia." *World Bank Economic Review* 9(3): 477–508.

———. 1997. "Education, Growth, and Inequality." In *Pathways to Growth: Comparing East Asia and Latin America,* edited by Nancy Birdsall and Frederick Jaspersen. Washington, D.C.: Inter-American Development Bank.

Birdsall, Nancy, and Richard Sabot. Forthcoming. "Virtuous Circles: Labor Markets and Human Capital in East Asia."

Brooker Group. 1999. "Socioeconomic Challenges of the Economic Crisis in Thailand." Report submitted to the Asian Development Bank and the National Economic and Social Development Board under an Asian Development Bank Technical Assistance on Capacity Building for Social Reform. Brooker Group, Bangkok (July).

Campos, José Edgardo, and Hilton L. Root. 1996. *The Key to the Asian Miracle: Making Shared Growth Credible.* Washington, D.C.: Brookings Institution.

Deininger, Klaus, and Lyn Squire. 1996. "A New Data Base for Income Distribution in the World." *World Bank Economic Review* 10(3): 565–91.

Deyo, Frederick. 1989. *Beneath the Miracle: Labor Subordination in the New Asian Industrialism.* Berkeley: University of California Press.

Diwan, Ishac. 1999. *Labor Shares and Financial Crises.* Washington, D.C.: World Bank.

Duryea, Suzanne, and Miguel Székely. 1998. "Labor Markets in Latin America: A Supply-Side Story." Working paper 374, Office of the Chief Economist, Inter-American Development Bank, Washington, D.C. Available at: *www.iadb.org/res/publications/pubfiles/pubwp-374.pdf.*

Fields, Gary. 1999. "The Employment Problem in Korea." Unpublished paper. Cornell University, Ithaca, N.Y.

Frenkel, Stephen, ed. 1993. *Organized Labor in the Asia-Pacific Region: A Comparative Study of Trade Unionism in Nine Countries.* Ithaca, N.Y.: ILR Press.

Frenkel, Stephen, and Jeffrey Harrod, eds. 1995. *Industrialization and Labor Relations: Contemporary Research in Seven Countries.* Ithaca, N.Y.: ILR Press.

Friedman, Thomas. 1999. *Lexus and the Olive Tree.* New York: Farrar, Strauss, and Giroux.

Goodman, Roger, Gordon White, and Huck-ju Kwon. 1998. *The East Asian Welfare Model: Welfare Orientalism and the State.* London: Routledge.

Graham, Carol, and Cheikh Kane. 1998. "Opportunistic Government or Sustaining Reform? Electoral Trends and Public-Expenditure Patterns in Peru, 1990–1995." *Latin American Research Review* 33(1): 67–104.

Gupta, Sanjeev, Calvin McDonald, Christian Schiller, Marijn Verhoeven, Zelika Bogetic, and Gerd Schwartz. 1998. "Mitigating the Social Costs of the Economic Crisis and the Reform Programs in Asia." IMF paper on policy analysis and assessment. Washington, D.C.: International Monetary Fund, Fiscal Affairs Department.

Haggard, Stephan. 1990. *Pathways from the Periphery: The Politics of Growth in the Newly Industrializing Countries.* Ithaca, N.Y.: Cornell University Press.

Hong Kong. Census and Statistics Department. 1999. "Hong Kong in Figures." Accessed November 3, 1999 at: *www.info.gov.hk/censtatd/eng/hkstat/index2.html.*

IMF (International Monetary Fund). 1998. "The Crisis in Emerging Markets, and Other Issues in the Current Conjuncture." IMF Occasional Paper. Washington, D.C.: International Monetary Fund.

Kittiprapas, Sauwalak, and Chectha Intaravitak. 1998. "Impacts of the Asian Economic Crisis: Case of Thailand." Paper presented at a conference Impacts of the Asian Economic Crisis, Thailand Development Research Institute. Bangkok (November 23–24, 1998).

Knowles, James C., Ernesto M. Pernia, and Mary Racelis. 1999. "Assessing the Social Impact of the Financial Crisis in Asia: Overview Paper." Paper presented at the Asian Development Bank Conference on Assessing the Social Impact of the Financial Crisis in Selected Asian Developing Economies, Manila (June 17–18).

Korea, National Statistical Office. 1998. Statistical Database (KOSIS). Accessed November 3, 1999 at: *www.nso.go.kr/eng.*

———. 1999. Statistical Database (KOSIS). Accessed November 3, 1999 at: *www.nso.go.kr/eng.*

Manuelyan-Atinc, Tamar. 1999. *Towards a New Social Contract.* Unpublished manuscript. World Bank, Washington, D.C.

Moon, Hyungpo, Hyehoon Lee, and Gyeongjoon Yoo. 1999. "The Social Impact of the Financial Crisis in Korea: Economic Framework." Unpublished paper. Seoul, Korean Development Institute.

Nelson, Joan. 1999. *Reforming Health and Education: The World Bank, the IDB, and Complex Institutional Change.* Overseas Development Council.

Park, Se-Il. 1999. "Labor Market Policy and the Social Safety Net in Korea: After 1997 Crisis." Unpublished paper. Brookings Institution, Washington, D.C.

Pongsapich, Amara, and Peter Brimble. 1999. "Assessing the Social Impact of the Financial Crisis in Selected Asian Developing Countries: Executive Summary (Thailand)." Asian Development Bank. Manila (June 17–18, 1999).

Poppele, Jessica, Sudarno Sumarto, and Lant Pritchett. 1999. "Social Impacts of the Indonesia Crisis: New Data and Policy Implications." Unpublished report. Jakarta, Indonesia: Social Monitoring and Early Response Unit (SMERU) (March).

Prescott, Nicholas. 1997. "Poverty, Social Services, and Safety Nets in Vietnam." World Bank Discussion Paper No. 376. Washington, D.C.: World Bank

Pritchett, Lant, Asep Suryahadi, and Sudarno Sumarto. 2000. "Qualifying Vulnerability to Poverty: A Proposed Measure with Application to Indonesia." Unpublished paper. World Bank and SMERU, Washington, D.C.

Ranis, Gustav, and Frances Stewart. 1998. "The Asian Crisis and Human Development." Paper presented to the Institute for Development Studies, Seminar on the Asian Crisis, Brighton, U.K. (July 13).

Rodrik, Dani. 1997. *Has Globalization Gone Too Far?* Washington, D.C.: Institute for International Economics.

SMERU. 1999. *Social Monitoring and Early Response Unit Newsletter* 6 (June–July). Available at: *www.smeru.or.id/news.htm*.

Statistics Singapore. 1999. Historical Data. Accessed November 3, 1999 at: *www.singstat.gov.sg/SDDS/data.html*.

Stiglitz, Joseph. 1999. "Reflections on Mobility and Social Justice, Economic Efficiency, and Individual Responsibility." In *New Markets, New Opportunities? Economic and Social Mobility in a Changing World,* edited by Nancy Birdsall and Carol Graham. Washington, D.C.: Brookings Institution Press and Carnegie Endowment for International Peace.

Thomas, Duncan, Elizabeth Frankenberg, and Kathleen Beegle. 1999. "Household Budgets, Household Composition, and the Crisis in Indonesia: Evidence from Longitudinal Household Survey Data." Paper prepared for the 1999 Population Association of America meetings. New York (March 25–27).

World Bank. 1993. *The East Asian Miracle.* New York: Oxford University Press for the World Bank.

———. 1997. *World Development Report 1997.* Washington, D.C.: World Bank.

World Bank, Thailand Office. 1999a. "Thailand Social Monitor 1: Challenge for Social Reform." Bangkok: World Bank, Thailand Office (January).

———. 1999b. "Thailand Social Monitor 2: Coping with the Crisis in Education and Health." Bangkok: World Bank, Thailand Office (July).

Chapter 4

Is There a Future for Social Policy in Latin America?

MIGUEL SZÉKELY AND RICARDO FUENTES

L ATIN AMERICA is a region with a tradition of investments in public health and education. The state has devoted considerable effort to providing labor protection and to implementing policies explicitly aimed at reducing poverty. Paradoxically, these traditions coexist with the well-known fact that Latin America has the highest level of income inequality in the world. How is this possible? Is the strategy followed so far simply wrong? Should the public sector do more, or should it do less?

This chapter seeks to provide some answers to these three questions, with special emphasis on new approaches for social policy for the future. We use information from a vast collection of household surveys to document some of the basic facts and rely on a growing body of research on inequality in Latin America to argue that this is the right time to redefine the scope and orientation of social policies in the region. The latest evidence shows that economic growth does not automatically reduce poverty or improve living standards for the whole population, so social policies are most likely to continue playing a central role in guaranteeing that the benefits of development accrue to all segments of society.[1]

The chapter is divided into three broad sections and a final section with some general conclusions. The first section discusses the paradox of relatively broad social policies coexisting with high inequalities. Our argument is that, in terms of social policies, Latin America's policies are of more limited scope than those of Western European countries with a long and well-established tradition of a welfare state and labor protection, but with a more established tradition of social policies and labor protection

102

than the countries of East Asia, which have had much more limited state intervention in these affairs. The second section takes an historical perspective to argue that one important reason why social policies and high inequalities have coexisted in Latin America during the past twenty-five years is that social policies and, in particular, poverty alleviation policies have been subject to the excess volatility of the macroeconomic environment. The third section outlines a new strategy for social policy in Latin America, arguing that there are ways of improving the current situation and of establishing the role of the state in the new context of a globalized world.

Traditional Social Policies and Social Inequalities

Social expenditure in Latin America has been historically high for the level of gross domestic product (GDP) of the countries in the region. Figures 4.1 and 4.2 plot expenditures on health and education as a share of GDP and show that, while Latin America is below the expenditure levels in Europe and Central Asia in terms of health, the region is above the

Figure 4.1   Education Expenditure as a Percentage of GDP by Region, 1988 to 1996

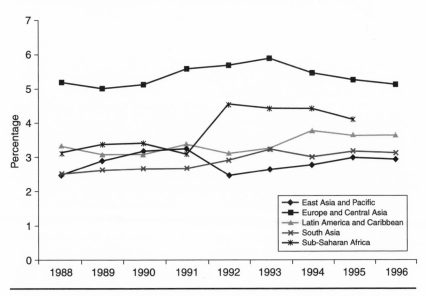

Source: World Bank (2000).

Figure 4.2   Public Health Expenditure as a Percentage of GDP, by Region, 1990 to 1997

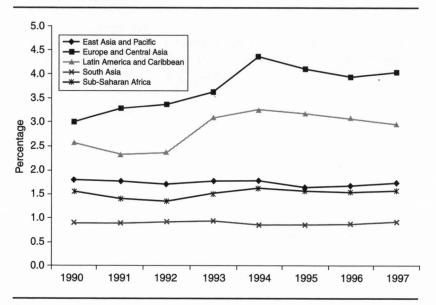

Source: World Bank (2000).

expenditure levels in South Asia and in East Asia and the Pacific in terms of education. Figure 4.3 plots the share of all social expenditures as a share of GDP in the ten Latin American countries with available data. Only two countries—Brazil and El Salvador—have levels well below 10 percent. Moreover, social expenditure in most of these countries increased during the period 1990 to 1999.

However, such high expenditures on health and education do not necessarily imply an efficient allocation of resources or a significant improvement in the welfare of the poorest members of society. According to the latest evidence, high expenditures have been accompanied by growing inequality and lack of distributive progress in the region (see Székely 2001). Of course, this mismatch may exist because social expenditure, when well targeted, does not affect social conditions right away. What is perhaps most interesting is that the data in figure 4.3 cover practically a ten-year period of growing expenditure with no signs of reversing income inequalities.

In the remainder of this section, we argue that the high average expenditures on health and education are not necessarily a sign of widespread access to services. We also refer to other kinds of policy interventions, namely labor protection and social insurance, mainly because these areas

Figure 4.3 **Social Expenditure in Latin America as a Percentage of GDP, 1980 to 1999**

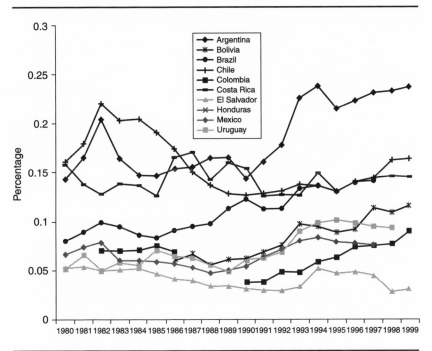

Source: World Bank (2000).

are traditionally identified as social policies. Even though our focus is on health, education, labor regulations, and social insurance, the public sector has many other mechanisms to improve the standard of living of the population, such as making electricity more accessible for households in the bottom of the income distribution.

Education Policies

As documented in figure 4.1, Latin America has relatively high average levels of education spending as a share of GDP. These high levels are not recent; they began several decades ago with the expansion of the schooling system during the initial stages of economic development.

The rapid expansion in coverage of the education system is documented in table 4.1, which plots the proportion of the population in select birth cohorts that has at least some primary schooling; that is, the share

Table 4.1   Proportion of the Population in Each Birth Cohort Completing at Least Some Primary School, by Country (Three-Year Moving Averages)

Country	Year of Birth					Change 1930 to 1950	Change 1950 to 1970	Change 1930 to 1970
	1930	1940	1950	1960	1970			
Honduras	39.3	58	72.5	84.2	87.9	33.2	15.4	48.6
El Salvador	45.2	59	68.6	81.4	85.6	23.4	17.0	40.4
Nicaragua	49.3	57.6	67.1	77.9	83.9	17.8	16.8	34.6
Bolivia	54.1	61.9	75.4	88.8	95.5	21.3	20.1	41.4
Mexico	59.7	71.5	83.1	91.1	94.8	23.4	11.7	35.1
Brazil	60.9	70.1	80	88	91.5	19.1	11.5	30.6
Venezuela	64.9	81.5	90.8	94.7	95.9	25.9	5.1	31.0
Ecuador	72.2	80.6	87.4	94.3	97	15.2	9.6	24.8
Colombia	74.1	82.4	89.2	93.9	96.3	15.1	7.1	22.2
Dominican Republic	75.3	79.2	88.5	92.1	93.6	13.2	5.1	18.3
Peru	76.2	82.8	89.4	96.4	97.4	13.2	8.0	21.2
Costa Rica	79.7	87	94.6	96.6	98	14.9	3.4	18.3
Panama	84.6	88.2	93.8	98	98.4	9.2	4.6	13.8
Paraguay	86.1	91.5	93.5	96.8	97.7	7.4	4.2	11.6
Chile	87.7	91.9	96.6	98.3	98.6	8.9	2.0	10.9
Jamaica	91.3	95.2	97	97.1	95.9	5.7	-1.1	4.6
Uruguay[a]	94.8	97.8	98.8	98.6	99.2	4.0	0.4	4.4
Argentina[a]	100	100	100	100	100	0.0	0.0	0.0
Average Latin American country	72.0	79.8	87.0	92.7	94.8	15.1	7.8	22.9
Korea	67.8	90.7	98.4	99.6	99.7	30.6	1.3	31.9
Taiwan	71.7	76.5	96.2	99.5	99.8	24.5	3.6	28.1
United States	99.2	99.5	99.5	99.7	99.8	0.3	0.3	0.6

Source: Authors' calculations from household survey data. Data from Korea was taken from the UNESCO *Statistical Yearbook* (1997).
[a] Surveys cover urban areas only.

of people who completed at least one grade of formal education at some point in their lifetime and therefore enrolled in school.[2] For example, among people born in 1930, who today are around seventy years of age, the average proportion of people who were enrolled in the schooling system in the region is 72 percent. For cohorts born ten years later (in 1940), who today are around age sixty, the proportion is 80 percent, while for those born in 1950, the share is 87 percent. For those born in 1970, who today are around thirty years old, the same share is 95 percent. This means that the schooling system expanded 35 percent in the course of forty years. The pace of the expansion is even greater than that registered in Korea or Taiwan, which are noted for making great strides in schooling during the postwar era.

Although this rapid expansion of access to schooling applies to the region as a whole, there are differences within Latin America. While Uruguay and Jamaica had already reached coverage rates of 95 percent for the cohorts born in 1940, it took Chile ten more years to reach this stage, and Costa Rica, Paraguay, and Peru another ten years. Brazil, El Salvador, Honduras, and Nicaragua did not even reach the stage of near-universal coverage for cohorts born in 1970. In any case, all Latin American countries have made considerable progress in expanding their schooling system and allowing the majority of their populations to enter formal education. This coincides with an active role of the state in channeling considerable public funds to the education system.

The problem arises when we go beyond averages and look at exactly who is benefiting from the public schooling system today. There are sharp inequalities in educational attainment, largely because the poor have very few years of schooling. Furthermore, there are large gaps in the returns to education.

In figure 4.4, we use household survey data to illustrate schooling inequalities by presenting the average difference in years of schooling among fifteen-year-olds living in the poorest and richest 10 percent, respectively, of the population in eighteen Latin American countries. The differences are striking, especially if we consider that, at this age, these children will most likely have few opportunities to close the gap. In Bolivia, Brazil, and Guatemala, fifteen-year-olds living in households belonging to the richest 10 percent of the population enjoyed three more years of schooling than fifteen-year-olds living in households in the poorest 10 percent of the distribution. And even in cases where the gap has closed, large inequalities *within* countries persist. In Mexico, for instance, the gap in years of education for fifteen-year-olds between the poorest 30 percent and the richest 10 percent closed slightly in the period from 1984 to 1996 (figure 4.5), but even so, the differences across states are striking. Figure 4.6 plots the years of education in Mexico by state in 2000.

Figure 4.4   Differential in Years of Education Among Fifteen-Year-Olds Living in the Poorest and Richest 10 Percent of Households, by Country

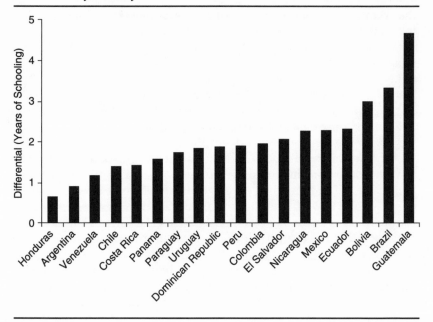

Source: Authors' calculations using household survey data.

While the richest states in the northern states and Mexico City are close to Chilean levels of education, which are the highest in Latin America, Chiapas and Oaxaca have an average below that of Guatemala, which is the lowest in Latin America.[3]

High public education expenditures have had only a limited impact on schooling inequality largely because education is a cumulative process. One can only benefit from the full "package" by passing through the whole system from primary to higher education. But to acquire the benefits, individuals also have to incur private costs, including lost wages. Furthermore, while the opportunity cost of attending school increases due to the higher wage that potentially can be earned in the labor market, the marginal short-run benefit of continuing in the schooling system generally increases at a slower pace. This provides incentives to poor families to exit the schooling system in order to increase their consumption level in the short run and, therefore, excludes them from the benefits derived from public expenditures in education at further stages.

Figure 4.5   Years of Education Among Fifteen-Year-Olds Living in the Poorest 30 Percent and Richest 10 Percent of Households in Mexico, 1984 to 1996

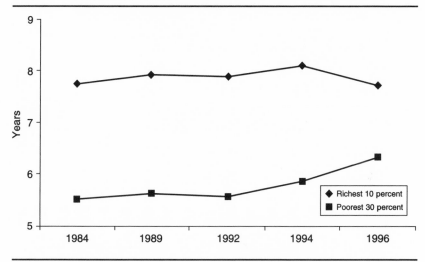

Source: Authors' calculations using household survey data.

The structure of public expenditures on education reinforces inequalities. Figure 4.7 shows the public expenditures per student in primary, secondary, and tertiary schooling during the 1990s in Latin America. The resources devoted to the higher levels of schooling are more than four times greater than those devoted to the primary levels. Since the vast majority of persons in the poorest income brackets attain only primary education, they do not benefit from the bulk of the benefits. In contrast, persons in richer households progress through the system and have access to the greatest expenditures per student.

Given the high inequality in access to the system, expanding the expenditures on public education is unlikely to eliminate schooling differences between rich and poor. Other support mechanisms directed specifically to the poor are necessary. Public policy can support the accumulation of skills by disadvantaged individuals in at least two ways. First, to be able to invest in the education of its members, a household has to be able to afford the private costs of schooling. To attend school, even when no tuition fees are involved (as with public education), one must finance transportation, clothing, food, and, most important for poor families, the opportunity cost of attending school. If households lack the means to finance even these basic investments, they probably will underinvest in

Figure 4.6   Average Years of Schooling by State, in Mexico, 2000

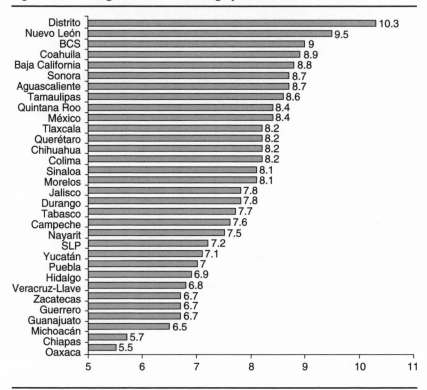

Distrito 10.3
Nuevo León 9.5
BCS 9
Coahuila 8.9
Baja California 8.8
Sonora 8.7
Aguascaliente 8.7
Tamaulipas 8.6
Quintana Roo 8.4
México 8.4
Tlaxcala 8.2
Querétaro 8.2
Chihuahua 8.2
Colima 8.2
Sinaloa 8.1
Morelos 8.1
Jalisco 7.8
Durango 7.8
Tabasco 7.7
Campeche 7.6
Nayarit 7.5
SLP 7.2
Yucatán 7.1
Puebla 7
Hidalgo 6.9
Veracruz-Llave 6.8
Zacatecas 6.7
Guerrero 6.7
Guanajuato 6.7
Michoacán 6.5
Chiapas 5.7
Oaxaca 5.5

Source: Authors' calculations from the Mexican Census 2000.

human capital. Educational support programs such as Progresa in Mexico or Bolsa Escola in Brazil, which provide direct financial assistance to households conditioned on their investment in the education of their family members, are one of the best policy options for enhancing the accumulation of human capital by the poor.[4] But even these programs would be more effective if they additionally offer students school supplies, meals, and transportation services to make the effect stronger.[5]

Second, to make investment in schooling an attractive option for a household, services of a certain quality have to be available. As discussed in recent Inter-American Development Bank reports (IDB 1996, 1998), resource allocation in the schooling system of most Latin American countries is shaped by payment commitments to large bureaucracies and not by the level and quality of educational results. Higher-income families may have the chance to escape to private schools where competition and standards for quality are in effect, but the poor have no option but to

Figure 4.7   Expenditure per Student by Educational Level in Latin America (Percentage of Gross Net Investment per Capita), 1990 to 1996

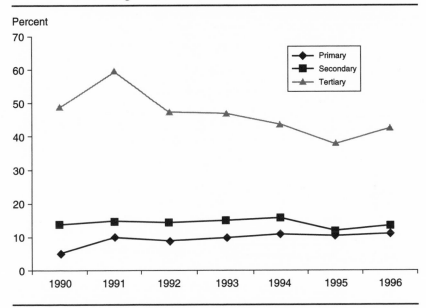

Source: Calculations from World Bank (2000).

attend the public system; when it is of low quality, differences in human capital are intensified. The government can play a decisive role by generating information, setting quality standards, and assuring that schools receive funds from public resources based on the quality and quantity of the education they provide, instead of focusing only on bureaucratic and budgetary controls.[6] There is also scope for introducing new ways of teaching for the disadvantaged. Education by television, for example, is an innovative way to reach the poor in remote areas, and it has not yet been exploited to its full potential.[7]

An additional problem is that many of the poor are already beyond school age and will not benefit from improvements in the standard schooling system. They are the ones who dropped out early because their families could not finance the investment any longer or who never attended more than a couple of years of school due to the poor quality of public schools and pressing household financial needs. Training policies may be one of the only ways to reverse the disadvantage these individuals face in the labor market. But here, too, there are problems of investment capacity and supply of training services since it is normally more costly to train individuals with lower levels of schooling than those with higher levels. One option could be to create Progresa-type programs that would give direct incentives in the form of cash transfers conditioned on training.

On the supply side, in Latin America technical education and training programs, especially those targeting the poor, became obsolete decades ago (see IDB 2000). Some countries are beginning to experiment with incentives to improve the operation of such programs. In some instances, the private sector has created its own training centers, supported by pay-roll taxes, but the quality of this option is not always good, and these centers are difficult to monitor. Perhaps the scope for action is in redefining the role of the government as regulator of the system rather than as service provider. If this is combined with income-support programs, the poor might have more and better opportunities to acquire the training they need to increase their income-earning power for the rest of their working life.

One of the main concerns in the provision of education is the extremely large amount of resources employed by ministers at the national level. This centralization of education policy poses problems for both efficiency and equity. Low levels of secondary education are the norm, but the organization of this service generally favors higher rather than primary and secondary education. This has a considerable effect on inequality, as only well-to-do individuals are able to attend college. As long as the systems are focused on the supply of resources—that is, the amount of money going into education—instead of the results, the inefficiencies will continue. There seems to be general agreement that more autonomy is needed at the state level in order to achieve a better assignment of resources and make the system more capable of internalizing feedback.

Health Policies

Latin America made undeniable improvements in the health sector during the twentieth century. During the past five decades, the gap in life expectancy between industrial countries and Latin America narrowed by more than a third, and infant mortality rates plunged from 106 to 31 deaths per 1,000 live births (IDB 2000). However, in broad indicators, such as disability-adjusted life years, which measure loss of productive life due both to mortality and to disease, Latin America stands well below the average of 120 in developing countries, with 220 person-years lost on average (IDB 2000, 8).

Furthermore, there is a sharp contrast between the high levels of expenditure on public health in Latin America (figure 4.2) and health outcomes. While public expenditure on health in Latin America is among the highest in the world, and increased from 2.5 percent of GDP in 1990 to 3 percent in 1997 (with a peak of 3.5 percent in 1994), in eight countries—Bolivia, Ecuador, El Salvador, Guatemala, Haiti, Honduras, Paraguay, and Peru—less than 40 percent of the total population has access to basic health services (IDB 1996, 315). Some countries, like Argentina, Barbados, Belize, Chile, Costa Rica, and Uruguay, are very similar to Southeast Asia in terms of life expectancy, but others, such as Bolivia, Guyana, and Haiti, are closer to Africa than to the rest of Latin America and are below the Asian countries (IDB 2000, 9).

At the core of the problem of health disparities is that centralized systems, which have predominated in the region, are more efficient when relatively homogenous groups need to be served, since central planning gives rise to economies of scale that allow extended medical coverage to large sectors of the population (Savedoff 1998). When a centralized system is introduced in the context of large initial inequalities, centralization can reinforce inequality. Mexico offers a good example. Census data show that, while life expectancy in Mexico City and the northern state of Nuevo León are practically the same as in Chile (the country with the highest life expectancy in the region, at seventy-five years), life expectancy in Oaxaca (the state with the lowest level, at sixty-eight years) is very close to that of Honduras (the country with the lowest life expectancy in the region). Similarly, while infant mortality rates in Mexico City and Nuevo León are around 20 per 1,000, which is practically the same as in Argentina (the country with the lowest infant mortality in Latin America), the states of Chiapas, Guerrero, and Oaxaca register rates of about 50 per 1,000, higher than the rate of 40 per 1,000 observed in Guatemala (the country with the highest infant mortality in the region). These differences in large part reflect the limitations of a centralized planning system that is unable to respond to the diverse needs of users with very different social characteristics across geographic areas.

Reforms in the health sector—principally decentralization—have been widespread in the region. In Brazil, for instance, a new policy regime was initiated in 1982 with the so-called health integrated actions, in which the administration and programming of health services became the responsibility of three levels of government: federal, state, and municipal. Further reform came in 1987 with the Unified System and Health Decentralization program, which gave different levels of government more autonomy in the decisionmaking process. By 1990 the Unified System had become the Single System, and the 1988 constitution granted the existence of single health units, which were run at the municipal level.

In Chile, reform started as early as 1979, when three institutions were given responsibility for three basic functions: control and policy issues were under the influence of the Ministry of Health, execution was an obligation of the Sistema Nacional de Servicios de Salud (SNSS), and funding was provided by the newly established Fondo Nacional de Salud. In 1981 management was transferred from SNSS to the municipal level, and the new pension system provided workers when the opportunity to obtain private health insurance plans managed by private administrators called Instituciones de Salud Previsional. Since then, few changes have taken place. The health system remains highly decentralized in execution, although the state is still in charge of supervision and design of the system, subsidy programs, payment mechanisms, and regulatory framework.

Colombia instituted a particular type of reform by conditioning decentralization on a certification process carried out by the Ministry of Health. Municipalities or districts fulfilled certain requirements in order to run the health system locally. These requirements included the development of a basic health information service, formulation of a local health plan, and creation of a local health fund. This system proved slow and not particularly fair, as it was not clear why some municipalities proceeded, while others did not.

What is the next step? As with schooling, there are two main reasons why the poor usually have more precarious health than the rich, even in the context of large public expenditures.[8] They have fewer means for financing the private costs of accessing the public health system, and they often lack appropriate health insurance and therefore have access only to lower-quality public services open to the whole population.

To address the lack of means, one option is to provide families with direct income support to finance health services. Mexico's Progresa program is a good example, but even actions of this type fall short because they do not normally include support for medication or preventive services for infants. Expanding income support to include these items would help to improve, or at least maintain, the health of the poor.

On the supply side, Latin American governments have usually ignored the private health insurance markets by building and financing hospitals to provide high-cost treatment directly. The problem is similar to that of public education in the sense that efficiency is low, and, in the end, it is not clear whether the objective is to provide health services or to support the huge bureaucracies that have grown around these institutions. As in the case of schooling, perhaps the main challenge is to create effective regulatory frameworks that guarantee access of the poor to basic health services. IDB (1996) acknowledges that resources for spending in the health sector are limited and that potential improvements could be achieved by enhancing efficiency. To do so, it proposes a set of measures to change the organization of public health services. These include increasing the autonomy of local providers, building mechanisms of accountability through information, empowering consumers through choice, and allocating resources on the basis of outcomes rather than budgetary needs. These changes are deep, but they have the potential to benefit the poor or at least to improve their access to health services.

Labor Protection

Latin America has highly inflexible labor markets. Although different benefits and programs were created to improve and preserve workers' rights and welfare, there are well-known costs as well: when a labor market is highly regulated, fewer people can enter into it, at least in the sector where all the benefits are provided.

Labor legislation in Latin America has evolved based on two principles: labor stability and worker protection (IDB 1996). Labor stability appears whenever the worker obtains ownership rights over his or her job position and thus is entitled to unemployment compensation. Different legislation exists in the region regarding which causes are just and which are not in case of dismissal and regarding the total amount of compensation and the notification period prior to termination of the labor relationship. The IDB argues that this legislation creates uncertainty for firms and distorts the labor market.

Heckman and Pagés (2000) describe labor market regulations in Latin America and the Caribbean and compare them with those in the Organization for Economic Cooperation and Development (OECD) countries (see table 4.2 for regulations in Latin America and the Caribbean). They compute an index measuring the firing costs that "summarizes the entire tenure-severance pay profile using a common set of dismissal probabilities across countries" and reflects the level of inflexibility. The computations of this index for 1990 and 1999 are shown in figure 4.8. The index is a cardinal measure showing that job regulation, or its expected costs, is almost twice as high in Latin America as in the industrial countries and 50 percent higher than in the Caribbean; these results hold in spite of the recent wave of structural reforms. Heckman and Pagés (2000) stress the difficulty firms face in terminating employees' contracts, the high cost of dismissal, and the requirement to pay forgone wages in case of strikes or legal processes.

During the 1990s, a shift toward deregulation created more flexibility in the Latin American labor markets. In the first half of the decade, Argentina, Colombia, Guatemala, Panama, and Peru reformed legislation in order to reduce the real or perceived costs of compensation. Several countries experimented with different approaches to cost cutting. Argentina, for instance, reduced the actual sums paid in compensation, while Colombia reduced the uncertainty involved in severance payments.[9]

Table 4.2 Labor Market Regulations in Latin America and the Caribbean

Country	Date of Reform	Advance Notice 1990	Advance Notice 1999	Seniority Premium 1990	Seniority Premium 1999	Compensation if Worker Quits 1990	Compensation if Worker Quits 1999	Compensation for Dismissal Due to Economic Reasons 1990	Compensation for Dismissal Due to Economic Reasons 1999	To Whom the Reforms Apply	Upper Limit to Compensation for Dismissal 1990
Argentina	None	1 to 2 months	1 to 2 months	0	0	0	0	$\frac{2}{3}m \times N$, min 2 months	No changes		Max. lim. in m
Bahamas	None	½ to 1 month	No changes	0	0	0	0	Negotiable	No changes		No
Barbados	None	Negotiable In practice 1 month	No changes	0	0	0	0	$0.41 \times m \times N$ if $N \geq 2$	No changes		Max. $m \times N =$ 3.75
Belize	None	½ to 1 month	No changes	0	0	$\frac{1}{6}m \times N$ if $N \geq 10$	No changes	$\frac{1}{4}m \times N$ if $N \geq 5$	No changes		Max. 42 weeks
Bolivia	None	3 months	No changes	0	0	$1m \times N$ if $N \geq 5$	No changes	$1m \times N$	No changes		No
Brazil	1988	1 month	No changes	Pension fund (8% wage $+ r$)	Fund (8% wage $+ r$)	0	0	$0.4 \times$ Fund	No changes		No
Chile	1991	1 month	No changes	0	0	No	$\frac{1}{2}m \times N$ (2) if $N \geq 7$	$1m \times N$ (3)	No changes	All workers	Max. $m \times N = 5$
Colombia	1990	45 days	No changes	$m \times N$ Double retroactivity given lack of inflationary adjustment of withdrawals	Fund (8% wage $+ r$)	Fund	No changes	$m \times 4$ if $N = 5$ $m \times 6.6$ if $N = 10$ $m \times 16.5$ if $N = 15$ $m \times 21.5$ if $N = 20$	$m \times 4$ if $N = 5$ $m \times 6.6$ if $N = 10$ $m \times 21.5$ if $N = 15$ $m \times 28.5$ if $N = 20$	All workers	No

Country											
Costa Rica	None	1 month	No changes	0	0	0	0	m × N	No changes	No changes	Max. m × N = 8
Dominican Republic	1992	¼ to 1 month	No changes	0	0	0	0	½ × m × N	.67 × m × N if N = 1–4, .74 × m × N if N ≥ 5	New employees	No
Ecuador	None	1 month	No changes	Pension Fund (8% wage + r)	Fund (8% wage + r)	Seniority premium	No changes	¼ m × N + 3 × m if N ≤ 3 + m × N if N = 3 – 25, N = 3 – 25 + pension if N ≥ 25	No changes		No
El Salvador	1994	0 to 7 days	No changes	0	0	0	0	m × N 0 if bankruptcy	m × N changes in max. m	All workers	Max. base wage = 4 wages (4)
Guatemala	None	0	0	0	0	0	0	2 days–4 months if bankruptcy m × N otherwise	No changes		No
Guyana	1997	½ month	1 month if N ≥ 1	0	0	0	0	Negotiable in practice, 2½ weeks per N	¼ × m × N if N = 1 – 5, ½ × m × N if N = 5 – 10	All workers	No
Honduras	None	1 day to 2 months	No changes	0	0	0	0	m × N	No changes		Max. m × N = 15
Jamaica	None	2 to 12 weeks	No changes	0	0	0	0	⅓ × m × N if m = 2 – 5 ½ × m × N if m ≥ 5	No changes		No
Mexico	None	0 to 1 month	No changes	0	0	0	0	⅔ m × N (min. 3 × m)	No changes		No
Nicaragua	1996	1 to 2 months	0	0	0	0	m × N if N = 1 – 3 3m × N + ⅔ m × N if N > 3	Negotiated in practice, 2m × N	m × N if N = 1 – 3 3m × N + ⅔ m × N if N > 3		No

(*Table continues on p. 118.*)

Table 4.2   Continued

Country	Date of Reform	Advance Notice 1990	Advance Notice 1999	Seniority Premium 1990**	Seniority Premium 1999	Compensation if Worker Quits 1990	Compensation if Worker Quits 1999	Compensation for Dismissal Due to Economic Reasons 1990	Compensation for Dismissal Due to Economic Reasons 1999	To Whom the Reforms Apply	Upper Limit to Compensation for Dismissal 1990
Panama	1995	1 month	No changes	$\frac{1}{4} \times m \times N$ if $N \geq 10$	$\frac{1}{4} \times m \times N$	$\frac{1}{4} \times m \times N$ if $N \geq 10$	$\frac{1}{4} \times m \times N$	$m \times N$ if $N \leq 1$; $3 \times m$ if $N = 2$; $3 \times m + \frac{3}{4} \times m \times N$ if $n \geq 2 \leq 10$; $9 \times m + \frac{1}{4} \times m \times N$ if $N \geq 10$	$\frac{3}{4} m \times N$ if $N < 10$; $7.5 \times m + \frac{1}{4} \times m$ if $N \geq 10$	New employees	No
Paraguay	None	1 to 2 months	No changes	0	0	0	0	$\frac{1}{2} \times m \times N$	$\frac{1}{2} m \times N$		No
Peru	1996 1995 1991	0	0	Determined by judge in legal proceedings	Pension fund (8% wage + r)	Pension fund (8% wage + r)	Seniority premium	$3 \times m \times N$	Funds + $1.5 \times m \times N$	1991 new employees 1995 all workers 1996 all workers	Max. $m \times N = 12$
Suriname	None	¼ to 6 months	No changes	0	0	0	0	Negotiated	Negotiated	New employees	No
Trinidad and Tobago	None	2 months		0 0	0	0 0	0	$\frac{1}{3} m \times N$ if $N = 1 - 4$, $\frac{1}{2} m \times N$ if $N \geq 5$	No changes		No
Uruguay	None	0		$m \times N$	No changes	0	0	$m \times N$	No changes		Max. $m \times N = 6$
Venezuela	1997	¼ to 3 months	No changes	$m \times N$	$2m \times N$	$m \times N$	$m \times N$	$\frac{2}{3} - 2m \times N$	$2m \times N$	All workers	No

Source: Heckman and Pagés (2000).

m = Monthly wages.

N = Years of tenure.

r = Real interest rate.

Figure 4.8   Job Security Index (Expected Discounted Cost of Dismissing a Worker, in Multiples of Monthly Wages), 1990 and 1999

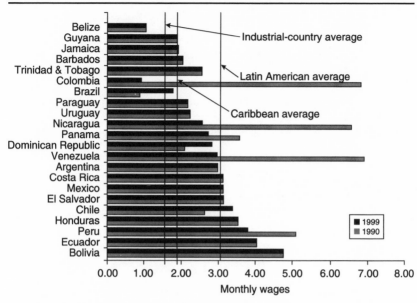

Monthly wages

Source: Based on data from Heckman and Pagés (2000).

At the same time, various programs were being implemented to minimize the impact of reforms on the labor market. Márquez (2000) points out three different types of programs in the labor market: employment generation, training, and unemployment insurance. According to Márquez, employment generation programs have been the most recurrent policy instrument used in times of economic or financial crisis, since they are generally self-targeted and can be implemented quickly in the face of economic turmoil. The problem, however, is that, by their nature, they provide only short-term support that tends to be inefficient when the crisis is prolonged. Short-term training programs are attractive because they may provide long-lasting benefits, but their use has been somewhat restricted.

With regard to unemployment insurance, there is little experience in the region. It is by no means a universal policy in Latin America, and, where it exists, its scope is very limited. According to Márquez (2000), Brazil has the largest system, with around 400,000 beneficiaries, but no other country in Latin America comes close to these numbers or to having the majority of the workforce under this type of scheme. Unemployment insurance also has well-known limitations, such as moral hazard problems and the generation of dependency among beneficiaries, but when it is well managed, unemployment insurance may constitute an efficient safety net for the poor. It is likely that the region will begin to use this policy instrument more intensively.

Minimum wages, on the contrary, are a common feature of labor markets in Latin America, despite the controversy around their usefulness. The problem is that minimum wages may lead to lower employment and can make it impossible for labor markets to clear.

One key aspect of labor markets in Latin America that tends to reinforce inequality is workers' self-organization. Unions can play an important role in the protection and decisionmaking of workers, but in Latin America, they tend to increase income inequality by protecting privileged groups of workers, including those in the public sector. Furthermore, even industrial unions tend to have close relationships with the state. This combination of powerful unions that negotiate through collective bargaining and inflexible labor legislation results in a small "club" of formal sector workers who benefit from the protection, stability, and benefits provided by the state. As a consequence, those who want to work but cannot access the formal sector are forced into informal sector activities, which tend to involve higher risks, less stability, and lower wages.

Table 4.3 documents the fact that labor force participation rates change systematically along the income distribution. Household survey data reveal that the poor participate systematically less than the rich in all countries. The difference in participation is overwhelmingly explained by female participation, which remains substantially below male participation throughout the region. The gap between genders is substantially higher than in the industrial countries. This difference is particularly large in the Central American countries, Chile, Mexico, Panama, and Venezuela.

While male participation is relatively constant and high along the income distribution, female participation varies strongly with income in all countries except Paraguay and Peru. Although on average in the region only 34 percent of women in the top decile are out of the labor force, among the poorest three deciles more than 55 percent are not working.[10]

When poor women participate, they do so mainly in the informal sector. This is clear from table 4.3, which presents the share of informal employment among women of working age. The proportions working in the formal and informal sectors change dramatically along the income distribution. For example, while poor women in Ecuador, Paraguay, and Peru have high participation rates, they are conspicuously absent from the formal sector. By contrast, women in the top decile, who participate twice as much as poor women, on average, have a much smaller presence in the informal sector and an overwhelming presence in the formal sector.

Table 4.3 Labor Force Participation Rates by Income Decile (Ages Eighteen to Sixty-Five)

				Total Labor Force						Informal Sector					
		Total		Top 10 percent		Bottom 30 percent			Total		Top 10 percent		Bottom 30 percent	
Country and Year	All	Males	Females	Males	Females	Males	Females		Males	Females	Males	Females	Males	Females
Argentina, 1996	65.5	83.2	48.8	88.5	68.1	80.9	39.6		35.1	22.2	18.0	12.8	48.2	27.6
Bolivia, 1995	63.4	76.2	51.5	80.2	57.6	72.8	44.6		38.0	36.6	21.0	20.7	45.0	38.5
Brazil, 1995	69.2	86.8	52.5	85.8	61.7	85.9	44.8		48.2	20.0	32.6	17.8	56.8	18.4
Chile, 1994	58.1	80.0	37.5	78.5	55.7	78.3	21.3		33.1	14.3	17.4	13.5	37.2	12.9
Colombia, 1995	62.3	84.5	42.1	87.2	52.2	82.8	27.2							
Costa Rica, 1995	62.0	86.0	38.0	86.0	57.0	82.0	25.0		42.0	17.6	21.2	10.9	52.8	17.0
Ecuador, 1995	72.3	89.1	55.8	90.2	69.6	87.7	50.4		54.7	44.4	29.7	27.9	68.5	52.0
El Salvador, 1995	61.4	82.4	43.4	84.2	62.4	78.3	23.1		46.3	30.2	24.4	23.4	60.6	23.9
Honduras, 1996	63.1	88.4	39.7	86.6	61.7	86.5	24.1		55.9	30.2	34.4	21.8	72.3	31.5
Mexico, 1994	N.A.	84.2	37.9	82.4	52.3	85.1	29.9		58.2	28.8	30.7	19.5	67.7	33.2
Panama, 1995	60.2	80.4	40.0	83.5	63.8	79.6	24.3		39.2	15.2	11.7	6.6	63.8	19.6
Paraguay, 1995	60.1	90.8	72.8	84.9	60.2	83.0	59.0		64.8	52.8	36.1	34.9	88.1	65.1
Peru, 1996	78.7	84.1	59.8	90.8	72.8	93.6	64.7		49.6	44.3	28.8	29.5	53.7	46.7
Uruguay, 1995	71.7	85.3	57.0	88.7	67.2	83.6	48.3		27.5	22.7	16.6	12.9	35.3	28.1
Venezuela, 1995	70.3	82.3	39.6	86.6	59.3	76.5	24.7		41.1	18.5	29.4	13.9	43.7	19.3
Industrial countries	61.2	94.0	73.0											

Source: Authors' calculations from household survey data.

These differences in labor force participation largely reflect differences in opportunities. For instance, figure 4.9 uses household survey data to document the rate of female participation by education level in the fifteen Latin American countries that appear in table 4.3. There is a strong and clear correlation between educational attainment and participation. In fact, the differences between educational levels are quite sharp. While only some 40 percent of women with four years or less of schooling participate in the labor market, over 78 percent of those with higher education do. The differences in participation by educational attainment are even larger in the formal sector.

One reason for the sharp difference between male and female labor force participation is that traditional labor legislation in the region was designed by men, for men. Its objective was to generate formal employment with benefits and with guarantees for stable jobs. But this induces discrimination against women, because these mechanisms impose higher implicit costs for hiring women (due to maternity leave and allowances, for instance) and because it restricts employment to full time and limits flexibility in hours, making employment prohibitive for women who work both inside and outside the home. In short, labor legislation induces much lower participation rates among poor uneducated women.

Figure 4.9   Female Labor Force Participation Rate by Level of Education in Latin America

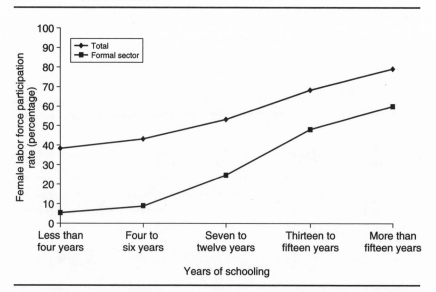

Source: Authors' calculations from household survey data for fifteen Latin American countries.

Public policy can help to support female participation in the workforce in at least four ways. The first is by providing access to basic infrastructure and services that lower the cost of household chores and free some time for women. The second is by enhancing child care services and preventive health services that create a network of support for females. These could be either subsidized by the state or promoted through appropriate taxes, or other schemes, for private firms. A third way is by socializing maternity costs. Rather than charging these costs to employers, the state could finance them through fiscal revenue, improving the incentives to hire women.

The fourth way is by designing labor legislation itself. As argued by IDB (1998), labor protection laws and regulations favor individuals who work in the formal sector, leaving the rest with few benefits. At least two types of actions could improve labor market opportunities for poor women in this respect. The first is to introduce greater flexibility into contracting conditions in order to allow for part-time or temporary workers. This would have to be accompanied by the corresponding (proportional) benefits enjoyed by full-time workers. The second action is to introduce unemployment payments to stabilize the incomes of workers who lose their jobs or are transiting between jobs. Many countries have established individual savings accounts that can be used as personal unemployment insurance, but this insurance is restricted to the formal sector of the economy. For those in informal employment, collectively financed social safety nets could be created that play the role of social insurance. Individual savings accounts could possibly be expanded to cover these groups.

Social Insurance

Even though the demographic transition has been much slower in Latin America than in industrial countries, Asia, or Eastern Europe, Latin America's population is starting to age, and it will age even more rapidly in the years to come. The share of population of working age is increasing; there is a steady decline in the share of children ages birth to fifteen years; and an increase in life expectancy is expanding the share of population over sixty-five years of age. Although social insurance mechanisms and, in particular, pension systems have not been at the heart of the social policy debate, they surely will be in the near future. These demographic changes are threatening the financial soundness of several systems because most of the region is covered by pay-as-you-go (PAYG) schemes. With the shift of the population toward the retirement age group, there will be fewer and fewer people of working age per pensioner, placing an excessive burden on social security for the generation where the working age group is smallest. IDB (2000) estimates that by 2050 a direct transfer of 50 percent of the wage from workers to pensioners will be necessary in countries with an advanced demographic transition, such as the Bahamas, Costa Rica, and Jamaica.

Chile, of course, has set the pace for pension reform in Latin America. Early in the 1980s, the Chilean government shifted from a state-run PAYG system to a privatized, individual accounts scheme. Following the Chilean example, many countries have moved from a common pension fund to a wholly or partially privatized pension fund. Pension reform has occurred in Peru (1993), Argentina (1994), Uruguay (1996), Mexico (1997), Bolivia (1997), and El Salvador (1998).

Many other governments in the region have also placed pension reform at the top of their social agenda. Venezuela has been planning an ambitious new system in the wake of the year 2000 constitution. This program consists of two parts: the Fondo de Solidaridad Intergeneracional (FSI) and Individual Accounts. Individual Accounts is a fund that provides a pension for those who did not accumulate enough capital in individual accounts during their working life span. The system will create incentives so that working people will be less willing to contribute to individual accounts because of the universality of the pension coming from the FSI. And, of course, the FSI eventually will face accounting problems due to the demographic transition.

In Panama, despite a current surplus in the existing PAYG program, there is growing interest in shifting toward individual accounts. But the biggest country in the region, Brazil, still runs a very complicated national pension system, which differentiates public from private workers. Disparities in the contribution, the deficits, and the benefits of these two subsystems create a new problem for social security reform; in 1999 the total deficit of the social security system as percentage of GDP was 4.7 percent, of which the public sector accounted for 3.7 percent.[11]

According to the IDB (2000), pension systems with individual private accounts seem to be the best choice for the region under the present circumstances. They create incentives for workers to make contributions and increase efficiency in the management of those funds. The IDB additionally suggests a shift in the state's role in pensions toward regulation, oversight, and provision of the necessary subsidies for poor workers with low levels of savings in their individual accounts when they retire.

Even if private accounts seem to be the best option at hand, they are not likely to solve the problem of social security on their own. The informal sector forms a considerable part of the economy, and as these employees do not pay or report to tax agencies, they do not participate in the standard formal pension scheme. This problem is not necessarily solved even by programs targeted to the informal sector, because they do not guarantee labor market participation. So, although it is clear that the way forward is to design schemes that give social protection to individuals who do not have access to the formal labor market, the exact way to do this is still a topic for analysis and debate.

Poverty Alleviation Policies in Latin America

A key element of social policy—some would argue *the* key element—is poverty alleviation programs. While education, health, labor protection, and social insurance are well-established policies and have been present in every country and type of government in Latin America, poverty alleviation programs came on the scene much later, and their resources, design, and scope have been highly volatile.

Despite variations from country to country, poverty alleviation programs can be broadly associated with four phases of economic development: the postwar era of import-substituting industrialization, the debt crisis of the 1980s, the structural adjustment packages of the mid-1980s to the early 1990s, and the incipient recovery of the mid-1990s.

The First Phase

The first phase covers the period between World War II and the late 1970s. These were the golden years of economic growth in Latin America. The industrial sector in most countries was expanding vigorously, fueled by the import substitution development strategy popular in those decades. The urban middle classes were expanding (see, for instance, Székely 1998 for a description of the case of Mexico). All kinds of subsidies were granted for industrial production under the belief that industrialization was the best engine for growth.

This first generation of poverty-focused social policies was characterized by the widespread provision of subsidies for goods and services open to the whole population. Its main beneficiaries were the expanding middle classes. Some of these subsidies, such as for food consumption, were justified as being an indirect subsidy to support industrial sector wages. Since high growth rates financed these widespread subsidies to consumption, there was a virtuous circle: on the one hand, the middle class contributed to economic growth by joining the industrial sector and migrating from rural areas. On the other hand, the policies introduced to facilitate import substitution improved the standard of living of vast sectors of the population by guaranteeing low prices for basic goods and by supplying subsidized services.

In essence, the poverty alleviation strategy and the wider development strategy were one and the same. The same was true for the rural sector. Rural areas provided primary goods and natural resources for industrial production at low prices as well as low-cost goods for the expanding middle class. This implied subsidizing rural production as well as land redistribution, since high priority was given to minimizing idle resources and the under-usage of land. Again, social policy was seen as a fundamental part of the overall development strategy.

In spite of the large declines in poverty and inequality, at some point this development strategy proved unsustainable (see Londoño and Székely 2000 for evidence on poverty and inequality trends for Latin America during the 1970s). During the late 1970s and early 1980s, declining international oil prices triggered the debt crisis that pulled Latin America into a deep recession. This marked the end of the first phase and the start of the second.

The Second Phase

Under the new macroeconomic constraints of the early 1980s, widespread subsidies to goods and services were simply prohibitive. Governments had to cut all expenditures, especially in social areas, which were not the priority, in order to reduce public deficits. With escalating inflation rates, devaluation, and declining GDP, the priority was to stabilize the economy at all costs. It was hoped that, once the macroeconomic situation was under control, growth would resume and, with it, the expansion of the middle classes and the social development of past decades. People would have to endure some sacrifices in order to return to the glory days, including substantial declines in living standards. The sacrifice, however, would only be temporary and would not discriminate according to a person's position in the social ladder.

Consequently, the second phase began by dismantling the previous strategy. It coincided with an identity crisis of the state, where it was unclear whether the government's role should go beyond setting the rules and perhaps intervene only when markets failed. In this context, widespread subsidies, poverty alleviation policies, and social policies became an obstacle to growth rather than a powerful engine of development.

Growth did not resume immediately. Latin America went through a period of economic reform, intense volatility, and stagnation that lasted nearly the entire decade, and this prolonged the population's sacrifice well beyond initial expectations. The previous social strategy of providing widespread subsidies to the population at large proved to be financially unsustainable. However, it became evident that dismantling the previous system and minimizing the role of the state could also be unsustainable from the social point of view. Toward the end of the decade, inequality was growing, and—most worrying—poverty was rising.[12] This marked the end of the second generation of policies and the start of the third.

The Third Phase

The third phase began with the acknowledgment that structural adjustment programs and economic reform could impose greater burdens on the poor. It was recognized that the poor generally have fewer means of protecting their incomes from unexpected shocks or from the erosion of liquid assets entailed by high inflation. It also was recognized that they have the worst chances of engaging in activities with higher productivity and higher probability of surviving external competition.

Compensatory policies were introduced through the implementation of safety nets. In a set of influential papers, Ravi Kanbur (1985, 1987a, 1987b) introduced the idea of targeting resources to the poor. The concept of targeting is quite simple. It suggests that when budgets are limited in times of economic hardship, the policy challenge is to allocate scarce means in order to obtain the largest possible poverty reduction per dollar spent. Since there are administrative costs of finding the people who are most in need, the population is generally classified into subgroups according to some characteristic (such as geographic location, gender, or schooling). To target specific subgroups, it is necessary to have the guidance of poverty maps or poverty profiles, which identify the population that has the highest poverty rates and is the most sensitive (in terms of poverty reduction) to the allocation of funds. If some subgroups will generate higher poverty reduction per unit of budget spent, funds should be allocated to them until other subgroups arise where the marginal dollar would produce greater poverty reduction.

This third generation of policies had two important features. The first is that they entailed a different way of distributing resources. In fact, they entailed new "costs," since to find the poor, one had to look for them. Thus administrative costs incurred while identifying the target population had to be balanced with the benefits of identifying them. Under this framework, the policies of the first generation induced high "leakage," since many of the nonpoor or the not-so-poor were benefiting from resources that perhaps should have been allocated only to the poorest of the poor. Most of the gains from targeting originate precisely in reducing leakage. However, this comes at a cost. Since finding all the poor is too costly, some of the poor inevitably are "missed." The main challenge is to find a balance between administrative costs, leakage, and undercoverage.

The second, and perhaps most important, feature is that there was a deep change in the spirit of social policy. Under the targeting generation, policies aimed at raising the standard of living of the poor or at protecting them against the unfavorable macroeconomic environment were compensatory, and they had to be small, specific, and tightly focused. The growth strategy of countries might well be totally disconnected from these policies. More often than not, social and macroeconomic goals in the third generation of social policies were *not* part of an integrated strategy and were regarded as having opposite objectives. Perhaps due to the profound scars of the lost decade of the 1980s, the main objective of governments was to keep tight budgetary controls; thus poverty alleviation programs, although perhaps necessary, were a potential threat to public deficits and to macroeconomic stability. Poverty-focused policies and a country's growth strategy became two separate things; they were opponents challenging each other for public resources.

Table 4.4 presents a thorough list of the main poverty alleviation programs by country in Latin America from the early 1980s to the late 1990s. During the mid-1980s, social investment funds, most of which were "emergency" targeted social safety nets, proliferated. The first were introduced in Bolivia, with the Fondo de Emergencia Social (Emergency Social Fund, EFS). Although quite successful in the efficiency and transparency of resource use, this approach did not offer a permanent solution to poverty and did not reach the poorest of the poor (Graham 1996, 3). Nonetheless, the model proved highly influential, and many other countries in the region soon created their own social fund programs. In the early 1990s, for example, the Chilean government promoted the Fondo de Solidaridad e Inversión Social. Its main goal was to involve beneficiaries in the poverty alleviation process. Most such programs were aimed at promoting participation in poor communities to support microenterprises and income generation, particularly in rural areas, and to support youth programs that assisted poor young people who had left school with little formal education.

At the same time, Peru's government developed the Fondo Nacional de Compensación y Desarrollo Social (Foncodes). This fund proved to be a good project executor, managing more than 300 projects during its first year, but as in the case of ESF in Bolivia, Foncodes presented a limited scope and reach and, in a later stage, was used as a political instrument by President Alberto Fujimori in the marginalized areas of Peru (Graham 1996, 9).

Mexico had its own initiative, the Programa Nacional de Solidaridad (Pronasol), which operated up to 1994. This program directed funds to municipalities based on the demands of the communities and municipal governments, with the active participation of citizens in the use of funds. Most of the financing for Pronasol came from the privatization of public enterprises (Hiskey 2000). As in Peru, later stages of the program were closely linked to the partisanship of the municipalities, and funds were politically manipulated.

Table 4.4 Poverty Alleviation Programs in Latin America

Country	Program	Year
Argentina	Materno Infantil (PROMIN)	1993
	Plan de Arraigo de "Villas"	1991
	Programa de Normatización y Evaluación Medico-Asistencial	
	Programa de Prevención, Promoción y Protección de la Salud	
	Programa de Protección del Menor y la Familia	
	Programa de Subsidios de Desempleo	
	Programas Compensatorios	
Belize	Belice Hospital Fee Waivers	
Bolivia	Fondo de Emergencia Social	
Brazil	Programa de Nutrición en Salud (PNS)	1975
	Programa de Complemento Alimenticio (PCA)	1977
	Proyecto de Adquisición de Alimentos Básicos en Zonas Rurales de Bajos Ingresos (PROCAB)	1977
	Programa de Abastecimiento en Zonas Urbanas de Bajos Ingresos (PROAB)	1979
	Programa de Alimentación Popular (PAP)	1985
	Programa de Suplemento Alimentario (PSA)	1985
	Programa Nacional de Leche para Niños Desprovistos (PNLCC)	1986 to 1991
	Programa de Alimentación de los Hermanos de los Escolares (PAIE)	1986
	Programa de Apoyo Nutricional (PAN)	1987
	Programa Nacional de Atenção Integral à Criança e ao Adolescente/Projeto Minha Gente PRONAICA	1986 to 1993
	Projeto VALE SABER	
	Plan de Combate al Hambre y a la Miseria (PCFM)	1993
	Programa Nacional de Salud y Nutrición	

(Table continues on p. 130.)

Table 4.4   *Continued*

Country	Program	Year
Chile	Fondo de Solidaridad e Inversión Social	1990 to the present
	Programa Nacional de Superación de la Pobreza	
	Subsidio Unico Familiar (CAS-SUF)	
	Pensiones Asistenciales (CAS-PASIS)	
	Viviendas Básicas (CAS)	
	Programa de Alimentación Escolar (PAE)	
	Programas Especiales de Empleo (PEM and POIH)	
Costa Rica	Centros de nutrición (CEN/CENAI)	
	Comedores Escolares	
	Pensiones no Contributivas	
	Informática Educativa	1988
Colombia	El Programa de Desarrollo Rural Integrado	Two phases: 1976 to 1982, 1983 to 1990
	Nacional de Rehabilitación	
	Programa de Desarrollo Integral Campesino	1991 to 1996, third phase of Programa de Desarrollo Rural Integrado
Ecuador	Programa de Mejoramiento de la Educación Básica Rural	
	Programa de Desarrollo de la Eficiencia y Calidad de la Educación Básica Urbano Marginal	
	Proyecto de Fortalecimiento de las Areas de Salud	
	Programa de Modernización de la Salud	
	Fondo de Solidaridad	
Honduras	Bono Materno-Infantil (BMI)	
Jamaica	Foods Stamps Program (Means Tested)	
	Foods Stamps Program (Health Services)	
	Nutribun Program	
Mexico	Programa Nacional de Solidaridad	

Table 4.4   *Continued*

Country	Program	Year
	Coordinación General del Plan Nacional de Zonas Deprimidas y Grupos Marginados	
	Programa Integral de Desarrollo Rural	1989 to 1994
	Leche Industrializada Compañia Nacional de Subsistencias Populares	
	Tortibonos	
Nicaragua	Programa de Empleo Temporal (PET)	
	Fondo de Inversión Social de Emergencia	
	Programa Nacional de Desarrollo Rural	
	Proyecto de Educación Básica (APRENDE)	
Peru	Estrategia Focalizada de Lucha contra la Pobreza	
	Fondo Nacional de Compensación y Desarrollo Social (FONCODES)	
	Plan de Mejora del Gasto Social Básico	1996 to 2000
	Comedores Populares	1991 to ?
	Programa de Alimentación y Nutrición para Familias de Alto Riesgo (PANFAR)	
	Vaso de Leche	
Dominican Republic	Hospital Fee Waiver	
	Proyecto Materno-Infantil (PROMI)	

Source: Information compiled by the authors from the following sources: Grosh (1994); UNDP (various years); and interviews with country economists at the Inter-American Development Bank.

Many other governments implemented their own social funds (for example, Nicaragua and El Salvador), and in many cases they proved helpful, but incomplete. Their main feature was that, rather than creating income-earning capacity, they provided temporary assistance to the poor.

The Fourth Phase

The early 1990s marked yet another shift in the macroeconomic environment in Latin America. On the one hand, the first years of the decade witnessed the recovery of positive economic growth in most countries in the region. Economic performance was far from spectacular—with Chile a partial exception—but governments could afford to start looking beyond the objective of macroeconomic stability. On the other hand, the world-wide trend toward globalization became apparent during the middle years of the decade. The economic reforms implemented in the 1980s implied opening up Latin American economies and exposing them to world markets; during the 1990s, this was combined with similar trends in other regions of the world. Globalization made it clear that, to survive in today's world, it was necessary to be competitive, and although this implied a smaller government with a lower tax burden, it also required a highly skilled labor force.

This change in the economic environment has had crucial consequences for poverty alleviation policies, mainly because it implied that having large sectors of the population living in poverty limited a country's competitiveness. Those at the bottom of the social ladder rarely have the means to be "productive" in the new economic order. For instance, if poor families have limited means of financing the education of their children and large sectors of the population live in poverty, the country will have limited human capital and may have difficulty attracting investment to finance development. To be competitive, countries must have some natural resources or human, physical, or other factor endowments that enable them to produce goods or services at relatively low cost. Having an army of unskilled workers with low wages does not necessarily solve the problem. Workers need to have at least some minimum skills (such as the ability to read or write) and be physically able to engage in economic activity. Moreover, the awareness of human rights imposes some restrictions on the use of labor, such as requiring minimum standards in working hours and wages.

The fourth generation of poverty alleviation policies has continued to use targeting mechanisms to allocate resources, but two key features distinguish them from earlier efforts. The first is that their primary aim is to attack the *causes* of poverty (lack of education) and not just its *consequences* (low incomes). If one of the reasons why the poor are poor is that they have scarce human capital, then helping them to improve their human capital endowments by supporting investments in schooling or health (as is the case of Mexico's Progresa program) may improve their situation well beyond the operation of the program. Even if these programs are discontinued in the future, they might achieve permanent improvements in the standard of living of their beneficiaries because they improve income-earning capacities.

The second key feature is that these types of programs are not totally disconnected from the overall development strategy, as is the case of traditional targeted safety nets. These new policies can even be viewed as contributing to economic growth in the long run. For instance, since education is an important requirement for faster GDP growth, if these programs raise education levels, then in some sense they are fueling the economic system with resources useful for expanding production and enhancing competitiveness (see Birdsall, Pinckney, and Sabot 1998).

Apart from Progresa in Mexico, Bolsa Escola in Brazil and Chile Joven in Chile also exemplify this fourth phase. They are centerpieces of their countries' social development strategies, which have shifted away from only having temporary safety nets. These programs, which are being replicated across the region, provide assistance to the poor, with strong incentives for the accumulation of human capital. They help the poor by equipping them with the tools that will allow them to help themselves in the new economic environment.

The fourth-generation policies are normally viewed as a separate set of programs aimed at specific subgroups of the population needing government assistance. They impose costs on the economic system and have to compete for public resources at a time when many voices are advocating a smaller state. They have not been institutionalized in any country so far, yet they are still viewed as a necessary cost for compensating the disadvantaged.

Furthermore, these types of programs also entail some risks. The main danger is lodged in the belief that their successful implementation will effectively substitute for a broader social strategy. That is not the case. Although these programs have the capacity to improve the well-being of the poor, they cannot solve the poverty problem. For instance, they may raise the level of schooling among poor children, but if there are no opportunities to put human capital to work, they will not have the expected impact on the income-earning capacity of individuals.

New Directions for Social Policy

In spite of considerable improvements in some social indicators on average, large segments of society in Latin America still have not benefited much from the four phases of social policy. Paradoxically, this situation persists even though governments have traditionally devoted important amounts of resources on areas such as health and education and have implemented various types of poverty alleviation programs and labor protection.

One important challenge for policymakers in the region is to define a strategy that provides long-term solutions to the poverty problem. This section discusses some elements that could provide the foundation for such a strategy. Our main objective is to argue that governments still have a key role to play in social development, even in the new economic environment of the twenty-first century.

The main idea behind our approach is that poverty and the lack of improvement in the social well-being of the poor are mainly due to the unequal distribution of resources. In turn, the high inequality is, to a large extent, a consequence of the unequal distribution of income-earning *assets,* such as human and physical capital, and of the unequal distribution of investment and labor market *opportunities* to use the assets productively. Therefore, in order to understand the causes of inequality—and of poverty—it is necessary to explore why the distribution of assets and opportunities is so unequal.

Income-earning assets are normally acquired through a process of accumulation. Why are some individuals able to accumulate such assets, while others are prevented from doing so? Our answer is that this is because some sectors of society are subject to *restrictions* for investing in the accumulation of assets due either to market imperfections or to the absence of markets. Therefore, public policies that affect or eliminate these restrictions will have a greater chance of addressing the underlying causes of poverty and inequality.

The same is the case with the distribution of opportunities. Some segments of society do not have access to the opportunities generated by the economic environment because they face restrictions for accessing the productive sectors of the economy. If the restrictions they face were identified, it would be possible to delineate and debate policies to eliminate them.

In sum, the scheme proposed here for guiding social policy consists of identifying the restrictions underlying social disparities and then implementing policies to eliminate them. Some of the policy instruments we propose are already operating in many countries, but other key instruments are absent and constitute gaps in the social policy strategy. Some of the instruments that enter into this scheme are not normally thought of as part of the social policy agenda, and one important conclusion is that they should be at its core rather than at the margins.

Going Beyond Income

The first step toward approaching the social policy challenge is to go beyond income and focus on the determinants of the income level of an individual. Income is a frequent indicator of standard of living and a measure of economic success. Even though it is clearly an imperfect measure, it is useful for our discussion. In general terms, incomes are the result of a combination of four main elements:

- The income-earning assets owned by an individual;
- The opportunities that each person has to use his or her assets to generate income;

- The market price of income-earning assets; and

- The transfers, gifts, and bequests that are largely independent of the income-earning assets owned.

To simplify the discussion, we classify income-earning assets into two groups: human capital and physical capital. Human capital endowments determine an individual's capability, knowledge, and expertise for producing goods or services. Two key components of human capital are formal education and health.

In our scheme, physical capital refers to the monetary value of any financial or liquid asset, property, rents, or other form of physical capital used in the production of goods or services. These types of assets can play different roles: they can be used as a stock to buffer the impact of unexpected shocks; they can be used for investment in productive activity; or they can be accumulated with longer-term objectives such as savings for retirement. For the purpose of our argument, we can classify physical capital in two groups: housing and a household's basic services, and savings.[13]

The ownership of these income-earning assets implies that an individual has the capacity to generate an income, but in reality, the income flows depend on the opportunities at hand to put the assets to work. For instance, in the case of human capital, an individual's years of schooling may be translated into income if the individual participates in the labor market. Physical capital generates income when it is invested and produces a return. Therefore, we consider two types of opportunities: labor market opportunities and investment opportunities.

The third element in our list refers to the prices that determine the market value of assets. In Latin America, the market price paid for assets is usually set by supply, demand, and institutional (for example, labor legislation) factors. In short, prices are established by the nation's economic environment. In a globalized world economy, it becomes increasingly difficult to modify and set prices by direct policy intervention, with positive and negative effects for the welfare of any particular individual. We do not develop this issue here.

In sum, if we go a step beyond income and ask why some sectors of the population are living in much worse conditions than others, one answer is that there are underlying inequalities in the ownership of income-earning assets, such as health, education, housing, and investment capacity, and in the access to labor market and investment opportunities.

A Scheme for Organizing Policy Ideas

If this is the case, the central question is why some individuals are able to accumulate income-earning assets and have opportunities for using them to generate income, while others are prevented from doing so? The answer that we offer is that most individuals want to have access to a larger stock of assets and opportunities, but an individual will find it impossible to accumulate assets or to access economic opportunities if he or she is subject to restrictions. The problem, then, consists of identifying such restrictions and thinking about policies to eliminate them. Székely (1998) and Attanasio and Székely (2001) have identified the following restrictions in the context of Latin America:

1. Supply restrictions

2. Survival restrictions

3. Liquidity constraints

4. Insurance constraints

5. Restrictions on access to labor markets

6. Restrictions on access to financial markets

Restrictions for Accumulating Income-Earning Assets   The first restriction refers to the lack or insufficiency of the basic services needed to accumulate assets. For instance, in the case of education, access to schools and teachers is needed to be able to invest in human capital. In the case of health, access to hospitals or medical services is needed. In terms of infrastructure, access to basic services, such as electricity, potable water, or drainage, is needed. When a household is subject to the supply restriction, the process of asset accumulation is difficult, if not impossible, because the basic elements are missing.

The *survival restriction* consists of the absence of the minimum food and nutrition necessary to function in society. When a household lacks these basic elements, it most likely will not be able to look beyond survival and, therefore, will not be able to have a longer-term planning horizon. For instance, if a family has an income that is barely sufficient to provide each of its members with the necessary food for survival, it most likely will not be able to invest in longer-term ventures such as the acquisition of human capital, simply because such investments will be prohibitive. Even in the case of health and education, which are normally provided publicly, it is necessary to finance some private costs to be able to access them. Therefore, the insufficiency of resources to look beyond immediate survival is a key restriction on the accumulation of income-earning assets.

The *liquidity constraint* refers to the lack of resources or lack of access to credit markets to finance investments in productive ventures. Even when the environment generates opportunities, investment capacity is needed to transform the opportunity into economic activity or profits.

A household that is subject to the supply and survival constraints, but has access to credit markets, will be able to invest and therefore will have the opportunity to finance investment and increase future income flows. On the contrary, when there is no access to credit—for instance, due to the absence of efficient financial markets—the investment capacity of households will be equal to their own resources; when these are low, investment possibilities also are low.

The *insurance constraint* refers to the lack of market mechanisms to cushion unexpected shocks. When an individual or household is not able to acquire insurance, it generally uses its own resources as a buffer. For instance, when the risk of falling into unemployment rises and there is no access to unemployment insurance, individuals will probably have to use their savings to fulfill the household's basic needs. These kinds of savings become a mechanism for smoothing consumption in the event of a negative shock rather than a means for investing in longer-term ventures with higher returns. Another common example is the risk faced by farmers or peasants in rural areas where no insurance mechanism is available. When this is the case, they tend to invest in lower-profit and lower-risk projects in order to ensure survival in the long run.

Restrictions for Taking Advantage of Opportunities   Restrictions on opportunities can be classified into two groups for the purpose of our discussion. The first group includes labor market restrictions. Perhaps the most common of these restrictions is the discrimination faced by some population groups. For instance, in Latin America employers tend to exclude women or to hire them under unfavorable conditions simply because of their gender. Moreover, indigenous groups are marginalized from the labor market due to their cultural and ethnic characteristics.

A related labor market restriction is the *monetary entry costs,* among which transport costs are perhaps the most common. If, in order to perform a job, an individual needs to travel long distances, sacrificing monetary resources and time, the net value of the wage received is lower than it would be without these sacrifices. One example is the case of migrants. If an individual inhabits a geographic area where employment opportunities are scarce and needs to travel in order to find them, he or she will only be able to do so if resources are available to finance the transportation costs involved.

In many countries, a further restriction on access to labor markets is labor legislation itself, especially in the case of women. In Latin America, for cultural reasons, women usually play a central role in the performance of household chores and childrearing. Therefore, in order to participate in the labor market and generate an income, women usually require flexibility in terms of hours worked, schedule, and even location of employment. By prohibiting this kind of flexibility, labor legislation restricts women's access to the labor market even though this is generally not its intention. In order to eliminate entry restrictions to labor markets, perhaps the best option, at least for women, is to promote labor legislation making the rules of the game more adequate for them.

The second group of restrictions includes *investment constraints*. In a world of perfect credit markets, in which the economic environment offers investment opportunities, in principle any individual who can obtain a loan or finance investment can have access to profitable activity. However, when formal credit markets are imperfect, or simply nonexistent, as is the case for large sectors of society in Latin America, the absence of an efficient financial market will restrict the ability of individuals to transform opportunities into income flows.

Restrictions and Public Policies

We believe that social policy should focus on eliminating these restrictions—and many more that we may have overlooked. An integrated approach to social policy would create programs and implement mechanisms that "free" the poor from these constraints. By eliminating such barriers, public policies could trigger a virtuous circle in which the accumulation of income-earning assets, combined with the emergence of new opportunities, would allow individuals to generate resources by their own means, without the need for additional income support or poverty alleviation programs.

In the case of the supply restriction, and especially in the case of electricity, potable water, drainage, and basic infrastructure, the state has a role to play in covering the deficits accumulated in the past by the poor. In the case of housing, there is scope for helping to create both financial markets and a regulatory framework suitable for the poor. In most countries, public or private mortgages are only available for "finished" housing, defined as units that have been completely built and have access to basic services. The house itself is normally the collateral, so it has to have some minimum value for banks or other creditors to engage in the scheme. The problem is that the poorest of the poor either do not have access to mortgages because they are employed in the informal sector or do not meet the minimum requirements to qualify for a loan for the full price of a house. Either a regulatory framework promoting the financing of "unfinished" units or the creation of a market for "unfinished" housing could improve the ability of the poor to acquire housing of acceptable quality as well as access to services.

In order to eliminate the survival constraint, perhaps the best option is to use mechanisms such as those found in existing antipoverty programs like Mexico's Progresa or even food subsidies or social investment funds. Since the primary objective of every individual and household must be to survive, policies need to be developed and implemented to address this goal. Such policies are an absolute necessity, but they should not—cannot—constitute the entire social policy strategy.

In the case of liquidity constraints, one option worth considering is the promotion of informal credit mechanisms such as family or other social networks. However, these resources are limited for the poor because their networks are poor as well. When family resources are restricted, people must resort to informal credit markets that charge high interest rates. This reduces the profitability of investment or makes it prohibitively expensive.

Policies in two areas can create savings capabilities. The first, and perhaps most obvious, is to promote the existence of small-scale financial institutions that provide the poor with safe ways to save through liquid savings accounts that yield some return even when the investment is low; banks can be encouraged to engage in such microfinance.[14] The second is to create insurance mechanisms, such as unemployment insurance or own-insurance through social security accounts, that reduce the risk of abrupt declines in income. Schemes of this type could allow the poor to invest with longer-term objectives, such as to accumulate income-earning assets and or earn higher yields, which would make their savings and investment more profitable.

In order to bolster credit markets, especially in support of microlending (and saving), several policy reforms are needed. The first requires setting clear rules of the game, including regulations that ensure the safety and soundness—and flexibility—of microlending institutions. But the problem is that microlending institutions are a minuscule part of the financial sector in Latin America. Altogether, they account for less than 1 percent of the credits that commercial banks provide to the whole economy. Policies are needed to generate widespread access to credit. The option of creating and managing state-owned banks that provide subsidized credit is not the solution, since historically this has been a disaster, as judged by their low rate of success and high inefficiency throughout the region. In order to determine the scope for state intervention, it is necessary to identify the obstacles that impede the credit relationship.

The credit relationship depends on the borrower's ability and willingness to repay loans. What can policy do to ensure ability and willingness to pay? Apart from introducing appropriate regulation and supervision of banking institutions, governments can use at least four mechanisms to create or expand competitive and efficient financial systems that reach the poor: punishment, collateral, reputation, and relationships.

Punishment is the effectiveness of the legal system to enforce the law. Although enforcing the law does not necessarily benefit creditors on a case-by-case basis, it does provide incentives for debtors to repay if they possibly can. For financial systems that serve smaller borrowers, there need to be additional ways of ensuring willingness to pay. Areas for improvement include lifting the operational restrictions on banks (in terms of flexibility of times and forms of operation), simplifying documentation requirements, and lowering capital requirements on loans.

Collateral is one of the key mechanisms that make financial systems work because it implies some guarantee of repayment. The problem in the context of poverty reduction is that the poor normally lack collateral. One option is to introduce new financial products such as leasing and factoring or at least to create the regulatory framework so that they can exist. These types of instruments are closer in spirit to the concept of renting rather than selling capital. For instance, in leasing, the lending institution normally retains ownership of the equipment or other form of capital, while the debtor pays a monthly rent (which includes interest and amortization) for its use and eventually becomes an owner. Public action can promote these types of arrangements by facilitating repossession of the leased equipment at rapid and low cost in case of default. Other options include the creation of tax schemes and the elimination of regulatory barriers.

Reputation can be an effective mechanism for lowering the costs of monitoring the ability and willingness to repay. One of the strongest advantages of reputation in the context of poverty reduction is that anybody can develop a good reputation, regardless of his or her socioeconomic condition. Credit bureaus introduce reputation mechanisms into the financial system by making credit histories available to creditors. By sharing information with creditors, they limit the ability of persons with a bad credit history to obtain credit in the future. Credit bureaus are a rare commodity in Latin America. One of the few places where they are found is where small banks provide microloans. In these types of institutions, credit is provided progressively in larger loans to an individual or group, with default resulting in loss of access. Rates of repayment of microloans are usually very high, largely due to this. Creating public credit bureaus on a larger scale would support the creation and expansion of credit markets.

Promoting *relationships* is another important way to promote the creation of financial institutions. For instance, one common credit mechanism is group lending, where default by one member results in the loss of access to credit for the entire group. These schemes take advantage of the relationship that borrowers have with each other by introducing self-monitoring mechanisms that dramatically reduce the cost of monitoring lending. Public policy can promote the use of group lending through fiscal incentives to entities or groups that provide these types of loans.

Additionally, there is scope for policy intervention in setting the regulatory framework or even creating insurance mechanisms that reduce the risk of default.

Is There a Future for Social Policy in Latin America?

It is time to start thinking about new ways of designing social policies in Latin America. We need policies that support the poor, while contributing to growth and being themselves engines of growth and development. This can only be done if social policy is at the heart of development strategy, rather than an opponent constantly competing for public resources and threatening to undermine macroeconomic stability. Therefore, the solution is not to create compensatory measures. Policies are needed that promote efficiency in the economic system and improve the productivity of the poor by eliminating the restrictions they face on accumulating income-earning assets and accessing economic opportunities.

If we go beyond income and ask what determines the income of each individual, it is possible to outline some of the elements of such a strategy. This discussion has been framed in terms of policies that generate income-earning assets and create opportunities. By creating assets and opportunities for the poor, such policies seek to raise their income and thus their standard of living.

But when we start thinking about what is needed to build up assets and generate opportunities, we end up talking about cash transfer programs such as Progresa or Bolsa Escola, health policy, incentives for saving, housing, and basic services, labor market regulations, credit bureaus to expand access to credit, and even alternative financial instruments, such as leasing to avoid the restrictions imposed by lack of collateral by the poor. We end up talking about the economic environment as a whole. Many of these items are not normally conceived of as part of social policy. They are normally viewed as part of the overall development strategy of countries.

By outlining this integrated strategy, it becomes obvious that poverty alleviation programs such as Progresa are important policy tools, but they cannot be regarded as *the* strategy for poverty reduction. If other elements of the economic environment are not modified, these types of government intervention will always be swimming against the tide. But if they are complemented by a wide set of policies that eliminate restrictions, generate assets, and create opportunities for the poor, their chances of contributing to our understanding of the poverty puzzle in Latin America may be multiplied.

Notes

1. See, for instance, the evidence in Foster and Székely (2001). This is still a highly controversial issue, where evidence that growth benefits the poor one-to-one also exists (see, for instance, Dollar and Kraay 2001).

2. The data are taken from Behrman, Duryea, and Székely (1999), who compute the proportion of population by birth cohort that completes primary schooling, by using household surveys for years close to 1998.

3. These are the authors' own calculations from the Mexican Census 2000 data.

4. Progresa is the Spanish acronym for the Mexican Programa de Educación, Salud y Alimentación (Education, Health, and Nutrition Program). The program provides cash transfers and a nutritional supplement to families in extreme poverty in rural areas. Cash transfers are conditioned on children's school attendance rates of at least 85 percent and regular attendance at health clinics for checkups and follow-ups. The cash transfer is given to the mother, who has to attend a series of talks and courses on health practices. Bolsa Escola is a similar program that provides scholarships for disadvantaged children. Part of the cash transfer is held in a special account, which the beneficiary can access after completing a schooling cycle. Chile Joven is also a program of cash transfers, but in this case the transfers are provided to young adults as an incentive to training. A detailed description and evaluation of the Progresa program can be found at: *www.ifpri.org/country/mexico.htm*. A description of the Bolsa Escola program can be found at: *www.mec.gov.br/home/bolsaesc/default.shtm*.

5. In the case of the Progresa program, a key issue is that, by definition, some of the poorest of the poor do not have access to benefits because they live in isolated and remote areas where no school or health clinic exists. If the program was accompanied by supply-side efforts, or by support for temporary reallocation (during the school year) or subsidies to transport costs, it could perhaps reach these sectors of society.

6. In the the future, demographic factors will make this even more of a challenge than before for Latin America. IDB (2000) estimates that to meet the demographic challenge of a changing age structure of the next ten years, the number of teachers in secondary schools will have to increase from 1.8 million to 2.6 million just to keep pace with higher demand.

7. As discussed by IDB (2000) there are already several examples of success in the region. The program Telecurso in Brazil and Telesecundaria in Mexico are among the most notable.

8. These are reflected in higher infant mortality, lower life expectancy, and higher incidence of disease.

9. A complete explanation of the reform is developed in IDB (1996, 197–98).

10. Household surveys ask individuals directly about how they use their time. The low participation rates among females presented in table 4.3 reflect

that when women were asked about their activities, a larger proportion of females in poor households declared that they use their time in activities other than performing a job in the labor market. Therefore, not participating does not imply that a woman does not work, and the differences between poor and rich do not mean that poor women work less hours than the rich. They only reveal that a higher proportion of the rich receives a remuneration in the labor market for the time they spend working. In fact, poor women tend to spend more time working in household tasks, which are not remunerated and therefore do not count as participation. It should be borne in mind that the participation rates will be underestimated when female respondents understate their work activities and that some types of activities such as working informally in family businesses, which are more common among the poor, are more prone to this problem.

11. So far, it seems that the social security reforms implemented in the region have had some impact on population coverage. Pagés-Serra and Lora (2000) show, for instance, that coverage increased from 26 to 31 percent in Peru and from 26 to 36 percent in El Salvador, while in Mexico coverage expanded almost 20 percent in three years. In Bolivia, the population covered with social insurance increased 40 percent in four years.

12. One of the documents that best articulate the worries that adjustment programs were causing excessive social distress, is the book by Cornia, Jolly, and Stewart (1987).

13. Another type of income-earning assets that is relevant for our discussion is social capital. Since this is a more elusive concept, we do not focus on it here.

14. There are many examples of this in Latin America. Perhaps the most successful are the Banco Sol and Caja los Andes in Bolivia and the Banco del Pacífico in Ecuador. The Grameen Bank in Bangladesh is perhaps the best-known case in the world of successful microlending for the poor.

References

Attanasio, Orazio, and Miguel Székely. 2001. "Going Beyond Income: Redefining Poverty in Latin America." In *A Portrait of the Poor: An Asset Based Approach*, edited by Orazio Attanasio and Miguel Székely. Baltimore, Md.: Johns Hopkins University Press.

Behrman, Jere R., Suzanne Duryea, and Miguel Székely. 1999. "Schooling Investments and Macroeconomic Conditions: A Micro-Macro Investigation for Latin America and the Caribbean." OCE working paper series 407. Washington, D.C.: Inter-American Development Bank, Research Department, October.

Birdsall, Nancy, Thomas C. Pinckney, and Richard Sabot. 1998. "Why Low Inequality Spurs Growth: Saving and Investment by the Poor." In *Social Inequality: Values, Growth, and the State*, edited by Andrés Solimano. Ann Arbor: University of Michigan Press.

Cornia, Giovanni Andrea, Richard Jolly, and Frances Stewart. 1987. *Adjustment with a Human Face*, 2 vols. Oxford: Clarendon Press.

Dollar, David, and Aart Kraay. 2001. "Growth Is Good for the Poor." Policy research working paper 2587. Washington, D.C.: World Bank, Development Research Group (April).

Foster, James, and Miguel Székely. 2001. "Is Growth Good for the Poor? Tracking Low Incomes Using General Means." Unpublished paper. Inter-American Development Bank, Research Department, Washington, D.C. (February).

Gallup, John Luke, Steven Radelet, and Andrew Warner. 1999. "Economic Growth and the Income of the Poor." CAER II discussion paper 36. Cambridge, Mass.: Harvard University, Harvard Institute for International Development.

Graham, Carol. 1996. *Gender Issues in Poverty Alleviation: Recent Experiences with Demand-based Programs in Latin America, Africa, and Eastern Europe.* Paris: International Labor Organization.

Grosh, Margaret E. 1994. *Administering Targeted Social Programs in Latin America: From Platitudes to Practice.* Washington, D.C.: World Bank.

Heckman, James, and Carmen Pagés. 2000. "The Cost of Job Security Regulation: Evidence from Latin American Labor Markets." Working paper 430. Washington D.C.: Inter-American Development Bank, Research Department.

Hiskey, Jonathan. 2000. "Does Democracy Matter? Electoral Composition and Local Development in Mexico." Unpublished paper. University of California, Riverside, Department of Political Science.

IDB (Inter-American Development Bank). 1996. *Economic and Social Progress Report: Making Social Services Work.* Baltimore, Md.: Johns Hopkins University Press.

———. 1998. *Economic and Social Progress Report: Facing up to Inequality in Latin America.* Baltimore, Md.: Johns Hopkins University Press.

———. 2000. *Economic and Social Progress Report: Development beyond Economics.* Baltimore, Md.: Johns Hopkins University Press.

Kanbur, Ravi. 1985. "Poverty: Measurement, Alleviation, and the Impact of Macroeconomic Adjustment." Discussion paper 125. Essex, U.K.: University of Essex.

———. 1987a. "Measurement and Alleviation of Poverty." *IMF Staff Papers* 34: 60–85.

———. 1987b. "Structural Adjustment, Macroeconomic Adjustment, and Poverty: A Methodology of Analysis." *World Development* 15(12): 1515–26.

Lloyd-Sherlock, Peter. 2000. "Failing the Needy: Public Social Spending in Latin America." *Journal of International Development* 12(1): 101–19.

Londoño, José L., and Miguel Székely. 2000. "Persistent Poverty and Excess Inequality: Latin America 1970–1995." *Journal of Applied Economics* 3(1): 93–134.

Márquez, Gustavo. 2000. "Labor Markets and Income Support: What Did We Learn from the Crises?" Washington, D.C.: Inter-American Development Bank, Research Department (June).

National Institute of Statistics, Geography and Informatics. 2000. *Mexican Census 2000.*

Pagés-Serra, Carmen, and Eduardo Lora. 2000. "Hacia un envejecimiento responsible: Las reformas de los sistemas pensionales América Latina." Washington, D.C.: Inter-American Development Bank, Research Department (October).

Pastor, Manuel, and Carol Wise. 1997. "State Policy, Distribution, and Neo-liberal Reform in Mexico." Working paper 229. Washington D.C.: Woodrow Wilson International Center for Scholars, Latin American Program (August).

Savedoff, William D., ed. 1998. *Organization Matters: Agency Problems in Health and Education in Latin America.* Washington, D.C.: Inter-American Development Bank.

Székely, Miguel. 1998. *The Economics of Poverty, Inequality, and Wealth Accumulation in Mexico.* London: Macmillan.

———. 2001. "The 1990s in Latin America: Another Decade of Persistent Inequality, But with Somewhat Lower Poverty." RES working paper 454. Washington, D.C.: Inter-American Development Bank, Research Department (June).

UNDP (United Nations Development Programme). Various years.

UNESCO. 1997. *Statistical Yearbook 1997.* Paris: UNESCO.

World Bank. 2000. *World Development Indicators.* Washington, D.C.: World Bank.

Chapter 5

Welfare State Policies in the Middle East and North Africa

ZAFIRIS TZANNATOS AND IQBAL KAUR

THIS PAPER reviews public social spending and programs in the Middle East and North Africa (MENA) region in light of the significant economic changes that have occurred since the early 1980s. At that time, economic growth rates, averaging 7 percent a year, were historically high, driven in large measure by booming oil revenues. Social policies benefited from the increase in state spending, as did employment opportunities. As a result, MENA had the lowest levels of poverty of all developing regions.

A reversal of fortunes in the 1990s was accompanied by significant policy changes. Public sector reform, greater openness to the world economy, and structural adjustment for the industrial sector placed greater pressure on the welfare state at a time when government expenditures were contracting. In addition, demographic change is leading to an aging population, creating in five to ten years the kinds of pressures other regions are already facing.

At the beginning of the millennium, the global economic slowdown during the first eight months of 2001 was accentuated by the New York events on September 11, 2001. This added greatly to global uncertainties and will have both direct economic impacts in some countries and indirect effects in others, as the expected recovery of the global economy is delayed. Countries in the Middle East and North Africa will be particularly hit if oil prices fall or regional tensions, already at a high point, are exacerbated. The region will be profoundly affected by its proximity to military action, and specific countries will be affected by the loss of tourism revenues resulting from heightened security concerns. Increased uncertainty in financial markets also is likely to depress foreign direct investment throughout the region, and the costs of trade could escalate because of war-risk premia. Increasing political tensions, as governments walk a tightrope between support for U.S. actions and latent anti-American sentiments, may also depress economic activity.

This paper argues that the state will need to remain a strong player in the area of social protection during this period of adjustment, globalization, and crises, but that its role will need to change to meet the challenges it now faces.

Overview

The economies in the MENA region are diverse in many respects:[1]

- Population ranges from the small state of Jordan, with only 4 million, to Egypt and Iran, with a population of more than 60 million each, both countries effectively accounting for almost half of the regional population.

- Incomes vary from Yemen, with annual per capita income of only $300, to Lebanon and the Gulf economies, with per capita income over $3,500.

- Countries differ in their composition and structure. Differences between the urban and rural population and between agricultural and nonfarm employment are marked, as are differences in the structure of output and in the characteristics of the oil and nonoil economies—60 to 75 percent of gross domestic product (GDP) accrues to services in Jordan, Lebanon, and West Bank and Gaza, whereas in Yemen, Egypt, and Iran agriculture is a sizable sector.

Countries also share some common characteristics in the economic and social spheres:

- The MENA economies are highly dependent on oil, and even the nonoil-exporting ones are affected by oil price volatility.

- They all suffer from scarce water resources. Less than 1,700 cubic meters of water are available annually per person, and in some countries the amount is substantially less.

- Population is growing faster than the international average of 1.5 percent.

- The unemployment rate is persistently greater than 10 percent in every economy in the region.

Another similarity is that MENA entered the 1990s with a high share of government employment in the labor force, high wages, and extensive involvement of the state in economic production. The rise in government employment was initially associated with a significant expansion in social services (education, health, social protection) and great improvement in social indicators. Living standards and health status improved significantly in the past thirty years, and the MENA region now has the lowest poverty rates in the developing world. Universal enrollment in basic education is within reach, and, although child labor exists, it lacks the scale and general conditions found elsewhere. By 1995, except in Yemen and Morocco, more than 90 percent of the population had access to health services, and mortality and morbidity rates had declined.

The situation reversed with the collapse of oil prices in the mid-1980s. Plummeting oil prices depressed disposable income, and this led to sharp decreases in the level of domestic and foreign investment. Nonoil countries also felt the effects of falling oil prices through lower migrant worker remittances and reduced foreign investment. In the decade beginning in 1985, virtually all countries in the region experienced GDP growth lower than that of the previous decade.

The policy emphasis on high capital-output ratios was associated with the decline in GDP. Many MENA countries behaved as capital-abundant countries when, in fact, factor proportions indicated a relative abundance of labor, stemming mainly from high population growth rates. Policies subsidized interest rates, which became negative in real terms, or investments, which provided incentives for distorted choices of capital-intensive technologies. This was exacerbated by the choice of state enterprises with large-scale capital-intensive units as the main modality for productive activities. This model allowed labor to be absorbed through employment in public enterprises, albeit some in nonproductive ways. By the same token, a large part of the industrial and urban labor force became eligible for formal modes of social protection, such as health benefits, retirement benefits, and unemployment insurance. In some cases, unions evolved to protect the interests of public enterprise employees, gradually extending to other urban and industrial workers. The limits of this model became apparent as the supply of labor surpassed the absorptive capacity of state enterprises and public employment. These conditions were compounded when economic conditions worsened. Market liberalization and the divestiture of public enterprises resulted in high unemployment.

Recovery was hindered by the countries' large and rigid public sectors, their marginalized—rather than leading—private sectors, and their relative isolation from global trade. Following the decline in the price of oil and the collapse of growth and investment, regional capital and labor markets collapsed, as did the growth of economywide productivity, or total factor productivity. All of these factors, along with high population growth, contributed to an average regional decline in real per capita income of 2 percent a year after 1986, the largest decline in any developing region during this period. In some oil-exporting countries, the average yearly decline was more than 4 percent. Expansion of the public sector during the 1980s led to the hiring of teachers, managers and workers for state-owned enterprises, and this over-recruitment played a substitute role in social protection. In essence, public sector employment created deficit-financed jobs to absorb the excess supply of labor as economic activity slowed, acting as a welfare program for those who could not be absorbed in the private sector. The role of government in economic production became increasingly significant, and MENA now stands out in world statistics on public sector employment (figure 5.1).

The Size of the State in MENA at the Start of the Twenty-First Century

In the late 1990s, civilian government employment accounted for about 11 percent of total employment worldwide, but for MENA countries it stood at 18 percent (table 5.1). This figure was much lower for other developing regions, for example, 9 percent for Latin America and the Caribbean, 7 percent for Africa, and 6 percent for Asia. In only Morocco and Lebanon was the share lower than the world average.

Figure 5.1   Public Sector Employment as a Percentage of Total Employment, by Region, 1974 to 1997

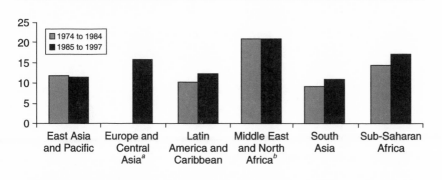

Source: Schiavo-Campo, de Tommaso, and Mukherjee (1997).
[a]Data not available before 1989.
[b]Most recent year is 1996.

Table 5.1   Public Sector Employment as a Percentage of Total Employment, Early 1990s

| | Civilian Government Employment | | | | | | |
| | Government Administration | | Social Sectors | | Total | | |
Country	Central Government	Noncentral Government	Education	Health	Civilian Government	Armed Forces
Algeria	8.7	4.9	7.5	3.8	24.9	2.7
Bahrain	5.9	0.0	4.0	2.6	12.5	n.a.
Egypt	7.2	11.1	3.8	3.0	25.1	3.1
Jordan	3.3	3.3	6.5	2.0	15.1	10.3
Lebanon	1.1	1.6	5	0.5	8.2	6.9
Morocco	2.9	1.7	3.2	0.5	8.3	2.7
Syria	4.2	1.2	7.1	1.1	13.6	n.a.
Tunisia	5.2	0.9	5.4	1.9	13.4	1.5
West Bank and Gaza	16.6	n.a.	7.6	2.0	26.2	n.a.
Yemen	14.5	4.4	1.9	1.3	22.1	1.9
MENA average	6.6	3.9	5.1	1.9	17.5	3.2

Source: Schiavo–Campo, de Tommaso, Mukherjee (1997).

Predictably, given the large size of the public sector, in the early 1990s the share of the government wage bill in GDP was highest in MENA, averaging almost 10 percent compared to a worldwide average of almost half that figure (Said 1995). This was exacerbated by the fact that public sector wages in MENA were significantly higher than private sector wages (table 5.2).

Finally, the share of public enterprises in economic production was high. In the late 1980s, it was generally below 10 percent in middle-income economies compared with more than 30 percent in Egypt and Tunisia and nearly 60 percent in Algeria (figure 5.2).

In short, the region reached the end of the twentieth century with the following characteristics:

* The public sector was sizable and rigid, the private sector was marginalized, rather than leading, and economies were relatively isolated from global trade. Following the decline in the price of oil, investment and growth rates collapsed, as did regional capital and labor markets. Over the past thirty years, growth of total factor productivity (TFP) declined, while population growth remained high. Declining productivity, high population growth, and falling oil prices contributed to an average regional decline in real per capita incomes of 2 percent a year after 1986, the largest decline in any developing region during this period. In some oil-exporting countries, the decline was more than 4 percent a year.

Table 5.2   Central Government Wages, by Region, Early 1990s

Region	Central Government Wages and Salaries as Percent of GDP	Average Central Government Wage as Multiple of Per Capita GDP	Ratio of Public to Private Sector Wages
Africa	6.7	5.7	1.0
Asia	4.7	3.0	0.8
East Europe and Central Asia	3.7	1.3	0.7
Latin America and Caribbean	4.9	2.5	0.9
MENA	9.8	3.4	1.3
OECD	4.5	1.6	0.9
World average	5.4	3.0	0.8

Source: Schiavo-Campo, de Tommaso, Mukherjee (1997).

Figure 5.2   Share of Public Enterprises in Economic Activity in Select Countries, 1986 to 1991

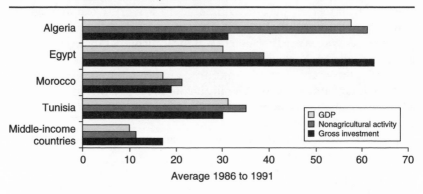

Source: World Bank (1995).

- Labor market characteristics, which were shaped by the macroeconomic and trade policies implemented during the oil boom, were out of tune with economic reality. Expansion of the public sector was partly fueled by an expansion of the activities of state-owned enterprises, while public administration played a substitute role for social protection through over-recruitment. These rigid institutional structures produced an inflexible response to labor market pressures.

- Urban unemployment was high and rising in many MENA countries. Unemployment in countries with major labor market imbalances, such as Egypt and Morocco, was worsening more quickly among older workers, shifting the center of the problem away from one of unemployed dependents and toward one of unemployed household heads. Rising unemployment among the less educated, as seen in Algeria and Morocco, was also of great concern, particularly from a poverty perspective.

As the new millennium proceeds, significant changes are being induced by an evolving role of the state and the associated economic reform measures. A series of adjustment and liberalization programs have been introduced that aim to enhance the efficiency of the economy by creating an environment for market mechanisms to work more properly and to facilitate the positioning of the economy in the context of globalization. Reforms are gathering momentum despite a slow start in the early 1990s.

During the early 1990s privatization proceeds were creating negligible amounts of public revenue (for example, less than $25 million before

1992), but they had reached more than $2 billion by the late 1990s. Tunisia is the regional pioneer in this area, and Algeria, despite its stop-and-go record with privatization, has sold or liquidated almost one-third of its public enterprises, and the government is expected to put another half of the remaining ones up for privatization. Significant changes are also under way in Egypt, Jordan, Lebanon, Morocco, and Yemen.

All of this creates efficiency gains in the economic sphere but results also in social dislocation. The issue goes beyond the question of winners and losers and individual interests. It relates also to the fact that the share of government employment in the labor force in MENA reflects the level of attention paid to health, education, and social protection policies. The new role of the state therefore calls for an adjustment of broad government employment in such a way as to provide some compensatory mechanisms in the short run for those who lose their jobs, while creating an economic environment that will enable faster labor absorption in the medium run. During this "transition" period, human capital must be developed through effective but fiscally affordable social policies.

Labor Market Challenges

Given the large size of government employment, efficient public sector downsizing in MENA will require a great number of labor redundancies. For example, in Egypt the initial estimate for labor redundancies in public enterprises was around 10 percent, but in practice this figure proved to be closer to 35 percent. In Morocco, 23 percent of public enterprises had very small returns (lower than 5 percent), 36 percent had losses, and the fourteen largest public enterprises produced an annual average loss that reached more than 2 percent of GDP by 1992. In Algeria, more than 500,000 employees were retrenched between 1990 and 1998, and the pace of adjustment has accelerated since then. Still, the large public sector awaits restructuring, despite an official unemployment rate that has risen to 29 percent.

Any downsizing of this magnitude will require political consensus, as voluntary separations reflecting compensation for accrued rights could amount to several thousand dollars per worker. A single downsizing operation may therefore go beyond the ability of the economy to bear such costs, since countries where public sector downsizing is most needed are usually strapped for cash.[2]

Coping with unemployment therefore remains a significant challenge. Although a flexible labor market facilitates the efficient deployment of labor and reduces unemployment in the longer run, unemployment remains high in most MENA countries, generally in excess of 10 percent (figure 5.3). This group of newly unemployed not only faces a high risk of falling into poverty but also constitutes a political tinderbox as well.

Most regional forecasts indicate that unemployment is likely to rise (and in some cases significantly). On some accounts, unemployment is not expected to start declining before 2010. This is only partly due to the underlying demographic transition. The key to enhancing labor absorption will be to increase effective investment and stimulate higher economic growth. In this respect, the role of government is to ensure that, while the drive to increase efficiency through adjustment continues, employment programs are not overly designed, and informal employment keeps expanding. For example, in Morocco, about half of all new employment has come from expansion of the informal sector, and in Egypt the figure is even higher. Although little is known about the behavior of informal wages over time, it is likely that these have fallen as the formal sector has become increasingly less able to absorb new entrants to the labor market. For example, in Egypt, agricultural wages fell by almost half between 1982 and 1995.

Despite the usefulness of the informal sector, there are no reliable data on its size and, by extension, on the shares of the formal and informal sectors in total employment. In general, a very large part of the agricultural

Figure 5.3   Unemployment Rate, by Region, 1990s

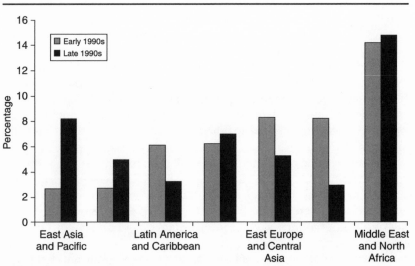

Source: World Bank (2002).

sector is informal, which ranges from 50 percent of total male employment in Yemen to 18 percent in Algeria. In many countries, the largest part of the formal labor market is in the public sector, ranging from 53 percent of all employment in Algeria, 47 percent in Jordan, 34 percent in Egypt, and 20 percent in Morocco. A large part of the formal labor market is the industrial sector, which is about 22 percent in Yemen and Egypt, 28 percent in Morocco and Jordan, 33 percent in Tunisia, and 38 percent in Algeria, where it is the largest (see table 5.3).[3]

As long as opportunities exist to expand the informal sector, unemployment will be lower and government budgets will be directed more effectively at measures targeted to the employed poor and those unable to work. This can enable governments to continue playing a useful role in education, health, and labor redeployment (for example, through compensation to retrenched workers).

In addition to offering compensation when redundancies occur, other policies have been called on to ease the cost of adjustment and enable the redeployment of affected workers. These policies, often lumped under the heading of active labor market policies (ALMPs), include the setup of counseling and placement services, training and retraining of displaced workers, support for entry into self-employment, public works, and wage subsidies. In some cases, as in Algeria, the introduction of ALMPs was accompanied by an unemployment assistance scheme.

An alternative approach to public enterprise restructuring is the employee shareholders associations (ESAs) that were formed in Egypt to enable workers to buy a stake in their company. This approach was expected to create an interest in the privatization program and incentives to improve productivity. Some empirical evidence suggests that this innovation has led to greater efficiency: in seven of the ten companies that were sold to ESAs in 1994, profits improved on average by more than 60 percent (Abrahart, Kaur, and Tzannatos 2002).

Table 5.3 Share of Employment in MENA Countries, by Selected Sector[a] (Percentage)

Sector	Algeria	Egypt	Iran	Jordan	Morocco	Tunisia	Yemen
Agriculture	18	32	30	10	35	22	50
Industry	38	23	26	28	28	33	22
Public	53	34	26	47	20	25	—
Informal	20	30	—	15	33	24	—

Source: Börsch-Supan, Palacios, and Tumbarello (1999); Charmes (1991); Said (1995).
[a] Male workers only.
— Not available.

ALMPs and ESAs are not, however, panaceas for the problem of low employment creation in the region (Dar and Tzannatos 1999). A survey of the evidence from more than 100 evaluations of ALMPs in developed and developing countries shows that such policies can only marginally mitigate structural problems in the labor and product markets and the macroeconomy at large and that some, if inappropriately designed, can produce negative economic effects in terms of fiscal implications and deadweight loss (OECD 1997). Equally, ESAs are not necessarily the most effective form of privatization. For example, in Hungary, the decision to privatize by selling state enterprises to strategic investors, including foreigners, has been largely successful, while privatization by selling state-owned enterprises to workers in some other transition economies has had much less effect on corporate governance and company performance. A critical factor in deciding whether to liquidate, privatize, or create ESAs is the presence of investor interest in the companies under question.

In addition to the introduction of ALMPs and ESAs, governments in MENA have started reforming labor laws and regulations in areas such as job security, separation awards, and wage regulations (such as collective bargaining and minimum wages). For example, in Tunisia, the labor code was revised both in the early and in the late 1990s. Measures have been taken to revise the representation of workers in the firm and the procedures for resolving conflicts. The costs of individual firings have been fixed between one or two months of the wage bill per year of service, with a maximum ceiling of thirty-six months of the wage bill. Labor legislation regarding layoffs has been simplified, and the time frame has been fixed at a maximum of thirty-three days from the time a retrenchment request is submitted to the inspectors of employment. Additional measures have been introduced, such as a distinction between abusive layoffs and the maximum amount of fines to be paid on breach of contract; fixed-term contracts for permanent employment have been set at a maximum of four years; the recruitment procedure has been simplified by allowing firms to advertise vacancies without the approval of the employment bureau; and a guaranteed fund has been created to finance severance packages for workers of bankrupt firms.

Public Social Spending

As economic conditions eroded and economic growth declined, the ability of the MENA countries to support social programs declined as well (table 5.4). Economic growth hardly kept pace with the increase in population, meaning that demand for social policy rose as the state's ability to supply it while maintaining fiscal soundness fell.

Table 5.4   **Annual Growth Rates of Real GDP for Select MENA Countries, 1976 to 1998 (Percentage)**

Country	1976 to 1985	1986 to 1995	1996 to 1998
Algeria	5.8	0.2	3.0
Egypt	8.5	3.8	5.6
Jordan	10.5	3.2	2.2
Lebanon	—	—	3.5
Morocco	4.8	2.8	4.2
Tunisia	5.3	3.5	5.2
Yemen	n.a.	5.6	4.6

Source: World Bank (1998).
— Not available.

By the 1990s, public social spending added up to a significant share of the gross domestic product (table 5.5). Excluding health and education, other social spending ranged between 1 and 11 percent of GDP around 1995. To these figures, one should add a significant part of (excess) public employment and benefits to civil servants, another de facto pillar of the welfare state in most MENA countries.

Political and economic considerations imply that, despite the tight fiscal constraints of recent years, social programs are difficult to reduce. In fact, some new measures have been added or expanded—such as unemployment insurance and income-generating activities for the poor in the form of public works and credit-based self-employment schemes. Public works programs provide immediate income, offering temporary employment with low salaries to unskilled workers in manual, highly labor-intensive activities. Credit-based livelihood programs facilitate income generation over the medium term by improving access for poor people to financial resources, thereby promoting their economic activity. (Appendix 5.1 summarizes existing public works programs in MENA and provides information on their impact, cost, coverage, and leakage.)

The attempt to adapt social programs to emerging realities is well illustrated by the case of consumer food subsidies, which are being phased out in most countries; pension systems, which have become unsustainable; social funds, which suggest the costs and benefits of a more targeted policy instrument; and microfinance programs. We deal with each in turn.

Consumer Food Subsidies

The design and objectives of consumer food subsidies vary across countries, ranging from universal subsidies to self-targeted systems and from rationed schemes to alternative targeted safety nets (see appendix 5.2 for

Table 5.5 Public Spending on Social Protection and Social Services in Select MENA Countries, Mid-1990s (Percentage of GDP)

Country	Food Subsidies	Cash and In-Kind Transfers	Public Works	Public Pensions	Housing	Public Health	Education	Total	Total Excluding Health and Education
Algeria	0.0	0.4	0.2	4.6	5.5	2.6	6.1	19.4	10.7
Egypt	1.3	0.2	0.3	2.5	2.0	1.8	4.8	12.9	6.3
Iran	2.7	1.2	—	1.5	1.5	2.4	4.0	13.3	6.9
Jordan	0.0	0.9	—	4.2	0.7	5.3	6.8	17.9	5.8
Lebanon	0.1	0.9	—	—	—	2.2	2.5	5.7	1.0
Morocco	1.6	0.1	0.2	1.8	0.1	1.2	5.9	10.9	3.8
Tunisia	1.7	0.5	0.1	2.6	1.7	3.0	6.9	16.5	6.6
Yemen	0.0	1.0	0.2	0.1	0.7	2.2	7.0	11.2	2.0

Source: World Bank (2002).
— Not available.

a summary of food subsidy reforms in MENA). In Morocco, subsidy programs were introduced to stabilize the price of strategic goods, with no explicit focus on the poor. This was achieved through subsidy, taxation, and a reallocation of resources among commodities to adjust for international price fluctuations. In Tunisia, the system aimed to stabilize the price of basic food staples, protect the purchasing power of the poor, redistribute income to the poor, and improve the nutritional status of the poor as well as that of the population at large, with multiple interventions along the marketing chain from importers to refiners to distributors. In Egypt, a ration scheme was introduced initially to ensure the supply of essential goods to the population at large, but over the course of the 1980s, policy objectives were reoriented toward poverty alleviation, and measures were adopted to reduce the number of goods subsidized and improve targeting by emphasizing inferior goods. In Yemen, the subsidy schemes were introduced through application of a preferential exchange rate for imports, and in Iran they were conducted through maintenance of multiple official overvalued exchange rates and controlled prices. Algeria and Jordan used to have food subsidy schemes but abandoned them in the late-1990s.

Subsidies have a relatively large impact on the poor, but the nonpoor absorb most of the public funds distributed in this way. Food commands a larger share of total spending by lower-income than by well-off households. Subsidized foods contribute about 40 percent of total caloric intake and thus constitute an important source of protein for the poor. In Tunisia in 1990, the share of subsidized foods in per capita expenditure was five times higher in the lowest quintile than in the highest. A 1987 Jordanian household survey showed that subsidies represented about 14 percent of expenditures for the lowest quintile, compared to 8 percent for the top quintile. However, higher-income groups benefit more in *absolute* terms than do the poor, because they consume greater quantities of subsidized goods (World Bank 1999b). In Morocco, for example, people in the top quintile consume twice the value of subsidized food as do those in the lowest quintile. In Yemen, the wealthiest 10 percent of the population spend ten times more than do the poor on subsidized wheat and flour—they benefit ten times as much. Clearly, reform of the subsidized food system should be a top priority in MENA. Already, many countries have reduced the amount of public resources going to subsidize food (see table 5.6).

Pensions

The MENA region faces the challenge of population aging like the rest of the world. The demographic structure suggests that in five to ten years the aging process will begin to accelerate in the region. Yet, pensions

Table 5.6   Food Subsidy Expenditure in MENA, as a Percentage of GDP 1990 to 1999

Country	1990	1995	1999
Algeria	4.3	0.9	0.0
Egypt	4.4	1.3	n.a.
Iran	—	2.9	n.a.
Jordan	3.4	1.4	0.3
Morocco	1.3[a]	1.7	1.7
Tunisia	2.4	2.1	1.2
Yemen	3.7[a]	2.6	0.3

Source: Razmara et al. (1999).
— Not available.
[a]1992.

pending as a percentage of GDP is already among the highest in the world (see figure 5.4), and in some countries, pensions are paid from deficit financing (see table 5.7). Therefore, the region should take this opportunity to reform the system before demographic pressures force cuts in benefits and or increases in contributions that are politically difficult and economically harmful. Although the rising proportion of old people in the

Figure 5.4   Pension Spending as a Percentage of GDP

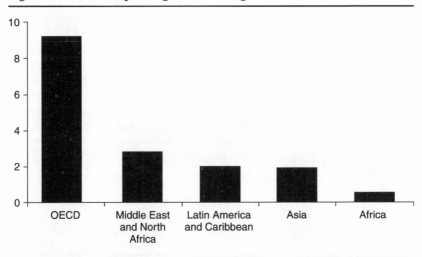

Source: Börsch-Supan, Palacios, and Tumbarello (1999).

Table 5.7   Financing of Pension Expenditures in Algeria (In 1995 DA)

	1992	1993	1994	1995	1996	1997	1998
Total pension surplus (deficit) in billions, DA	2.2	0.5	0.5	−1.1	−6.4	−9.6	−19.0
As percentage of GDP	0.1	0.0	0.0	−0.1	−0.3	−0.4	−0.8

Source: World Bank (1999a).
Note: DA = Algerian dinar.

population will be important in the long term, in the short term, the number of people taking early retirement and the ratio of dependents to working population may also rise (Börsch-Supan, Palacios, and Tumbarello 1999).[4]

As the number of elderly rises compared to the working-age population, the need for better family, societal, or public-based support mechanisms also increases. In MENA, by 2025, the number of elderly is expected to rise by an annual rate of 4 percent, while the rest of the population is expected to grow by 1.4 percent.

Countries in the region have mandatory pension schemes. These schemes are based on partially funded systems and operate as pay-as-you-go systems with defined-benefit plans. However, in most countries, the schemes are poorly designed, and reserves are inappropriately managed. In addition, evasion of contributions is widespread, unequal treatment of individuals occurs, and the systems are rigid and offer little choice.

The parameters of pension schemes are poorly designed from a public policy point of view. For most workers in the MENA economies, the benefit formula *appears* generous, promising 70 to 80 percent of the worker's wage at the end of his career. However, because none of the schemes has a formal indexation mechanism, benefits are actually dependent on inflation and discretionary adjustments. The absence of formal indexation and rules increases the level of uncertainty related to the value of the ultimate benefit, and workers often perceive contributions as a tax.

Payroll taxes for pensions are set at fairly high levels, compared to international benchmarks. This is done in order to generate surpluses and smooth the long-run contribution rate under the scaled premium concept. Payroll taxes for pensions as a share of total labor costs (gross wages plus employers' payroll contributions) vary between 8 and 9 percent in the main schemes of Algeria, Libya, Morocco, and Tunisia to more than 23 percent in Iran and Egypt. If other social insurance contributions are taken into account, the range is between 13 and 36 percent of total labor costs. Important differences emerge, however, when considering details such as whether or not there is a ceiling on taxable earnings.

Based on eligibility criteria, it is relatively easy to obtain a pension in the MENA region. The normal retirement age is particularly low for women in the main schemes of Algeria and Jordan. In Egypt the ratio of pensioners to older persons is extremely high (241 percent with small agricultural pensions or 133 percent without agricultural pensions, compared to 111 percent in Jordan, 73 percent in Tunisia, 49 percent in Iran, and 36 percent in Morocco), which suggests that early retirement (along with broad survivorship rights) is also available and often used.

Although coverage rates are low, they are comparable to what is found in countries with similar levels of income per capita. In MENA countries, coverage rates range from 20 percent of the labor force in Morocco to about half in Egypt (in Yemen, where data are poor, the coverage is likely to be even lower than in Morocco).

Pension finances are deteriorating because the dependency ratio in the pension system (the ratio of pensioners to contributors) is not in line with the old-age dependency ratio (the ratio of old to working-age persons). Available data suggest that there are more than ten persons between ages twenty and fifty-nine for every person over sixty. At the same time, the system dependency ratio in the region varies between three and five workers per pensioner.

The other reason for the deteriorating situation of pension finances is the inefficient public management of reserves. Many of the MENA countries' pension systems have substantial reserves, which tend to dominate local capital markets. In most instances, the return from the investment is lower than private investments with comparable risk, and in some systems, the rate of return is even negative. In Tunisia, Egypt, and Yemen, returns have been significantly negative for long periods of time.[5] This is due largely to the use of pension reserves for subsidizing other government priorities, a phenomenon found in many countries around the world (for example, in Algeria pension reserves finance social assistance programs; in Tunisia they financed social housing until 1992, and they are still financing a small unemployment assistance program).

Most pension systems in the region create labor market distortions. Due to poorly designed benefit formulas and large implicit taxation on labor force participation after a certain age, the system provides incentives for workers to move into the informal sector, which is less productive, and encourages experienced workers to retire early (see table 5.8 on the vesting period). Most MENA pension systems give full benefits at a relatively early age, with no incentives to retire later, so the incentives to retire early are quite high. These negative incentive effects come in addition to a lack of actuarial fairness with respect to retirement age. This lack of actuarial

Table 5.8   Vesting Periods in Select Countries, 1990

Region	Vesting Period (Years of Work Required to Qualify for Benefits)
MENA average	13
OECD average	18
Eastern Europe average	25

Source: World Bank (1994).

fairness also creates strong incentives to retire early in the Organization for Economic Cooperation and Development (OECD) countries.

Large informal sectors are also a serious public finance problem. Given the design of the system, a large fraction of the workforce is not paying taxes and is not contributing to the pension system. For instance, a very large part of the agricultural sector is informal (ranging from 50 percent of total male employment in Yemen to 18 percent in Algeria), and in many countries, the largest part of the formal labor market is in the public sector. Among nonagricultural workers, around 57 percent in Morocco, 47 percent in Tunisia, and 40 percent in Egypt are in the informal sector.

The ways in which pensions are funded can generate poor microeconomic incentives that discourage labor supply for those workers who cannot avoid being in the formal sector. A common feature is that contributions, particularly in the early stages of working life, have little or no value for the contributor and therefore are perceived as pure taxes, with the associated labor supply disincentives. The associated labor market distortions appear to be even larger in MENA than in developed countries, where they have been studied in great detail (Börsh-Supan 1992; Disney 1996; Gruber and Wise 1999). The perception of a weak link between lifetime contributions and benefits is also created by the absence of formal indexation rules. This increases the level of uncertainty related to the value of the ultimate benefit. To the extent that the contribution falls on the worker and is perceived as a tax, the worker will supply less labor than would have been the case otherwise.

There are two reasons to believe that the behavioral responses in the MENA countries are even larger than those in the OECD countries for which some empirical evidence is available. First, although inadequate in some cases, actuarial adjustments with respect to retirement age exist in most OECD countries. These are typically nonexistent in MENA countries. Second, benefits are closely linked to contributions in most OECD countries, while the link is very weak or almost absent in the MENA pension systems. Third, the relevant elasticities are probably lower in OECD countries than in MENA, where it is much easier to move between the formal and informal sectors. With stronger incentives to escape pension contributions (and smaller transaction costs of doing so), deadweight losses are likely to be huge.

A final point relates to the mobility of workers across sectors of the economy, which may be severely restricted in MENA as pension rights are not especially portable. For example, a civil servant may be reluctant to shift to the private sector if the defined-benefit rights that have been accumulated so far during his career would be lost or devalued when he changes employment. Again, pension reform is a clear priority for most MENA countries.

Social Funds

Many economies in the MENA region have social funds, although their relative importance in safety net programs ranges from negligible to moderately important (see box 5.1).[6]

Social funds have been used to mitigate shocks and their effects on the most vulnerable groups and to increase access to, and improve the quality of, basic services used by the poor. Social funds are increasingly common in the region's social protection portfolio. Social funds cover a range of programs, including public works, community development projects, and microfinance, which previously had been undertaken as stand-alone programs.

To date, social funds have been instrumental in transferring resources to target groups. Poor communities and beneficiaries receive a far greater degree of government support than they would in the absence of social funds. However, the operations are small compared to the magnitude of poverty. In terms of total level of resource transfers, as a percentage of GDP, Egypt's Social Fund is the most important, but its annual expenditures still amounted to only 0.2 percent of GDP from 1993 to 1996. Egypt also has the largest per capita transfers, as well as the largest total transfers per poor person, estimated between $83 and $125. However, if every poor person received an equal value of social fund transfers, the annual amount transferred would represent less than 4 percent of the average income.

Social funds within the region use a variety of intermediaries. For instance, in community infrastructure, Egypt works mainly with governorates, Yemen works with nongovernmental organizations and community groups, and the West Bank and Gaza works with a combination of the two. Within the project cycle, funds differ widely in the extent to which projects are demand-driven and participation is built into operating procedures. In general, there are very few mechanisms for involving beneficiaries in the identification and supervision of social fund investments, except where local project committees are eligible as sponsors.[7]

Box 5.1   Social Fund Operations in MENA

The main social funds in the MENA region are the Egyptian Social Fund for Development, the Yemen Social Fund for Development, the West Bank and Gaza Community Development Project (CDP) and nongovernmental projects, and the Algerian Social Development Agency. In addition, several projects are either in the pipeline or very similar to social funds, such as the proposed Moroccan Social Fund and the ongoing Jordan Community Infrastructure project (for its targeted nature rather than its operational mechanism).

The weight of social funds in the overall safety net varies from one country to another: it is of moderate importance in Egypt and is negligible in Algeria. Social funds have been successful in terms of generated outputs. The Egypt Social Fund for Development, SFD, for its size and number of years of operation, has generated the largest level of outputs. As of June 30, 1998, the small business support program had assisted more than 63,000 small businesses with loans, averaging $5,000, and more than 40,000 microentrepreneurs were receiving smaller loans (averaging $500) through the Community Development Project. About 30 percent of small business loans went to women. Over 1 million adults benefited from literacy training. Communities were given greater access to better-quality infrastructure and services. Even in countries with newer and smaller social funds, significant benefits were delivered.

In Yemen, most targets have been surpassed. By the end of 1998, 269 communities had received support compared to an expected 25, and the Social Fund for Development had supported 2,168 microentrepreneurs compared to an expected 2,000.

In West Bank and Gaza, the Community Development Project—a follow-up to the first-phase project—will continue to improve infrastructure services. Nevertheless, the strategy will be redefined to target marginal and poor communities with emphasis on identifying poor areas and focusing on labor-intensive microprojects that will preserve capital assets as well as promote local job opportunities.

Source: Based on World Bank (2002).

Moreover, coordination and collaboration with beneficiary communities and intermediary organizations are central to the impact and effectiveness of social fund investments. Gaps in coordination have reflected poorly on the sustainability of certain social fund investments.

Social funds have been able to absorb foreign assistance in a number of ways. With their emphasis on locally driven investments, funds have offered an innovative approach for building a modern civil society and promoting self-help mechanisms. They have mitigated risk—or reduced the variability of income in the case of a shock—through support for

diversification of household and community portfolios and have supported asset accumulation through the provision of social and economic
infrastructure improvements and microenterprise development.

Social funds have created employment, although the exact amount is
debatable, as little is known about the permanence of jobs created. In
Algeria, West Bank and Gaza, and Yemen, the amount of employment
generated is far below 1 percent of the total labor force. The Egypt Social
Fund for Development accounted for an estimated 25 percent of the
nonagricultural jobs generated in the nation between 1993 and 1996.
This would have absorbed about 10 percent of the estimated 2.2 million
unemployed.

Efficiency in generating these jobs is difficult to estimate. Public works
under social funds have opted largely for medium labor-intensity projects, because they have been as concerned about the type of infrastructure created as about the employment benefits generated. For instance,
improving access to services has often meant new construction, usually
far more capital-intensive than routine repair and maintenance. In addition, wage rates are administratively set at levels comparable to those
prevailing in the labor market. Therefore, unit costs appear to be higher
than those of other national programs that may prescribe lower wages,
particularly in countries such as Algeria that regulate social benefits and
minimum wages. In addition, there has been little systematic evidence
on the impact of social funds on living conditions of beneficiaries, such
as income, skills development, or health indicators.

The sustainability of social funds depends heavily on donor money. To
date, there has been little provision for maintaining social funds from
domestic finance, should international donor money be exhausted. Lever-
aging community and local resources could help to sustain social funds.
In the West Bank and Gaza, such resources constitute 25 percent, on
average, of the Community Development Program, higher than initial
appraisal estimates. In Egypt and Yemen, the average is about 10 percent
in the public works program. At the initial stages, social funds are concerned more with responding to an emergency and producing outputs
than with ensuring their own sustainability.

Microfinance

Microfinance is potentially useful, and the main bottleneck is not the lack
of funds for on-lending, but rather the lack of local capacity to deliver
microfinance services efficiently. There are more than 7.5 million poor
households in MENA (over 60 million poor people), of which less than
2 percent have access to financial services.[8] The gap in outreach—people
needing financial services and willing to pay for them, who nevertheless
lack access—is estimated to be between 2 million and 4 million house-

holds. The gap in funding—funds needed for on-lending—is estimated to be between $750 million and $1.4 billion, less than 1 percent of total lending of the region's formal financial sector. There are more than sixty microfinance programs, the majority run by nongovernmental organizations. Together, these programs serve more than 112,000 active borrowers, 75,000 of which live in Egypt. Of active borrowers, 14 percent live in rural areas, and 36 percent are female. Of the sixty programs, only two are fully sustainable (the Alexandria Business Association program and the National Bank for Development program, both in Egypt), and eight are well under way toward sustainability.[9] Another seven are designed and implemented according to best practice guidelines, but it is too soon to evaluate their sustainability. The seventeen best practice programs together serve the majority (70 percent) of current active borrowers. However, most of the remaining forty-three programs are funded by the government, charge subsidized interest rates, lack sustainability, and perform poorly.

Programs that are part of a larger socioeconomic program are difficult to implement. In general, it is very difficult to implement a best practice microfinance program as a component of a larger, more socially oriented program such as a social fund or relief program. Although the initial umbrella of a larger organization ensures financial and institutional support, "culture" clashes can occur as the microfinance program adheres to sound business and banking practices, while the larger program does not.

Programs that target both men and women tend to marginalize women. However, programs that target women exclusively not only reach the poorest but also achieve sustainability.

Banks have a mixed role in the delivery of microfinance. Banks may be the most effective institutions in filling and funding the outreach and funding gap because they have a wide branch network, have systems in place, and usually have a business orientation. Subsidized lending programs through banks—often imposed under political pressure—have proven largely unworkable in, for instance, Egypt, Morocco, and Tunisia. Banks often select borrowers based on their poverty or unemployment status and not their entrepreneurial capability, and banks did not receive technical support to develop the loan screening and monitoring systems required for successful lending to micro and small businesses. As a result, repayment rates are low, and banks incur high loan losses.

At the program level, some micro programs are already being spun off from their larger, socially oriented mother organizations, and a similar strategy should be developed at the country level. Microfinance should be a joint responsibility of financial and social development policymakers and a joint responsibility of the financial sector and donors. In the medium term, microfinance can deepen and widen the financial system in a country, and development of the microfinance industry should be part of a country's financial sector development strategy.

Concluding Remarks: Expectations and the Way Forward

The economic decline has created daunting challenges with regard to the labor market in terms of generating productivity, employment, and incomes; public policy in terms of determining the optimal mix of formal and informal mechanisms to protect the welfare of the poor and decrease the vulnerability of both the poor and the fragile middle class; economic policy in terms of restoring sustainable growth in the region; and fiscal policy in terms of ensuring that the benefits of growth are distributed equitably among the population. With this downward pressure on economic and social conditions, MENA economies have a pressing need to reduce the vulnerability of their populations.

The economic decline of the region during the late decade of the twentieth century and the welfare state's inability to protect the population are putting pressure on the social contract. The events in New York of September 11, 2001, will affect the regional economies in both direct and indirect ways. As one effect of the crisis, the number of refugees and internally displaced persons in Afghanistan and its neighboring countries, and possibly farther afield, is expected to increase as a consequence of political disturbances. After years of civil war and chronic drought in Afghanistan, 3.5 million Afghani citizens are living in neighboring countries, including Iran; this figure will swell with the arrival of new refugees, straining public services and possibly even generating major health threats. The influx of refugees may also put significant pressure on the budget and food security of receiving countries.

Receipts from tourism are being hit exceptionally hard as heightened security concerns exacerbate the adverse effect on consumer spending of the economic slowdown in the United States and other high-income countries. Many tourism destinations are likely to suffer sharp declines during the coming seasons and years. Perceptions of risk could have a significant effect on tourism in Egypt, Jordan, Morocco, and Tunisia.

If recovery is delayed in industrial economies, most commodity prices—which have never recovered to the levels attained before the East Asia crisis of 1997 and 1998—will fall even further. As of October 2001, oil prices were at $21 a barrel, almost $5 lower than just before September 11. Oil futures, which were above $24 on September 10, dropped below $22 on October 9, reflecting the expectation of prolonged slowdown in global growth and the absence of immediate threats to oil supplies. Prices of nonoil commodities also declined after September 11, about 6 percent for agriculture and 3 percent for metals (excluding gold and silver). Particularly steep declines in both cash prices and one-year futures were registered for sugar, cotton, and coffee. While the unit value index of manufactures exported from industrial countries to developing countries also declined in 2001, it is projected to increase by about 4 percent in 2002, in part because of changes in the valuation of major currencies. These price forecasts imply different terms-of-trade changes for different countries, depending on whether they are net exporters or net importers of oil, nonoil commodities, or manufactures.

Projected slower global growth in the wake of September 11 is also expected to affect remittance flows. Although the impact is likely to be significant for only a limited number of countries, the Middle East can be affected in two different ways. On the one hand, remittances from the Middle East are potentially at risk in the Philippines. On the other, a loss of remittances from the Gulf states and Western Europe could exacerbate possible balance of payments difficulties next year in Jordan, Morocco, and Tunisia.

The predicted effects on the world economy are summarized in table 5.9. Although the slowdown in global economic activity is being led by the industrial countries, aggregate growth for developing countries is also being adversely affected and is expected to weaken from 5.5 percent in 2000 to 2.9 percent in 2001. Delayed recovery in the OECD countries is likely to restrain the growth in developing countries in 2002 to 3.7 percent, about 0.6 percentage point lower than projected prior to September 11. The subsequent recovery in high-income countries should ignite a strong rebound to 5.2 percent growth in developing countries in 2003. Although the global slowdown is the main underlying cause for the poor outlook in 2001 and 2002, higher perceptions of risk are also at work, reflecting both the flight to quality of investors and financial tensions in large emerging markets such as Argentina, Brazil, and Turkey.

Amid these expectations, MENA will have to find resources for financ-

Table 5.9   Forecasts of GDP Growth, 2001 to 2003
              (Annual Percentage Change)

	Actual Growth	Before September 11			After September 11		
Region	2000	2001	2002	2003	2001	2002	2003
High-income countries	3.4	1.1	2.2	2.8	0.9	1.1	3.5
Developing countries	5.5	2.9	4.3	5.0	2.9	3.7	5.2

Source: World Bank calculations.

ing the adjustment and reform costs of social programs. Some resources can come from the proceeds of privatization, as total revenues from privatization appear to be rising. Although several MENA countries, including Egypt, Tunisia, Morocco, and Algeria, launched privatization programs in the late 1980s or early 1990s, the approach was cautious and gradual because of political constraints. As a result, of the more than $162 billion worth of state-owned enterprises sold worldwide in developing countries from 1988 to 1996, only about 3 percent of revenues was generated in MENA countries. The share of MENA countries in infrastructure privatization and private provision of infrastructure projects was similarly small. Meanwhile, deficiencies in the public provision of a variety of goods and services—notably infrastructure services—became increasingly apparent, as provision failed to keep pace with rapidly growing populations.

Recent trends are more encouraging, however. Over the past few years, there has been a clear shift in the role of the state in several MENA countries from one of "player" to one of "referee." Privatization of state enterprise appears to be gaining momentum. In Egypt, Jordan, Lebanon, Morocco, Tunisia, West Bank and Gaza, and several of the Gulf countries, competitive bidding for the provision of certain infrastructure services is being successfully put into practice (Page, Saba, and Shafik 1997). At the same time, the need for stronger regulations and clear legislation is becoming more pressing, as governance issues rise to the fore.

Indeed, broad-based cross-regional measures that attempt to capture the quality of public sector institutions, such as the index of overall institutional quality (figure 5.5), suggest that, although MENA countries lagged behind other developing countries in the early 1980s, by 1990 they had improved and closed the gap.[10] Performance in Maghreb (North Africa) exceeded that in Mashreq (Middle East), while—because of strong performance on rule of law and freedom from the risk of expropriation—the Gulf countries had the highest measure of institutional quality in the region.

This improvement in governance can have a significant effect on the economy. For example, efficient bureaucracies and greater transparency can have a positive impact on foreign direct investment. Figure 5.6 illustrates this point, even though some of the fall in foreign direct investment can be explained by political instability and the decline in petroleum sector investments. Still, the economic effect of public sector performance in MENA countries has yet to be investigated systematically. In-depth diagnostic survey work has not yet been carried out, although efforts in this direction are envisaged in Lebanon, Jordan, Morocco, West Bank and Gaza, and Yemen.

Therefore, the state has an important function that cannot be under-

Figure 5.5   Index of Institutional Quality in the Public Sector, by Region, 1982 and 1990

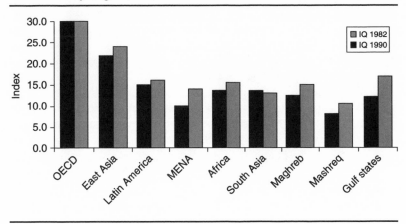

Source: Page and Van Gelder (1998).

Figure 5.6   Foreign Direct Investment in the MENA Region, 1980 to 1995

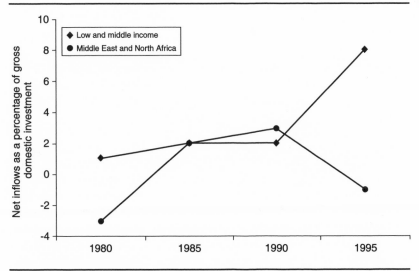

Source: World Bank (1998).

played. The growing demands of globalization, which calls for more efficiency and good governance, may change the role of state from one of producer and provider of services to one of regulator (enforcing competition rules and maintaining a level playing field among public and private providers, such as in the areas of social services). If governments follow policies that reduce legislative and fiscal uncertainty, they could "crowd in" the private sector, making corporations more efficient. The state has the ability to enhance growth and redistribute its benefits. This may call for a different role, but not necessarily a smaller one, and could strengthen the synergy between the public and the private spheres. Formal mechanisms of social protection will address social risks more effectively if they build on, enhance, and do not crowd out informal mechanisms.

The findings, interpretations, and conclusions expressed in this chapter are entirely of the authors and should not be attributed in any manner to the World Bank, to its affiliated organizations, or to the members of its board of executive directors or the countries they represent.

Appendix

Appendix tables begin on p. 174.

Notes

1. According to the World Bank, the MENA region consists of Algeria, Djibouti, Egypt, Jordan, Iran, Lebanon, Morocco, Tunisia, West Bank and Gaza, and Yemen (which are active borrowers) in addition to Bahrain, Iraq, Kuwait, Libya, Malta, Oman, Saudi Arabia, Syria, and United Arab Emirates. This paper focuses primarily on the former group.

2. It is in this context that multilateral agencies have increased their support for mass retrenchment, often by modifying their rules to allow lending for severance pay, provided it is aimed at restructuring the public sector, allows government to quickly reduce budget deficits, and is treated as investment and not recurrent expenditure.

3. Older estimates for the informal sector in urban areas are even higher and reach almost 60 percent in Egypt and Morocco (for 1976 and 1982, respectively). See Charmes (1998).

4. The ratio of working-age workers to pensions counts only workers in the formal sector.

5. Although data on returns are not available for the rest of the countries, in

Iran and Algeria reserves have been channeled to socially desirable purposes, with predictable consequences.

6. This review uses the broad definition of social funds as agencies that finance small projects in several sectors targeted to benefit a country's poor and vulnerable groups based on a participatory manner of demand generated by local groups and organizations and screened against a set of eligibility criteria. Social funds are second-tier agencies in that they do not directly execute projects, but rather support demands channeled to the social fund via nongovernmental organizations, local governments, private agencies, line ministries, or community organizations.

7. These general conclusions do not apply to the programs to support small and microenterprise, where the nature of working with individual clients is by definition highly demand-driven and participatory.

8. Microfinance practitioners prefer to use the household as the unit of analysis because household activity and microenterprise activity are highly intertwined. It is also a common rule that no more than one member of a household should be eligible for a microloan.

9. These include the spun-off Save the Children programs in Lebanon, West Bank and Gaza, and Jordan (respectively, Al Majmoua, JDWS, and Faten), the UNWRA program in West Bank and Gaza, Zakoura and Al Amana in Morocco, and two programs in Egypt (Cairo, Sharkia) designed along the lines of the Alexandria Business Association.

10. The index of overall institutional quality is based on International Country Risk Guide indicators, namely government repudiation of contracts, risk of expropriation, rule of law, corruption in government, and quality of bureaucracy; data are drawn from Political Risk Services.

Appendix 5.1   Public Work Programs in the MENA Region[a]

Country and Program Name	Year of Start	Source of Financing	Workers per Year	Workers per Year (Percentage of Labor Force)
Algeria Programme d'Activites d'Interet General	1994	Budget	190,000[b]	2.1
Travaux d'Utilite Publique	1996	30 percent budget, 70 percent International Bank for Reconstruction and Development	10,000[c]	0.1
Rural Employment Project	1997	13 percent budget, 87 percent donors	10,000	0.1
Egypt Public Works (part of the Social Fund)	1993	Social Fund: (10 percent budget, 90 percent donors)[d]	60,000[e]	0.4[f]
Morocco Promotion Nationale	1960s	93 percent budget, 7 percent donors	50,000[h]	0.6[i]
Tunisia Chantiers Nationaux and Chantiers Regionaux	1960s	Budget	75,000[j]	2.7[j]

Total Cost as Percentage of GDP (One Year)	Cost per Job (U.S. Dollars per Year)	Program Wage	Percentage of Wage Cost in Total Cost	Remarks
0.4	610	Half minimum wage	80	Temporary works; relatively high educated beneficiaries; primarily urban oriented; activities not always labor intensive; only one member per household can participate
0.07	2,650	Market or minmum wage	40 to 50	Project just implemented
0.07	1,580	Market wage	55	Project just implemented; mainly directed to the northwestern area of the country
0.3[g]	1,400	Unskilled or semi-skilled wage	30	Temporary unskilled workers; rural areas; labor intensive; workers employed in infrastructure building
0.26[j]	950	Minimum rural wage	75	Temporary, seasonal, and emergency works; unskilled workers; mainly (70 percent) in rural areas; labor intensive; workers employed in infrastructure building
0.4[k]	170	Below minimum wage	80	Temporary, seasonal, and emergency works; unskilled workers; mainly (two-thirds) in rural areas; labor intensive

(Table continues on p. 176.)

Appendix 5.1   *Continued*

Country and Program Name	Year of Start	Source of Financing	Workers per Year	Workers per Year (Percentage of Labor Force)
West Bank and Gaza				
Civil Works (part of the Community Development Project)	1997	10 percent budget, 90 percent donors	8,000	—
Yemen				
Public Works Project	1997	90 percent International Development Association, 10 percent domestic	3,500[f]	0.07
Public Works (part of the Social Fund)	1997	Social Fund (9 percent budget, 81 percent donors)	2,000	0.04

Source: Authors' compilation.
[a] All types of programs are cash for work except in Morocco where in addition to cash for work, there is also the provision for food for work.
[b] 1996. After 1995, as a result of improving targeting criteria, the number of beneficiaries was largely reduced; in 1995 they were still 430,000.
[c] So far only about 2,000 have been created.
[d] 1993.
[e] Average 1993 to 1996.
[f] Average.

Total Cost as Percentage of GDP (One Year)	Cost per Job (U.S. Dollars per Year)	Program Wage	Percentage of Wage Cost in Total Cost	Remarks
0.4	—	—	Min. 25	Short-term, semi-unskilled workers; small villages and municipalities; labor intensive; workers employed in infrastructure building
0.15	—	Unskilled wage	30 to 40	Just implemented; poor rural areas; workers employed in infrastructure building
0.08	1,000		35	Just implemented; poor rural areas; workers employed in infrastructure building; projects are demand driven

[g]1994.
[h]On average since its creation.
[i]1992 labor force.
[j]Average of the period 1987 to 1991.
[k]1989.
[l]Calculated on the basis of a six months average duration of job.

Appendix 5.2. Summary of Food Subsidy Reforms for MENA Countries

Country	Status of Reforms	Remaining Reform Options
Algeria	• Food subsidies have been eliminated gradually since 1992 • Safety nets were introduced in 1994 to compensate for the increase in food prices.	• Improve targeting and efficiency of the existing safety nets

Egypt	• Food subsidy costs were reduced by raising prices, reducing the number of ration book holders, and reducing the number and quantity of subsidized food items
	• A self-targeted mechanism has been adopted for bread and wheat flour through lower-quality products such as baladi bread and flour
	• Sugar and edible oil are subject to quotas and distributed through ration cards
	• Food subsidy is still general, untargeted, and open to all Egyptians through a system of no quantity restrictions or subsidized baladi bread and a monthly ration quota for subsidized sugar and edible oil
		• Continue reducing food subsidies costs through two possible options:
		  Adopt an administratively targeted or means-tested food subsidy system through establishing an efficient administrative system to screen the poor from the nonpoor
		  Eliminate current subsidies on edible oil or sugar or double the price of a loaf of subsidized baladi bread

Iran	• Reforms were launched in 1992 to reduce fiscal costs by lowering the exchange rate and making fewer commodities eligible for coupons • Cash transfers were introduced to replace coupons on chicken and eggs	• Increase prices on subsidized commodities; • Assess impact of different option reforms
Jordan	• Food subsidies were gradually removed: in 1996 they were replaced with food coupons available to everyone; in 1997 the food coupons were replaced by cash transfers, and the general cash transfers were eliminated in 1999	• Adopt further means testing to achieve better targeting • Monitor the impact of the transfer programs and the elimination of cash transfers on poverty

Country		
Morocco	• Food subsidies were virtually eliminated (0.3 percent of GDP in 1999, 0 percent in 2000) • Quantity restrictions on subsidized commodities were replaced by custom tariffs • All crop production and intermediary prices were liberalized • Consumer prices on sugar, cooking oil, and national flour are fixed by government • Flour is self-targeted via low-grade quality to favor the poor and middle class • Cost of food subsidies has remained unchanged (about 1.7 percent of GDP)	• Remove subsidy and reduce customs protection for all three products (eliminate tariffs on cooking oil and maintain moderate tariffs for substantially domestically produced crops, mainly soft wheat and sugar crops) • Introduce a compensatory targeted scheme for the consumers and small farmers and producers affected by the removal of custom protection • Finance cost-effective instruments focused on the basic needs of low-income groups
Tunisia	• Food subsidies are self-targeted in the form of quality differentiation: semolina, pain (bread) unique, generic grain oil, less-refined brown sugar, and pasteurized-reconstituted milk • Cost of food subsidies was reduced from 3 percent of GDP in 1990 to 2 percent in 1993, then dropping to 1.7 percent since 1995 • Food subsidy is still general, untargeted, and open to all Tunisians	• Strengthen the "inferior goods" approach by tailoring the selection of subsidies based on the consumption patterns of the poor • Liberalize prices on unsubsidized goods • Continue increasing retail prices on goods consumed by higher-income groups • Define targeted group and monitor progress of reforms • Reduce customs protection for all subsidized products and introduce compensatory targeted schemes to protect poor local producers
Yemen	• Food subsidies were reduced (3.6 percent of GDP in 1998, 5.2 percent in 1997, and expected to reach 0.3 percent in 1999) • Wheat pricing and marketing were liberalized in 1999.	• Assess the impact on poverty of reducing food subsidies • Monitor progress of reform and assess impacts on poor in both rural and urban areas • Increase investment in basic social services targeted to low-income groups

Source: Razmara et al. (1999); World Bank (1999b).

References

Abrahart, Alan, Iqbal Kaur, and Zafiris Tzannatos. 2002. "Government Employment and Active Labor Market Programs in MENA." In *Employment Creation and Social Protection in the Middle East and North Africa*, edited by Heba Handoussa and Zafiris Tzannatos. New York and Cairo: American University in Cairo Press.

Börsch-Supan, Axel. 1992. "Population Aging, Social Security Design, and Early Retirement." *Journal of Institutional and Theoretical Economics* 148(4): 533–57.

Börsch-Supan, Axel, Robert Palacios, and Patrizia Tumbarello. 1999. *Pension Systems in MENA*. Washington, D.C.: World Bank.

Charmes, Jacques. 1991. "Employment and Income in the Informal Sector of Maghreb and Mashreq Countries." Cairo papers in social sciences. Cairo: American University in Cairo Press.

———. 1998. "Progress in Measurement of the Informal Sector: Employment and Share of GDP. In *Handbook of National Accounting. Household Accounting: Experiences in the Use of Concepts and Their Compilation*." New York: United Nations Statistics Division.

Dar, Amit, and Zafiris Tzannatos. 1999. *Active Labor Market Programs: A Review of the Evidence from Evaluations*. Social protection discussion paper series 9901. Washington, D.C.: World Bank, Human Development Project, Social Protection Team.

Disney, Richard. 1996. *Can We Afford to Grow Older? A Perspective on the Economics of Aging*. Cambridge, Mass.: MIT Press.

Gruber, Jonathan, and David Wise, eds. 1999. *Social Security and Retirement Around the World*. Chicago: University of Chicago Press.

OECD (Organization for Economic Cooperation and Development). 1997. *OECD Employment Outlook*. Paris: OECD.

Page, John, Joseph Saba, and Nemat Shafik. 1997. "From Player to Referee: The Changing Role of Competition Policies and Regulation in the Middle East and North Africa." Paper presented at Arab Monetary Fund/Arab Fund for Social and Economic Development Seminar (1997).

Page, John, and Linda Van Gelder. 1998. *Missing Links: Institutional Capability, Policy Reform, and Growth in the Middle East and North Africa*. Washington, D.C.: World Bank.

Razmara, Setareh, et al. 1999. *MENA Consumer Subsidy Paper*. Washington, D.C.: World Bank, Middle East and North Africa Region, Human Development Department.

Said, Mona. 1995. "Public Sector Employment and Labor Markets in Arab Countries: Recent Developments and Policy Implications." Workshop on labor markets and human resources development, Economic Research Forum, Cairo.

Schiavo-Campo, Salvatore, Giulio de Tommaso, and Amitabha Mukherjee. 1997. "An International Survey of Government Employment and Wages." Policy research working paper 1806. Washington, D.C.: World Bank, Policy Research Department.

World Bank. 1994. *Averting the Old Age Crisis.* Washington, D.C.: World Bank.

———. 1995. *World Development Indicators 1995.* Washington, D.C.: World Bank.

———. 1998. *World Development Indicators 1998.* Washington, D.C.: World Bank.

———. 1999a. "Algeria Social Protection Note." Unpublished paper. Washington, D.C.: World Bank, Middle East and North Africa Region, Human Development Department.

———. 1999b. "Consumer Food Subsidies in MENA Region." Washington, D.C.: World Bank, Middle East and North Africa Region, Human Development Department.

———. 1999c. "The Employment Crisis in the MENA Region." Unpublished paper. Washington, D.C.: World Bank, Middle East and North Africa Region, Human Development Department.

———. 2002. "Reducing Vulnerability and Increasing Opportunity: Social Protection in the Middle East and North Africa." Washington, D.C.: World Bank, Middle East and North Africa Region, Human Development Department.

———. Various issues. *World Development Indicators.* Washington, D.C.: World Bank.

PART II

CONCLUSIONS AND POLICY RECOMMENDATIONS

Chapter 6

What Drives Social Spending?
1780 to 2020

PETER H. LINDERT

S OCIAL spending is mainly a twentieth-century phenomenon. As shown in table 6.1 and figure 6.1, which present the share of social transfers in gross domestic product (GDP), hardly any taxes went into social spending in Western Europe or America in earlier times. Historically, the main kind of social spending was in the form of poor relief, which was stretched thin to cover the poor and disabled of all ages. There were no mass public school systems, no tax-based health insurance, and no unemployment compensation beyond seasonal poor relief. It is only in the nineteenth century that we begin to see the rise of mass public schooling and a slow upward creep in tax-based poor relief on the continent. Figure 6.2 illustrates the rise and fall of Britain's poor-relief tax effort.

The stirrings of a movement toward comprehensive social programs became evident after 1880. As I have argued elsewhere (Lindert 1994), Bismarck's famous social insurance innovations of the 1880s and 1890s look less pioneering if one is interested in the rise of distributive transfers across income brackets. The 1880s versions of the Bismarck insurance schemes were generally contributory schemes, making workers and their employers, not general taxpayers, pay for the insurance. A truer pioneer in social transfers from the 1880s on would be Denmark, followed by the early pension schemes of Australia and New Zealand.

The real boom in all sorts of social programs came after World War II. It is interesting that the overall data in table 6.1 and figure 6.1 make the rise of social spending look more monotonic than one would have thought from the tone of public discourse after 1980. For all the often reported

Table 6.1 Social Transfers as a Percentage of GDP at Current Prices in Select OECD Countries, 1880 to 1995

Country	1880[a]	1890[a]	1900[a]	1910[a]	1920[a]	1930[a]	1960[b]	1970[b]	1980[b]	1980[c]	1995[c]
Australia	0	0	0	1.12	1.66	2.11	7.39	7.37	12.79	10.90	14.84
Austria	0	0	0	0	0	1.20	15.88	18.90	23.27	23.43	21.39
Belgium	0.17	0.22	0.26	0.43	0.52	0.56	13.14	19.26	30.38	22.45	27.13
Canada	0	0	0	0	0.06	0.31	9.12	11.80	14.96	12.91	18.09
Denmark	0.96	1.11	1.41	1.75	2.71	3.11	12.26	19.13	27.45	26.44	30.86
Finland	0.66	0.76	0.78	0.90	0.85	2.97	8.81	13.56	19.19	18.32	31.65
France	0.46	0.54	0.57	0.81	0.64	1.05	13.42	16.68	22.55	22.95	26.93
Germany	0.50	0.53	0.59			4.82	18.10	19.53	25.66	20.42	24.92
Greece	0	0	0	0	0	0.07	10.44	9.03	11.06	8.67	14.43
Ireland						3.74	8.70	11.89	19.19	16.20	18.30
Italy	0	0	0	0	0	0.08	13.10	16.94	21.24	17.10	23.71
Japan	0.05	0.11	0.17	0.18	0.18	0.21	4.05	5.72	11.94	10.48	12.24
Netherlands	0.29	0.30	0.39	0.39	0.99	1.03	11.70	22.45	28.34	26.94	25.70
New Zealand	0.17	0.39	1.09	1.35	1.84	2.43	10.37	9.22	15.22	16.22	18.64
Norway	1.07	0.95	1.24	1.18	1.09	2.39	7.85	16.13	20.99	18.50	27.50
Sweden	0.72	0.85	0.85	1.03	1.14	2.59	10.83	16.76	25.94	12.97	19.01
Switzerland	..	..	..	..	..	1.17	4.92	8.49	14.33	..	18.87
United Kingdom	0.86	0.83	1	1.38	1.39	2.24	10.21	13.20	16.42	11.43	13.67
United States	0.29	0.45	0.55	0.56	0.70	0.56	7.26	10.38	15.03	21.36	22.52

Source: Lindert (1994); OECD (1985).

0 = known to be zero. Blank = not yet a sovereign state. .. = known to be positive, but number is not available.

[a] Welfare, unemployment, pensions, health, and housing subsidies.

[b] OECD old series.

[c] OECD new series.

Figure 6.1   Social Transfers as a Share of GDP, 1880 to 1995

A. From 1880 to 1930

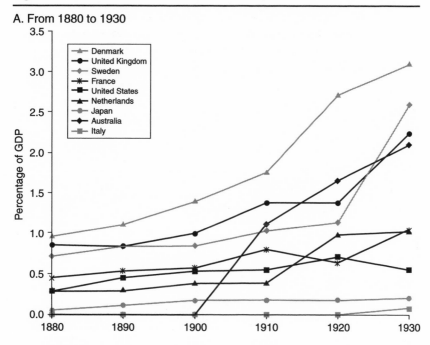

B. From 1930 to 1995

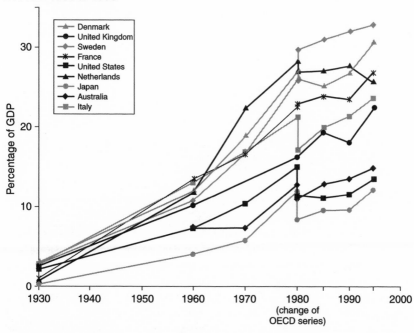

Source: Author's configuration.

Figure 6.2   Poor Relief and Pension Spending as a Share of National Product, England and Wales, and the United Kingdom, 1688 to 1987

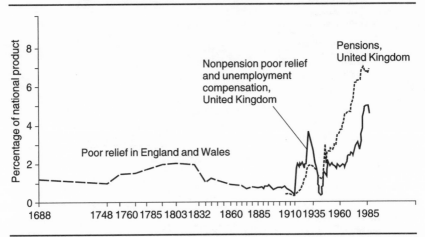

Source: The national product denominators for England and Wales, 1688 to 1811, are from Lindert and Williamson (1983) and O'Brien (1988). Those for 1830 on are based on the estimates of Deane (1968), Feinstein (1972), and the Central Statistical Office. The national product of England and Wales for 1830 to 1936 was assumed to be 0.813 times that of the United Kingdom, a ratio implied by Baxter (1868) for 1867. (This may be too low for the interwar period, after the separation of southern Ireland.)

The poor relief expenditures for 1688 to 1803 are from King (1936 [1695]), Davies and the official returns. Later figures for England and Wales are from Williams (1981, 145–234). All expenditures for the United Kingdom are from the Central Statistical Office. Pension expenditures include all public sector pension programs as well as social insurance pensions and include both contributory and noncontributory pensions. Nonpension poor relief in the twentieth century includes employment insurance, family allowances, and supplemental benefits.

"demise" of the welfare state, all one really sees after 1980 is stasis, not decline, in the shares of GDP taxpayers put into such programs.

Familiar as the broad rise of social transfers may look, it should also seem curious. Why should it have been delayed for so long? Why did it march so far by 1980? Why has it stabilized since then? What difference did its rise make to economic growth? This essay seeks to answer such questions, through an examination of several important conclusions that may be drawn from analyzing the comparative data on social spending.

The first curiosity to note from a historical perspective is how poorly social spending fits the role usually assigned to it (Lindert 1991, 2000). This leads me to the first of six observations: *History reveals a "Robin Hood paradox," in which social spending targeted to the poor is least present when and where it seems most needed. Further, that policy paradox has probably been inefficient, in that aid to the poor probably has the most positive effect on labor supply and GDP where it is least given.*

Poverty policy within any one jurisdiction might be expected to aid the poor more, the lower is the average income and the greater is the income inequality. Yet over time and space, the pattern is usually the opposite. Although there are exceptions to this general tendency, the underlying tendency itself is unmistakable. Today's global cross section of nations shows stark contrasts in the shares of GDP devoted to "social security," or social insurance, programs of central governments. From 1985 to 1990, they absorbed about 16.3 percent of GDP in the rich Organization for Economic Cooperation and Development (OECD) countries and only 2.7 percent in developing countries (United Nations 1994, 196), where poverty and inequality are much greater. Similarly, in the United States, support for the poor takes a smaller share of income in states with higher pretax inequality and poverty (especially in the Southeast).

What table 6.1 and figures 6.1 and 6.2 add is the reminder that this is also a basic paradox of history. In the poorer and more unequal world that existed before World War II, the least was given to those in the bottom quintiles—or, conversely, in today's prosperous world with relatively lower pretax income inequalities, the poor get the most generous support by historical standards.

Indeed, less was given in those earlier days even by private and religious charities. Although there are few data on charity for the poor, the few numbers I have gleaned suggest that private and church charity seldom reached even half a percent of national product in the absence of government programs (Lindert 1998).

Why does the paradox arise? The main forces that operate over time and across units of government are as follows:

1. The income effect, meaning the higher is the average income, the higher is the minimum level of living the country can tolerate for its poorest residents.

2. Democracy, since higher-income settings are ones in which political voice extends further down the income ranks.

3. The rise of human capital, because the return from investing in the poor rises as more workers with more skills are demanded.

In essence, the option of just turning the poor out becomes increasingly unattractive as their poverty is transmitted to succeeding generations in a skills-based world. Recent studies of today's developing countries have found that aid to the poor can bring significant gains in labor supply by improving health and nutritional status (Mehrotra 2000; Mehrotra and Delamonica forthcoming).

This suggests that social spending is driven not just by changing economics, but by changing politics as well. Specifically, democratization has played a key role in creating the welfare state. This leads to my second observation: *There was so little social spending of any kind before the twentieth century primarily because political voice was so restricted.*

If all residents had equal vote, and if the only way one could influence a political outcome was by using that single vote, the rich would be heavily taxed to support redistributive social programs (see, for example, Peltzman 1980; Meltzer and Richard 1981; Alesina and Rodrik 1994; Persson and Tabellini 1994). Of course, the distribution of pretax income and wealth is particularly skewed in less-developed settings, both historically and at the present time (for example, Kakwani 1980; the Deininger-Squire database), with the median income well below the mean income, creating a golden opportunity for a Robin Hood. That he fails to appear in such settings must relate to political economy problems stemming from a large concentration of political power in the hands of the rich.

Power was indeed more concentrated in the past than in today's industrial democracies. Voting rights were restricted by laws limiting the franchise to persons who owned some minimum value of land, earned some minimum income, or paid some minimum value of direct taxes. The retreat of such restrictions opened the initial door for a shift toward progressive taxation. Table 6.2 illustrates with some rough estimates just how restrictive Britain's franchise was before the reform acts and secular mass education set the stage for Lloyd George's assault on the rich just before World War I.[1]

The importance of historical shifts in who had voting power transcends the simple linear idea that the rich fight redistribution and lose that fight as voting rights march down the income ranks. Political historians would rightly insist that the issue is much more complex, since people generally do not vote on a single issue—outside the occasional referendum—and must elect representatives who trade influence on multiple issues. Yet the link between economic self-interest and political voice cannot be overlooked.

A good illustration is the strange rise of English poor relief after 1780, when only a small landed elite had the right to vote. Why should such a society vote to tax itself 2 percent of GDP to support the poor, when it had not done so earlier? Why did Britain move back toward toughness after the Reform Act of 1832 had extended the franchise?

The whole pattern makes good sense, in time and in space, once one understands the self-interest of England's farmers and wealthy rural landlords and combines it with Boyer's (1990) implicit-contracts model

Table 6.2   Declining Exclusiveness of the British Franchise, 1688 to 1911

Time Period and Location	Percentage of Household Heads Having the Right to Vote	Relative Income of Franchised Voters (Ratio of Median Household Income of the Franchised to Median Income of All Households)
1688, England and Wales	15.3	2.75
1759, England and Wales	20.0	2.40
1803, England and Wales	13.5	2.73
First Reform Act, 1832		
1867, England and Wales	19.0	1.37
1867, United Kingdom	4.2	1.46
Second Reform Act, 1867 to 1868		
Third Reform Act, 1883 to 1884		
1911, United Kingdom	74.2	1.13

Source: Author's estimation, using the sources cited in Lindert and Williamson (1982; 1983) and the House of Commons historical volumes. Unpublished revisions were used to improve the 1867 and 1911 estimates to put them on the same household, or "family," basis as the estimates for earlier benchmark years.

of their approach to poor relief. As seasonal hirers of farm labor in an industrializing and urbanizing economy, they had strong incentive to ensure that laborers stayed in their area across the low-income winter months instead of emigrating to cities and industrial centers. The richer the farmer or landlord was, the more he or she hired labor. Local poor relief became a way of making the less-landed households pay a share of local "poor rates" to retain a seasonal labor force they used very little. In fact, Gilbert's Act in 1782 tilted local voting power slightly more in favor of the top landowners by apportioning voting rights to the value of owned land. Conversely, the Reform Act of 1832 shifted voting rights toward rich industrialists in the rising centers, who saw little merit in a system that kept workers in the stagnating rural Southeast.[2] The spatial pattern of generous poor relief in the rural Southeast and greater toughness in prospering cities and the Northwest fits the same model of self-interest (although it is an exception to the Robin Hood paradox).

Similar reasoning about voice and economic interests also helps to explain a curious pattern in the rise of tax-based mass public schooling. In the first half of the nineteenth century, the wave of mass schooling started in the German states, most visibly in Prussia. After 1860, the leadership shifted to North America and Australasia. England and Wales, the Workshop of the World, lagged behind, before catching up quickly in the period 1891 to 1914. Why?

Although every nation's educational history has its unique elements, two systematic causal forces emerge from the comparative political economy of mass schooling before 1914 (Lindert 2001).

The first causal force was democracy. Abstracting from the specific character of ruling elites, we find a systematic influence of the spread of voting rights on primary school enrollments. Other things being equal, democracies—countries where a majority of adults voted—had a significantly greater share of children in school than either non-democracies or elite democracies where only a propertied minority could vote. The effect of extra votes on primary school enrollment was very similar to their effect on social transfer spending as a share of GDP. Thus North America and Australia and even France were ahead of Britain in school enrollments between 1850 and 1900, in part because they were more democratic. Within North America, the same democracy effect holds, in that the educational backwaters were those regions still controlled by a landed elite or by a single religion. The backwaters were the U.S. South (Kaestle 1976; Margo 1990) and Quebec, whereas Upper Canada and the United States outside the South were world leaders in schooling.

The second causal force was decentralization. Unlike Britain, France, and most other industrializing countries, Germany and North America left the decision of how much tax to pay for schools up to the localities. In Germany's case, one could even say that primary education was a matter left to local democracy, even though the national government was decidedly undemocratic. Localities raised most of the taxes for schools, and locally elected and appointed officials ran the schools. The landed Junker elite could, and did, keep down the level of schooling only in its own localities. Similarly, plantation owners in the U.S. South could influence educational spending and taxes only in their own states. A decentralized approach to school finance, as in most of Germany and North America, brought about a world in which localities competed for migrants and business by providing attractive tax-based schools. Although there is no easy theorem on this matter, decentralized local finance appears to raise taxes and spending for schools, relative to national approaches like those followed by Britain and France. In this context, it is of interest to note that decentralization of government functions has been a key policy recommendation of the World Bank and other international financial organizations in recent years, driven in large part by this competitive framework.

This leads to my third observation: *The administrative and incentive costs of taxation and social spending may actually drop with economic development. They dropped until about World War II, at least.* To illuminate the dawn of rising social spending and the dawn of statistics measuring it, we should first note a trend in its cost, a trend that does not square with prevailing assumptions about trends in the cost of social programs. Here "cost" means the average and marginal rates of (net national) deadweight cost per dollar transferred from taxpayers to others, a cost implying a reduction in gross domestic product.

The two main kinds of deadweight (net national) costs associated with government budgets are their administrative cost percentage and the percent ratio of their incentive costs to the amounts taxed and spent. We can measure trends in the first of these and conjecture plausibly about the second.

Administrative cost percentages have declined historically, both in tax collection and in the administration of welfare and pension programs. Tables 6.3 and 6.4 sketch the tax collection side, and tables 6.5 and 6.6 sketch the welfare administration side for Britain and America. Britain's tax collection system, which was already a recognized model of efficiency by 1780 (Brewer 1989), became increasingly cheap to administer, per pound collected, across the nineteenth and early twentieth centuries. So did the U.S. Customs Service and the Internal Revenue Service. These cost savings implicitly reduced the cost of any programs on which the tax revenues were spent, such as the social programs that are our focus here.

The cost of administering poor-relief programs also dropped, especially in the great twentieth-century expansion of the welfare state, but its cheapening was less a drop in price and more a shift in "quality" than the cheapening on the tax-collecting side of the budget. Tables 6.5 and 6.6 show why, presenting administrative cost shares from England and New York in the eighteenth and nineteenth centuries. In the age in which it was called "poor relief" and not "welfare," it was very expensive to administer. Administrative costs often ate up 25 percent of the budget, unlike today's welfare and social security programs, which can use as little as 2 to 3 percent of their budget for administration.[3]

The old way of helping the poor, the sick, and the elderly was so much more expensive in those days because taxpayers wanted so much more monitoring of the behavior of the poor than they do today. To see the role of monitoring costs, note the strong contrast in tables 6.5 and 6.6 between the administrative cost shares in "indoor" (poorhouse, workhouse) and "outdoor" (at-home) relief. Wherever the share of "outdoor" aid given to persons in their own homes was higher, as shown in the figures for rural towns and cities in 1772 to 1774, costs were lower and more of the budget was at the disposal of the poor themselves. By contrast, indoor relief was very expensive, because the poor had to be supervised so intensely, in an attempt to reform their behavior and keep them out of public view. As the tables show, both England and New York moved *toward* that tough and

Table 6.3   Tax Collection Costs as a Percentage of Central Government Revenue, United Kingdom, 1787 to 1986

| | | | Main Revenue Services | | |
| | | | | Inland Revenue | |
Year	All Collections[a]	Customs[b]	Total	Excise	Stamps	Direct Taxes
1787 to 1796		6.7	4.7	5.1	5.1	3.5
1803	5.0					
1820	6.4					
1830		6.1	4.8	5.4	2.6	5.3
1840	5.6	5.5	5.0	6.5	2.2	4.6
1850		5.8	5.0	6.5	2.2	4.6
1860	4.1	4.1	3.6			
1873		4.3	3.7			
1880	3.7					
1883		4.4	3.7			
1890		3.9	3.3			
1900	2.2	2.9	2.6			
1926		—[b]	1.6			
1927	1.5					
1937	1.5					
1960		0.9[b]	1.6			
1970		1.0[b]	1.4			
1980		1.4[b]	1.8			
1986		1.1[b]	1.8			

Source: For all collections other than post, telephone, and telegraph, Mitchell and Deane (1962, 392–99).

Notes: Figures for years before World War I divide the official estimates of collection costs by gross receipts, while those after World War I divide it by what are called "net receipts." The change in official convention matters little, since adding the collection costs themselves to the denominator would change the ratio by only about one percent of itself.

For 1787 to 1796, the figures were calculated from The Fourth Report of Great Britain, Select Committee on Finance, July 19, 1797. The collection costs are described only as the "charges of management" on the "collection of revenues" and are compared to gross receipts. For 1830 to 1860, the main source is a special return in House of Commons, Sessional Papers, 1862, vol. xxx, 601. Each figure from this source refers to the single fiscal year starting in the year listed. However, the customs percentages for 1840, 1850, and 1860 are five-year averages centered on that same fiscal year. For 1873 to 1900, annual reports of the Commissioners of Customs and Inland Revenue. The figures for Inland Revenue are again single-year figures for fiscal years starting April 1 and those for the Customs service are five-year averages centered on that year. The customs figures for years between 1855 to 1856 and 1876 to 1877 had to be adjusted upward to correct the temporary exclusion of the Coast Guard costs. For 1926 to 1986, single-year figures were calculated from the Annual Reports of the Customs Commissioner and the Commissioner of Inland Revenue.
[a] Other than post, telephone and telegraph. The figures for 1803, 1820, and 1840 are for the fiscal year ending January 5 of the following year. The figures for all other years are for the fiscal year starting on April 1 of the stated year.
[b] Customs and excise beginning in 1926.

Table 6.4   Tax Collection Costs of Main Revenue Agencies as a Percentage of Central Government Revenue in the United States, 1860 to 1970

Year	Customs	Internal Revenue
1860	6.8	..
1870	3.4	4.3
1880	3.5	3.0
1890	3.2	2.7
1900	3.5	1.6
1929	3.4	1.2
1960	3.7	0.4
1970	3.9	0.5

Source: All cost percentages are five-year averages calculated from the annual reports of the U.S. Secretary of the Treasury. The underlying data series on costs were discontinued in 1980.

costly regime across the nineteenth century, raising the share of administrative costs in their central government budgets. Only after World War I, with welfare support given to the poor more abundantly and with fewer strings, did the welfare costs drop to today's rates.

Like administrative costs, the incentive cost of social programs probably also declined, at least on the tax-collecting side. The incentive cost share is the ratio of the marginal deadweight costs (as in the classic welfare triangles) to the amounts transferred. The prevailing historical shift in tax collections was the same one we observe when scanning from lower-income to higher-income countries in today's global cross section—a shift from border taxes on foreign trade to direct taxation on income and wealth. The famous incentive effects of today's direct taxation on the supply of labor and other factors are real enough, but they are tied to elasticities that tend to be lower than the elasticities of foreign trade and other behavior subject to the older kinds of taxes. Lower elasticities of the taxed activity mean lower deadweight costs per dollar transferred, at least under most realistic initial conditions. Although this point cannot be quantified here, it seems likely that the incentive costs of the rising social programs have declined relative to the amounts spent.

One might imagine that an exogenous drop in the cost of social tax-and-spend combinations was a key historical source of the rise of the welfare state. Yet caution is in order here. As we saw for the old poor-relief programs, lowering costs—by giving more generous outdoor relief—was not really an exogenous price drop. Rather it was a policy shift toward a "quality" of poor relief that cost less to administer by failing to

Table 6.5   Administrative Costs of Poor Relief in England and Wales, 1772 to 1912

Location and Years	Administrative Costs as a Percentage of Expenditures on Poor Relief	Outdoor Relief as a Percentage of Number of Value of Transfers to the Poor	Paupers Relieved
English parishes with workhouses, 1772 to 1774			
Rural East Anglia	29.2	10.5	
London	23.6	27.4	
Towns	15.6	32.8	
Cities, excluding London	10.1	47.5	
All reporting parishes	19.4	32.5	
England and Wales, 1851 to 1912			
1851	12.8	64.7	87.3
1871	15.1	53.6	84.2
1879	18.1	42.1	78.2
1887	20.1	38.9	76.5
1895	22.0	33.4	74.1
1905	22.1	30.8	68.9
1911	24.7	22.6	60.4

Source: For 1772 to 1774, calculated from House of Commons, Cd. 3247 (1775). The data were edited to eliminate cases of poor reporting and correct obvious small errors. Administrative expenses consist of salaries and other incidentals, excluding medical salaries (a transfer in kind) where possible. Transfers consist of food, clothing, shelter, occasional outdoor relief, and a very incomplete accounting of the rental value of occupied real estate.

For 1851 to 1912 (years ending March 25), expenses for 1851 to 1852 are calculated from House of Commons, Sessional Papers, 1852 to 1853, vol. Lxxxiv, 394–97. For this year, the item "all other expenses immediately connected with the relief of the poor," equalling 9.7 percent of total expenses, was judged to be transfers to the poor rather than administrative costs. Expenses for 1871 to 1905 were calculated from Sessional Papers, 1909, vol. xxxvii, 43. The other-expenditures item was broken between buildings-repairs-furniture (largely a transfer) and other expenses (assumed administrative) according to the proportions prevailing in 1911 to 1912. Expenses for 1911 to 1912 are calculated from Sessional Papers, 1912 to 1913, vol. Lxxiii, 860, and 1913, vol. xxxvii, 43.

The counts for indoor and outdoor paupers are from the Annual Abstract of Statistics. Those for 1851 and 1871 are for January 1 only, while those for later years are the averages of July 1 and January 1.

Table 6.6   Administrative Costs of Poor Relief in New York State,[a]
1840 to 1895

| Years | Administrative Costs as a Percentage of Expenditures on Poor Relief | | | Outdoor Relief as a Percentage of | |
	Poorhouse	Outdoor	Total	Value of Transfers to the Poor	Number of Paupers Relieved
1840 to 1844	21.2	14.7	18.3	47.4	63.1
1846 to 1850	20.6	14.2	17.5	49.9	69.6
1851 to 1855	12.9	10.0	11.6	46.0	73.0
1856 to 1860	18.4	8.9	13.8	50.8	78.9
1870 to 1874	25.7	3.8	16.0	50.7	74.8
1875 to 1879	25.6	9.4	17.7	53.7	81.3
1880 to 1884	25.3	8.3	17.8	49.3	73.4
1885 to 1889	27.0	8.3	20.0	43.2	64.8
1891 to 1895	32.0	9.1	24.7	38.6	69.6

Source: All figures are calculated from Hannon (1986, app. A). There is a slight change of series between 1860 and 1870, when an attempt was first made to include building repairs in total expenditures. With these estimates as with the British, it is likely that building costs were incompletely imputed, although their inclusion probably would not have affected the administrative-cost share greatly.
[a] Excluding New York City.

give taxpayers the heavy hand of behavioral control over the poor that many taxpayers would prefer. That is, part of the decline in costs was an endogenous response to other changes, such as income growth.

Let us now turn to these other changes and my fourth observation: *The slow advance of all kinds of social spending in the century from 1880 to 1980 is well explained by the same political-voice motif, helped by population aging, income growth, and differences in religion.*

What best explains the rise of government social transfers and public schooling between 1880 and 1980 is a combination of economic, demographic, social, and political forces that lends itself well both to measurement and to interpretation. We can sort these forces out with the help of the sketch in figure 6.3 of the simultaneous-equation system linking a nation's average income with its tax-based social spending expressed as a share of GDP. That income affects the share spent on such programs is well known, although still not well explained. This effect is represented by the downward arrow in the middle of figure 6.3. The social budget shares, in turn, affect income growth, as shown by the upward arrow. To sort out these mutual effects requires a simultaneous-equation system with enough separate influences on the two kinds of endogenous variables to allow their sources to be identified statistically.

**Figure 6.3   Simultaneous System Linking GDP and Social
Spending Shares**

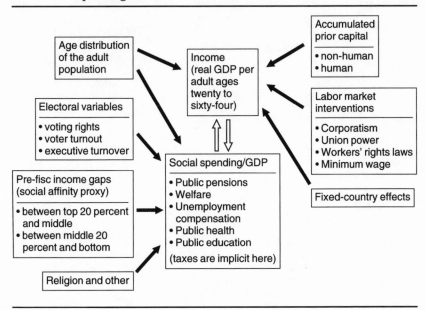

Source: Author's configuration.

The mutual feedbacks between income and social budgets have been
identified by instrumental-variable GLS (generalized least squares) estimates (Lindert 1994, 1996, forthcoming), using six different data sets:

- 1880 to 1930, a pool of data from twenty-one countries over six
  prewar benchmark dates (1880, 1890, 1900, 1910, 1920, and
  1930), introduced in two earlier writings (Lindert 1994, 2001);

- 1962 to 1981, a pool of data consisting of nineteen OECD countries over the five four-year periods from 1962 to 1965 through
  1978 to 1981, which draws on the OECD (1985) estimates of
  social spending for 1960 to 1981, as explained in Lindert (1996);

- 1978 to 1995, a pool of data for twenty-one OECD countries
  over the six three-year periods from 1978 to 1980 through 1993
  to 1995, using the newer OECD (1999) social expenditure database;

- 1975 to 1990, all countries, a pool of data for thirty-nine nations
  over the four dates 1975, 1980, 1985, and 1990, based on Kuo
  (1999);

- 1975 to 1990, Third World, a subset of data for twenty non-OECD countries from the same Kuo data set;

- 1975 to 1990, a pool of data for the nineteen OECD countries from the same data set.

In all these historical experiences the changes in total social transfers are partly explained by four main sets of systematic forces: income, electoral democracy, population aging, and social affinity. In all countries, part of the rise was explained by income growth, in the spirit of the somewhat-vague Wagner's Law, which can be construed as saying that, as average income rises, the share of national income taxed and spent by government rises.

The second force is a set of electoral variables—whether this was a democracy, the rate of voter turnout at the last election, and whether women were granted their voting rights—that have a strong positive effect on the rise of social transfers (and taxes). Of these, the distinction between democracies and other political systems has a less clear effect on social spending and taxes than the distribution of voice within democracies or the political interests of rulers within systems other than democracies. The clearest opposition to most social programs seems to come in elite democracies, where fewer than 40 percent of adults are permitted to vote. Such elite democracies have less political will to tax and transfer toward the poor than many other governments. Heavily voting democracies tax more and spend more on social insurance, especially those democracies that have granted women the vote.[4] The set of electoral-democracy variables has less visible impact on social transfers in the postwar era than in 1880 to 1930. The potential impact of electoral democracy on social spending probably remains strong but is hidden in the postwar samples. In the postwar samples confined to the OECD countries, electoral democracy cannot show its influence because it is practically universal. In the 1975 to 1990 samples including developing countries, the available indexes of democracy are probably too crude to show its influences.

Population aging plays the third main role, which becomes the starring role in explaining postwar trends and international differences in social transfers.[5] An older society seems to want higher tax-based social insurance. So say tests on all six samples—the early 1880 to 1930 sample, the postwar OECD samples, and the more global postwar samples for 1975 to 1990, which include several Asian and Latin American countries outside the OECD.

To give a sense of how population aging stands out among determinants of social transfer spending, table 6.7 summarizes the causal influences found in the 1975 to 1990 global sample. As is evident there, population aging stands out. The other outstanding influence is the eth-

Table 6.7 Determinants of Social Transfers in a Global Sample of Thirty-Nine Countries, 1975 to 1990

Is There a Significant Positive Effect of	In an Equation to Explain the Share of GDP Spent on				
	Public Pensions	Unemployment Compensation	Public Assistance to the Poor	Other Social Expenditures	Total Social Expenditures
Program existence (years of social insurance program existence)	—	Yes, +	—	—	—
Real income per capita?	—	Yes, +	—	—	—
Aging of the adult population?	Yes, +	Yes, +	Yes, +	Yes, +	Yes, +
A democracy index?	—	Yes, +	+ᵃ	—	—
Ethnic fractionalization?	No, –	—	No, –	No, –	No, –
Protestant share of population?	Yes, +	No, –	Yes, +	—	—
Catholic share of population?	—	No, –	—	—	Yes, +
Muslim share of population?	—	No, –	—	—	—
Military spending/GDP?	—	—	—	Yes, +	—
Openness, measured by (X + M)/GDP a year earlier?	Yes, +	+ᵃ	—	—	Yes, +

Source: The original source is Kuo (1999, tables C1 to C7, 27–30) for detailed definitions of most of the variables.

Note: Kuo also tested for several variations of the openness hypothesis, often confirming a significant positive link to social transfers. His sample consisted of fifty-three countries, some of which are dropped here due to insufficient comparability and completeness of data. The thirty-nine countries used here are nineteen OECD countries, other Asian countries, and several Latin American countries. There are no countries from Africa or the Middle East other than Turkey. The pooled sample consists of these thirty-nine nations for four years (1975, 1980, 1985, and 1990), or 156 observations. The detailed results are shown in Lindert (in progress).

— Coefficient not statistically significant from zero at 5 percent threshold in a two-tailed test. Where polynomials were used (years of social insurance program existence, aging), the confidence interval is measured at the low levels typical of the twenty developing countries in the sample.

ᵃSignificant only at the 7 percent level.

nic fractionalization index, which ethnographers have developed to quantify the division of a country into separate ethnic groups.

The age effect has some dimensions that need emphasis. First, we must remember that it is a reliable statistical result in search of an underlying mechanism. Is it gray power that demands more social insurance (and, implicitly, taxes)? What share of that power has arisen as lives lengthen because younger voters either want government help in handling their parents or see that they too face a long retirement? Or is the aging effect getting credit for other forces that happen to be correlated with aging?

A second point to emphasize is that the underlying regressions show that (up to a point) an older population seems to prefer higher social spending *of all kinds*, not just age-targeted public pensions and health care.

Finally, and most important, the effect of an older population on social transfers is *not linear*, despite the simplification in table 6.7. This finding is key to any projections of social transfer trends into the future. Figures 6.4 through 6.7 show what the six historical data sets suggest about the effects of aging on social budgets, holding other forces constant. Let us begin with the portrayal in figure 6.4 of how a rightward shift toward an older population affects total social transfers. Different samples yield different estimates, especially when the estimates are extrapolated out of the historically observed range, in which 2 to 18 percent of the national population consists of persons over sixty-five. Yet five of the six samples agree on the key point already introduced: an older population politically prefers higher tax-financed social transfers.[6]

Naturally, an older population's preference for social transfers favors those transfers received by the elderly. Figure 6.5 shows the upslope we would expect, meaning that an older society devotes a greater share of GDP to public pensions. There is also a hint that this aging effect decelerates, or curves downward, in the older-population ranges to the right. Yet the pressure for more pensions does not necessarily exceed the pressure for total social transfers. As figure 6.6 shows, the pressure on social transfers other than pensions rises with age in some settings and declines with age in others. For now we can only say that there is no clear direction of effect on social transfers other than pensions.

The key nonlinearity relates to the effects of aging on the relative generosity of pensions *per elderly person*. This relative generosity is measured by the ratio of public pension spending per elderly person to GDP per capita. Figure 6.7 shows what looks at first like a bewildering set of patterns in the effects on this support ratio. Yet with one exception (the 1975 to 1990 OECD subsample), there is an inverted-U pattern. In young populations, like in today's developing countries, a rise in the share of elderly in the total population actually raises the generosity of relief per elderly person. The rise in pensions as a share of GDP shown back in fig-

Figure 6.4   Effect of Population Aging on Total Social Transfers

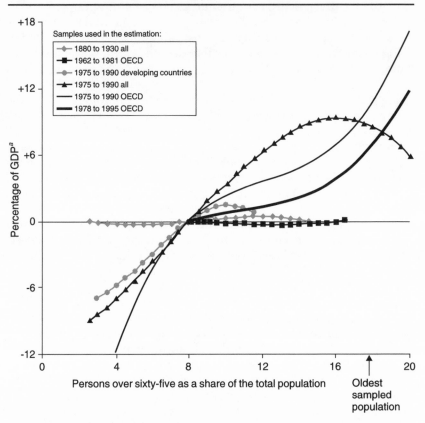

Samples used in the estimation:

- 1880 to 1930 all
- 1962 to 1981 OECD
- 1975 to 1990 developing countries
- 1975 to 1990 all
- 1975 to 1990 OECD
- 1978 to 1995 OECD

Persons over sixty-five as a share of the total population   Oldest sampled population

Source: Author's configuration.
[a] Percentage of GDP by which a country's total social transfers are estimated to depart from those of a country with 8 percent of its population over the age of sixty-five (other things held equal).

ure 6.5 is therefore not just a by-product of applying the same set of entitlement rules to a growing elderly population. Rather figure 6.7 suggests an early success for "gray power" lobbying, which gains momentum as a young and developing society ages. Later on, however, as the population ages toward the Scandinavian extreme, the effect on the generosity of pensions turns strongly negative. The implied effects are big. The rise (fall) of 40 percent in the ratio graphed in figure 6.7 means that if a middle population with 8 percent over the age of sixty-five gives its elderly an average of 60 percent of GDP per capita, as often has happened, then that 60 percent support ratio rises from (falls toward) only 36 percent in the youngest (oldest) societies.

Figure 6.5   Effect of Aging on Public Pension Spending

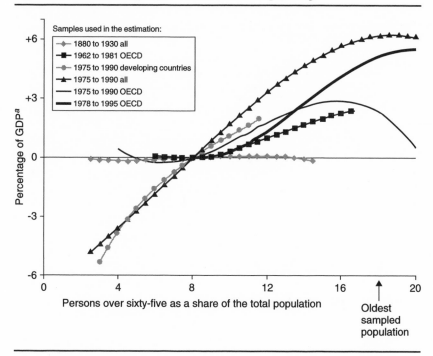

Source: Author's configuration.
[a]Percentage of GDP by which a country's public pension spending is estimated to depart from that of a country with 8 percent of its population over the age of sixty-five (other things held equal).

Such a rise and fall of gray power, as judged by the pension support ratio, does make sense. As one might have predicted from the public goods literature, being a larger share of the population does not help your redistributive fight forever. In the early stage toward the left in figure 6.7, having more elderly persons gives them more political voice. Eventually, however, raising the share of elderly in the population over 20 percent must erode the amount that each elderly person can extract from the political system.

Another force becomes visible in the postwar data, yielding my fifth observation: *The social affinities felt by middle-income voters, proxied by ethnic homogeneity or by their income distances from the bottom income ranks, are an important determinant of tax-based social spending.* The fourth and last main force determining the share of social spending in GDP is social affinity, including ethnic homogeneity as one source of affinity. The opposite of this homogeneity, or ethnic fractionalization, is a strong neg-

Figure 6.6   Effect of Aging on Public Nonpension Transfers

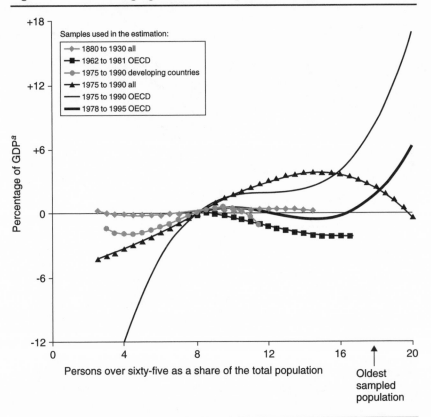

Source: Author's configuration.
[a]Percentage of GDP by which a country's public nonpension transfers are eliminated to depart from that of a country with 8 percent of its population over the age of sixty-five (other things held equal).

ative influence on social budgets and the taxes to pay for them. As shown in table 6.7, ethnic homogeneity strongly promotes every kind of social transfer program through government. Stated the other way around, ethnic fractionalization is a strong negative influence on the political will to raise taxes for social spending and related public investments. This result stands out in global data sets as well as in recent studies of Africa and U.S. local governments (Easterly and Levine 1997; Alesina, Baqir, and Easterly 1999).

Aside from its ethnic dimension, social affinity probably also has an income distribution side. It makes sense that social transfers and public education derived much of their political success from the willingness of swing voters, presumably middle-income voters, to identify with the

Figure 6.7   Effect of Aging on Public Pension Support Ratio

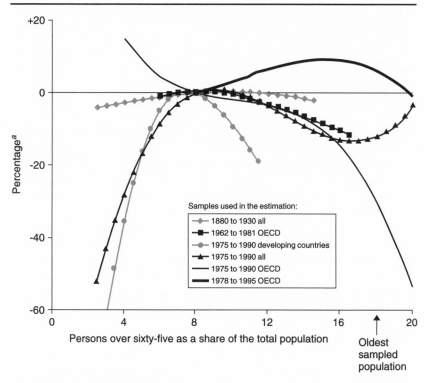

Source: Author's configuration.
[a]Percentage by which the public's pension support ratio, or (pensions per elderly)/(GDP per capita), departs from the ratio when the elderly are 8 percent of the whole population.

need for such tax-based programs. The economic stake of middle voters is likely to depend on their social affinities, as modeled elsewhere (Kristov, Lindert, and McClelland 1992). For which group do middle voters say, "That could be me": the tax-burdened rich or the poor to be caught in safety nets? There is no easy way to measure such affinities, aside from being alert to whether middle voters share the same language, religion, and race with those at the top or bottom. A recent study of panel data in seven OECD countries shows that greater inequality in children's fortunes in the U.S. and Britain has combined with a lower tendency for children to be able to move between income ranks over the years, relative to five other countries (Bradbury, Jenkins, and Micklewright 2000, 12–28). In such settings, we would expect less inclination of middle-income voters to look at the poor and say, "That could be my child."

An alternative measure of social affinity, one that works only weakly, is income skewness, measured as the difference between upper and lower gaps in the overall income distribution. We might imagine that perceived income intermobility should matter, so that the politics of social transfers will depend on whether those in the middle see more chance of rising, than of falling, in the ranks. I have used two pre-fisc (pre-tax and pre-transfer) income gaps as crude proxies: an upper gap (log of Y_{80-100}/Y_{40-60}) and a lower gap (log of Y_{40-60}/Y_{0-20}). These gaps vary across countries, especially the lower gap between those in the middle and those at the bottom. Among OECD countries, the lower gap is widest for the United States, followed by Australia. This basic fact about the lower income gap in a few countries partly explains why they differed decade after decade in their belief in social programs (Lindert 1996). However, the income-skewness proxy for social affinity is not very robust statistically, as shown in Kuo's global results (1999).

This brings me to my final observation: *The effect of population aging, which explains much of the growth of social spending in OECD countries in recent years, implies near-stagnation in this share up to at least 2020. For most developing countries, by contrast, population aging will not check, and will probably raise, the share of social transfers in GDP.*

Given the apparent role of aging, income, and other variables in explaining countries' levels of social transfers over the century from 1880 to 1995, we should ask what the patterns would predict about the near future. The usual dangers of forecasting apply, of course. Yet some cautious extrapolation is possible, since tests on all six of our historical samples seem to give a large role to the age distribution of the population, which can be projected into the future more reliably than economic variables. A likely improvement over most projections into the future is the nonlinearity of the effects highlighted in figures 6.4 through 6.7. It helps to know not only which countries will age faster than others in the years ahead but also that the implications of aging are different between young populations and already old ones.

Table 6.8 suggests where the inevitable aging will most strain public social budgets and the taxpayers by the year 2020. Strain should show up in a forecast that aging will noticeably cut the generosity of pension support, again measured as that ratio of pensions per elderly person to GDP per capita. Let us look first at young OECD populations, then at the most aging OECD countries, and finally at the non-OECD countries of Asia and Latin America.

The first set of countries is the younger set of OECD countries, ones that still will not have much more than 20 percent of their populations older than sixty-five by the year 2020. The estimates suggest that some of these might not have a crisis in social budgets, either for the elderly or for

Table 6.8   Pension Support and Social Transfers Projected to 2020, Using the Aging Effect Alone

Country	Share of Total Population Older Than Sixty-Five		Predicted Change Due to the Rise in the Share of the Population Over Sixty-Five in Total Population, 1990 to 2020			
	1990	Projected to 2020	Public Pensions as a Percentage of GDP	Ratio of Pensions Per Elderly to GDP Per Capita	Total Social Transfers as a Percentage of GDP	Nonpension Transfers as a Percentage of GDP
OECD countries with the elderly approaching 20 percent of the population by 2020						
Australia	11.2	15.9	3.2	3.7	2.7	-0.6
Austria	15.0	18.7	1.9	-5.0	5.5	3.6
Belgium	15.1	20.0	**2.0**	**-9.9**	**8.8**	**6.9**
Canada	11.2	18.1	4.4	0.5	6.0	1.7
Denmark	15.6	19.0	**1.6**	**-5.9**	**5.7**	**4.1**
Germany	15.0	20.0	**2.0**	**-9.9**	**8.9**	**6.9**
Ireland	11.4	15.9	3.1	3.3	2.6	-0.5
Netherlands	12.8	20.1	**3.6**	**-8.8**	**10.5**	**6.9**
New Zealand	11.1	18.2	4.4	0.4	6.2	1.8
Norway	16.3	18.2	0.9	-3.1	3.1	2.2
Portugal	13.6	19.0	**3.0**	**-5.2**	**7.1**	**4.1**
United Kingdom	15.7	19.1	**1.5**	**-6.2**	**5.8**	**4.3**
United States	12.4	16.3	2.7	1.6	2.8	0.0

(Table continues on p. 208.)

Table 6.8 *Continued*

Country	Share of Total Population Older Than Sixty-Five		Predicted Change Due to the Rise in the Share of the Population Over Sixty-Five in Total Population, 1990 to 2020			
	1990	Projected to 2020	Public Pensions as a Percentage of GDP	Ratio of Pensions Per Elderly to GDP Per Capita	Total Social Transfers as a Percentage of GDP	Nonpension Transfers as a Percentage of GDP
OECD countries with the elderly surpassing 20 percent of the population before 2020						
Italy	14.5	19.2[a]	2.4	-6.5	7.1	4.7
Japan	12.0	18.6[a]	4.0	-2.1	6.8	2.8
Greece	13.7	19.4[b]	3.0	-6.8	8.1	5.1
Finland	13.4	19.0[c]	3.1	-5.1	7.2	4.1
France	14.0	18.9[c]	2.7	-5.2	6.7	4.0
Spain	13.4	19.0[c]	3.1	-5.1	7.2	4.1
Sweden	17.8	20.0[c]	0.4	-7.3	5.3	4.9
Switzerland	14.3	18.7[c]	2.4	-4.8	6.0	3.6
Non-OECD countries						
Argentina	8.9	11.5	1.4	-16.0	-0.1	-1.5
Bolivia	3.6	5.4	2.2	34.8	2.4	0.2
Brazil	4.3	8.7	3.9	26.7	6.1	2.3
Chile	6.1	11.0	3.1	-11.7	4.0	0.8

China[d]	5.6	10.8	**3.5**	**−5.9**	**4.9**	**1.3**
Colombia	4.2	8.0	3.6	31.0	5.5	2.0
Ecuador	4.1	7.3	3.2	33.7	4.7	1.5
El Salvador	4.3	6.4	2.2	26.6	3.1	0.9
Guatemala	3.2	4.5	1.8	32.6	1.5	−0.3
India	4.3	7.2	2.9	29.2	4.3	1.5
Indonesia	3.9	7.0	3.2	38.0	4.6	1.3
Israel	9.1	13.4	**2.4**	**−22.4**	**−4.2**	**−6.5**
Malaysia	3.7	7.0	3.5	43.0	4.8	1.3
Mexico[e]	4.0	7.9	3.8	35.7	5.7	1.9
Panama	5.0	9.0	3.2	12.8	5.4	2.2
Philippines	3.3	6.0	3.3	49.4	3.7	0.4
Singapore	5.6	15.6	**6.7**	**−7.8**	**−10.0**	**−16.7**
Thailand	4.3	10.0	4.6	19.5	6.9	2.3
Turkey[e]	4.3	8.5	3.7	−7.5	6.0	2.2
Uruguay	11.6	12.8	**0.7**	**−5.6**	**−2.1**	**−2.8**
Venezuela	3.6	7.7	4.2	46.2	5.9	1.7

Source: Author's compilation.

Notes: Boldface numbers signify predictions for a country where the age effect predicts a drop in the pension support ratio by more than 5 percent by 2020, thus implying political tension with the elderly and their historical preference for safety net programs in general.

The percentages of persons over sixty-five are from United Nations, Population Division (1998).

The age effects on pensions/GDP, the pension support ratio, and total social transfers are based on cubic functions of the elderly share, in equations like those sketched in the causal diagram, but using Kuo's (1999) expanded global sample. I have used a 1978 to 1995 twenty-one-country regression (without full fixed effects) for OECD countries, and a third-world subsample of twenty of Kuo's (1999) countries, 1975 to 1990, for non-OECD countries.

[a] 2005.

[b] 2010.

[c] 2015.

[d] Outside the sample.

[e] Admitted to OECD since 1990.

others. One such country may be the United States, despite the heavy public prediction of a social security time bomb. True, when an already aged society gets older, something has to give: either the young get taxed more, or the elderly have to work longer or receive less in retirement. The United States, however, does not have a particularly old population, and the UN projections show only relatively mild aging by 2020. The more the Americans receive immigrants, the more they can attenuate an aging crisis. Something similar may hold for the young national populations of Australia, Canada, Ireland, and New Zealand, according to table 6.8.

A second set of OECD countries is likely to face a deeper aging crisis, primarily because the elderly will reach up to 25 percent of the population by 2020. To mobilize the regression-based estimates with due caution, I have restricted table 6.8 to a view of populations where people over sixty-five are not above 20 percent of the population. In the historical samples used in this study, that share never exceeded 18 percent, and it seems foolhardy to use the regression equations to forecast aging effects up to an elderly share of 25 percent. The countries with the greatest likelihood of experiencing a major social budget crisis by 2020 are the ones that are safely projected only to 2005 and 2010—Italy, Japan, and Greece. These countries will have switched from being relatively young before 1990 to being the world's oldest national populations by 2020. Taken at face value, the estimates say that the burden of the crisis in Italy, Japan, and Greece will be borne by pensioners (lower support ratio) and taxpayers (higher social transfers as a share of GDP), not by the recipients of transfers other than pensions. That remains to be seen, of course, since the prediction crosses the boundary of historical experience. Yet that is the prediction for social budget strain in these three countries. Pensioners and taxpayers probably will also have to face the music in Finland, France, Spain, Sweden, and Switzerland.

Most of the developing countries of Asia and Latin America probably will not face the same kind of crisis. Indeed, they will probably go on expanding the share of social transfers in GDP as they age (and as their incomes rise, a factor not quantified here). Scanning down the support ratio column in the middle of table 6.8, one sees that only six out of the twenty-one non-OECD countries are predicted to suffer declining support for the elderly and related strains. Those six are the ones whose populations will, in fact, have become relatively old by 2020: Argentina, Chile, China, Israel, Singapore, and Uruguay. Some of them have already begun to anticipate the budgetary strain. Chile has largely privatized its pensions, Argentina is cutting social budgets, and Singapore has changed its laws to make it easier for elderly parents to sue their adult children for inadequate private support. The other fifteen countries of Asia and Latin America, however, are likely to expand the generosity of their pensions and other social programs because they are young and still developing.

Thus for social transfers as a whole, and for public pensions in particular, the upshot of the extrapolations to 2020 is that the crisis will be severe in just a few OECD countries. Perhaps more important, the reason why the growth of social spending as a share of GDP has stalled appears to relate to population aging—not to any spreading discovery that the GDP costs of social transfers are soaring. The GDP costs are questionable, and newly industrializing countries are likely to accept the growth of social spending as a share of GDP for a long time to come.

Notes

1. A fruitful area for further research on the relationship of voting rights to redistribution is the possibility that economic growth and political competition interact to endogenize the spread of the franchise itself. Part of this feedback from the economy to voting rights could be an automatic by-product of economic growth, which pulls more people up over the income and wealth thresholds for having the right to vote, even if laws are static. Part may also come from the effects of economic growth on political parties' incentives to pass suffrage reforms. The latter has been modeled, with applications to nineteenth-century Britain, by Acemoglu and Robinson (2000).

2. The passage of the 1834 Poor Law Reform was not a simple direct result of the shift toward urban votes in the 1832 Reform Act, however. As past authors have rightly stressed, the early 1830s had brought a shift in the aristocracy's own attitude toward poor relief. Instead of thinking of it as an investment in preventing sedition, as in the stormy French War era, they came to view poor relief as an instigator of riot, as in the Swing riots of 1830 to 1831. In terms of the minimal political economy framework proposed here, the 1834 Reform mixed an extension of the franchise to groups less sympathetic to poor relief with a shift in the landed perceptions about the elasticity of cooperation by the poor.

3. On the administrative cost shares for social security programs in various countries, see Estrin (1988) and later issues of the same publication.

4. The significance of the positive effect of female suffrage on taxing and social insurance needs careful interpretation and further study. We do not know that a voting pattern by women themselves caused the change. In the postwar era, for example, direct poll results show that women vote more for social-insurance-oriented parties in the United States and Sweden, but definitely not in West Germany or in Britain (especially not in Britain before Thatcher).

5. Striking effects from the age distribution have also turned up in the quantitative sociological literature on comparative welfare states (Pampel and Williamson 1989; Hicks and Misra 1993; Hicks 1999, chs. 6–7).

6. Even the 1880 to 1930 sample shows a significantly positive effect of aging, although the levels of social spending in that era were too small to show the slope clearly in figure 6.4. The one sample without any clear age effect on total social transfers was the 1962 to 1981 sample.

References

Acemoglu, Daron, and James A. Robinson. 2000. "Why Did the West Extend the Franchise? Democracy, Inequality, and Growth in Historical Perspective." *Quarterly Journal of Economics* 115(4): 1167–1200.

Adema, Willem. 1997. "What Do Countries Really Spend on Social Policies? A Comparative Note." *OECD Economic Studies* 28(1).

Alesina, Alberto, Reza Baqir, and William Easterly. 1999. "Public Goods and Ethnic Divisions." *Quarterly Journal of Economics* 114 (4): 1243–84.

Alesina, Alberto, and Dani Rodrik. 1994. "Distribution, Politics, and Economic Growth." *Quarterly Journal of Economics* 109(2): 465–90.

Annual Abstract of Statistics. Great Britain, Central Statistical Office. Various years. London: His/Her Majesty's Stationery Office.

Baxter, R. Dudley. 1868. *The National Income*. London: Macmillan.

Boyer, George R. 1990. *An Economic History of the English Poor Law, 1750–1850*. Cambridge: Cambridge University Press.

Bradbury, Bruce, Stephen Jenkins, and John Micklewright. 2000. *Child Poverty Dynamics in Seven Nations*. Florence, Italy: UNICEF, Innocenti Research Centre.

Brewer, John. 1989. *The Sinews of Power: Money, War, and the English State, 1688–1783*. New York: Alfred Knopf.

Davies, David. 1975. *The Case of Labourers in Husbandry*. Bath: R. Crutwell.

Deane, Phyllis. 1968. "New Estimates of the Gross National Product for the United Kingdom, 1830–1914." *Review of Income and Wealth* 14(2).

Easterly, William. 1995. "Comment on 'What Do Cross-Country Studies Teach about Government Involvement, Prosperity, and Economic Growth?' " *Brookings Papers in Economic Activity* 2: 419–24.

Easterly, William, and Ross Levine. 1997. "Africa's Growth Tragedy: Policies and Ethnic Divisions," *Quarterly Journal of Economics* 112(44): 1203–50.

Estrin, Alexander. 1988. "Administrative Costs for Social Security Programs in Selected Countries." *Social Security Bulletin*. 51(88): 29–31.

Feinstein, C. H. 1972. *National Income, Expenditure and Output of the United Kingdom, 1855–1965*. Cambridge: Cambridge University Press.

Hannon, Joan Underhill. 1986. "Dollars, Morals and Markets: The Shaping of Nineteenth Century Poor Relief Policy." Paper prepared for the All-University of California Conference on Poverty, Old Age and Dependency in the Nineteenth Century, Laguna Beach.

Hicks, Alexander. 1999. *Social Democracy and Welfare Capitalism: A Century of Income Security Politics*. Ithaca, N.Y.: Cornell University Press.

Hicks, Alexander, and Joya Misra. 1993. "Political Resources and the Growth of Welfare in Affluent Capitalist Democracies, 1960–1982." *American Journal of Sociology* 99(3): 668–710.

Kaestle, Carl. 1976. " 'Between the Scylla of Brutal Ignorance and the Charybdis of a Literary Education': Elite Attitudes toward Mass Schooling in Early Industrial England and America." In *Schooling and Society*, edited by Lawrence Stone, 177–91. Baltimore, Md.: Johns Hopkins University Press.

Kakwani, Nanak C. 1980. *Income Inequality and Poverty*. New York: Oxford University Press for the World Bank.

King, Gregory. 1936 [1695]. "Natural and Political Observations and Conclusions Upon the State and Condition of England." In *Two Tracts by Gregory King*, edited by G. E. Barnett. Baltimore: Johns Hopkins University Press.

Kristov, Lorenzo, Peter Lindert, and Robert McClelland. 1992. "Pressure Groups and Redistribution." *Journal of Public Economics* 48(2): 135–63.

Kuo, Chun Chien. 1999. *The Determinants and Sustainability of Social Insurance Spending: A Cross-Country Examination*. Ph.D. diss. in Economics, University of California, Davis.

Lindert, Peter H. 1991. "Toward a Comparative History of Income and Wealth Inequality." In *Income Distribution in Historical Perspective*, edited by Y. S. Brenner, H. Kaelble, and M. Thomas. Cambridge: Cambridge University Press.

———. 1994. "The Rise of Social Spending, 1880–1930." *Explorations in Economic History* 31(1): 1–36.

———. 1996. "What Limits Social Spending?" *Explorations in Economic History* 33(1): 1–34.

———. 1998. "Poor Relief before the Welfare State: Britain versus the Continent, 1780–1880." *European Review of Economic History* 2(August): 101–40.

———. 2000. "Three Centuries of Inequality in Britain and America." In *Handbook of Income Distribution*, edited by A. B. Atkinson and François Bourguignon. Amsterdam: North-Holland.

———. 2001. "Democracy, Decentralization, and the Rise of Mass Schooling before 1914." Working paper 104. University of California, Davis, Agricultural History Center (April).

———. Forthcoming. *Growing Public: Social Spending and Economic Growth Since the Eighteenth Century*.

Lindert, Peter H., and Jeffrey G. Williamson. 1982. "Revising England's Social Tables, 1688–1812," *Explorations in Economic History* 19(4): 385–408.

———. 1983. "Reinterpreting Britain's Social Tables, 1688–1913." *Explorations in Economic History* 20(1): 94–109.

Margo, Robert A. 1990. *Race and Schooling in the South, 1880–1950*. Chicago: University of Chicago Press.

Mehrotra, Santosh. 2000. "Integrating Economic and Social Policy: Good Practices from High-Achieving Countries." Innocenti working paper 80. Florence, Italy: UNICEF, Innocenti Research Centre (October).

Mehrotra, Santosh, and Enrique Delamonica. Forthcoming. *Integrating Economic and Social Policy: Public Spending and the Social Dimensions of Poverty*. Book submitted for publication.

Meltzer, Allan H., and Scott F. Richard. 1981. "A Rational Theory of the Size of Government." *Journal of Political Economy* 89(5): 914–27.

Mitchell, Brian R., and Phyllis Deane , eds. 1962. *Abstract of British Historical Statistics*. Cambridge: Cambridge University Press.

O'Brien, Patrick K. 1988. "The Political Economy of British Taxation, 1660–1815." *Economic History Review*, Second Series, 41(1): 1–32.

OECD (Organization for Economic Cooperation and Development). 1985. *Social Expenditure 1960–1990*. Paris: OECD.

———. 1999. "Social Expenditure Database, 1980–1996." CD-ROM. Paris: OECD.

Pampel, Fred C., and John B. Williamson. 1989. *Age, Class, Politics, and the Welfare State*. Cambridge: Cambridge University Press.

Peltzman, Sam. 1980. "The Growth of Government." *Journal of Law and Economics* 23(2): 209–88.

Persson, Torsten, and Guido Tabellini. 1994. "Is Inequality Harmful for Growth?" *American Economic Review* 84(3): 600–21.

Select Committee on Finance. 1797. *Fourth Report of Great Britain*. London: Select Committee on Finance (July 19).

United Nations Development Programme. 1994. *Human Development Report 1994*. New York: United Nations.

———. Deininger and Squire. *World Income Inequality Database*. Accessed July 2, 2002 at: *www.undp.org/poverty/initiatives/wider/wiid.htm*.

United Nations, Population Division. 1998. *World Population Prospects: The 1996 Revision*. New York.

Williams, Karel. 1981. *From Pauperism to Poverty*. London: Routledge & Kegan Paul.

Chapter 7

Conclusions

Ethan B. Kapstein

Social policy now holds a prominent place in serious discussions of international economic policy. This reflects growing public economic reform, including liberalization, privatization, and globalization. It is the workers affected by these changes who have felt increasingly vulnerable in light of the loss of job security and the host of state-provided social benefits they once enjoyed. From Latin America to East Asia, questions are being raised about the costs and benefits of the neoliberal prescription.

This chapter seeks to make policy recommendations for governments and international institutions based on the empirical findings presented in the regional studies and to provide some suggestions for further research. By virtue of the loans and aid it supplies, the policies it recommends, and the data and ideas it generates, the international community will undoubtedly play a prominent role in shaping social policy within developing countries. Precisely what that role will be remains a matter fraught with considerable uncertainty. On one level, the international community may determine that its role will only be modest, given the overwhelming political and economic difficulties associated with introducing redistributive measures in most domestic societies. On another, the international community could determine that some minimum set of social standards of various kinds needs to be established or even that tax levels must be harmonized in order to prevent a competitive "race to the bottom" from undermining fiscal resources. More likely, the international community will find its role between these two extremes. Specifically, we can expect social policy concerns to remain part of conditional lending packages and perhaps to rise in importance.

Beyond its lending packages and broader global policies for trade, finance, and investment, international institutions will be among the major producers of data and ideas about social policy. Clearly, they have a significant amount of work to carry out in both domains. In terms of data, the comparable sets of numbers on social expenditure that we have are limited in quantity and quality, and we still know next to nothing about the incidence of such spending—that is, how much is being spent, who is being targeted, and who is being reached, by existing social programs. We have no comparative measures of programmatic efficiency. Overall, a major effort at data collection and analysis is required.

With respect to ideas, we believe that current research must look much more closely at the historical development of those social policies actually in place and the political and economic forces that have led to their creation and maintenance. In an important sense, the question that has led much of the work in this field has been a normative one: what can "we" do to help the poor in poor countries? To be sure, a great deal of useful research has emerged in the search for answers. But an analytical focus on the programs that exist and their beneficiaries would be useful, with policy recommendations aimed at making such programs more efficient. Tzannatos and Kaur, for example, provide a careful empirical report on social policy in the Middle East, supplying the necessary backdrop to any discussions of policy reform.

In sum, this volume has argued that economic change has indeed increased the demand for social spending in emerging markets from Latin America to Eastern Europe to Asia. Governments and international institutions are responding to that demand by putting into play a series of policy measures aimed at compensating those workers who may experience job displacement and falling incomes in the early stages of the reform process. Still, a mismatch between supply and demand remains. For better or worse, social policies have been designed largely to help formal sector workers cope with these shifting fortunes, in large part because of this group's organizational capacity; those in the informal sector, and the poor, have perhaps seen less benefit from the social policy innovations of recent years. The East Asian case presented by Birdsall and Haggard provides compelling insights into the political economy of social policy.

Yet excessive pessimism about the possibility of generating broad-based social policy would not be warranted. The chapters by Birdsall and Haggard and by Lindert suggest the important role that democracy can play in promoting equitable social policies. Further, in their contribution, Székely and Fuentes remind us that new ideas can promote policy innovation in settings that are ripe for change, as existed in Latin America following the debt crisis of the 1980s.

Still, some of our authors, such as Barr, express skepticism with regard to at least a few of the ideas for social policy reform now floating around the corridors of government ministries and international organizations. Here we highlight two concerns that appear in several chapters.

Rethinking Pension Reform

In recent years, pension reform has become something of a magic bullet for public officials, international bureaucrats, and academics. It promises to increase national savings, deepen capital markets, promote the development of the private sector, and provide an adequate retirement for the aging. Given all these benefits, it would also seem to be the social policy reform that is most capable of overcoming political and economic obstacles to its implementation.

Of course, that is not the case, and in most countries around the world pension reform has proved difficult to advance. This is because such reform usually entails raising the retirement age, increasing the contribution rate, and privatizing at least one pillar. Each of these policy recommendations may be contested. Raising the retirement age in countries where the life expectancy for males at retirement age is short and has decreased further during the recent period will undoubtedly seem unfair to those who have worked for the bulk of their adult life. Increasing contributions will, of course, be resisted, like most tax hikes. Finally, privatization of pensions is unlikely to produce good results unless it is accompanied by a host of supporting measures, including financial regulation, the creation of a vibrant capital market and service industry, and the maintenance of a state-supported scheme that ensures a minimum retirement benefit. Although these objectives may not seem overly ambitious on paper, in practice they may well be beyond the reach of many small, emerging market economies.

Indeed, even the most "successful" cases of pension reform have not been unblemished, as the Chilean case suggests. Despite competition among pension companies, fees remain much higher than expected, eating into the returns on worker portfolios. National savings rates have not increased according to projections, and many employers have failed to make their required contributions. Most important, as Székely and Fuentes point out, is the absence of universal coverage, given that the Chilean scheme only pertains to those at work in the formal sector.

Thus, although there are undoubted advantages to privatizing at least one pillar of the pension scheme, important problems remain unresolved and leave a large—potentially enormous—role and obligation for the state. The potential failure of private pension funds to achieve adequate returns (for example, adequate to provide more than a minimal annuity), the need to provide pensions to those outside the privatized scheme, large upfront transition costs, and the requirement that the state allocate scarce resources to insurance regulation and act as lender of last resort to failed providers are among the chief concerns that would-be privatizers need to take into account.

It needs to be emphasized that there is no consensus on what type of pension reform best maximizes social welfare. The most important reforms are those that introduce fairness and efficiency into the system, and while privatization may help to achieve those goals in many cases, reform of the public, defined-benefit pillar could be the sounder starting point.

Our own assessment, influenced largely by Barr, is that the first step in pension reform should be to shore up the existing, defined-benefit system. To be sure, this will require more transparency in pension fund management and a clearer link between taxes paid and benefits earned. For those outside formal employment, a minimum pension must be defined, likely to be funded out of general revenues; given the fiscal problems of most emerging economies, reforming the public scheme in a way that is expressly redistributive is likely to encounter severe objections from taxpayers.

Of course, in many emerging market economies, the elderly do not receive any pension benefit whatsoever at present. This is even the case in several East Asian countries, where old age is often associated with poverty, a point made by Birdsall and Haggard. Countries wrestling with the introduction of a pension scheme have a large menu of options before them and a considerable number of political and economic variables to consider. Should the scheme be defined contribution or defined benefit? Should it be universal or means tested? Today, many academics and international bureaucrats would urge countries to consider selective, defined-contribution schemes, augmented by minimum pensions for those outside formal employment.

Yet universal, defined-benefit schemes still have much to recommend them. Although they seem to be more costly to government budgets, they also have a number of attributes that should not be overlooked. Universal schemes are easier to administer, are more likely to receive broad political support, do not depend on the creation of capital markets, service providers, and regulatory bodies, and in some respects are more equitable, in that they provide coverage to women and persons who have worked outside the formal sector. In sum, both schemes can lead to problems. Sustainability of one depends on the evolution of the labor force and the total wage bill out of which current contributions are paid; sustainability of the other depends on the performance of the stock market. In neither case can sustainability be guaranteed.

This recommendation does not mean that we are opposed to privatization or defined-contribution schemes. To the contrary, we fully recognize the abuse that state-run systems have suffered, in transition economies as elsewhere. In Russia, for example, the pension amounts to nothing more than a pittance, and even that has often gone unpaid for many months on end. But that being said, we do have doubts that privatization should take precedence over reform of existing pension systems. Again, privatization involves implementation of many different policies, some of which may be beyond the capacity of states to implement in a relevant time horizon. As untrustworthy as many governments have proved to be in terms of meeting their obligations to the elderly, there is even less evidence that these same governments can provide the market oversight necessary to ensure the protection of an individual's life savings.

A more radical alternative is to consider what might be called "globalization" of the pension scheme. That is, in states that lack adequate capital markets, service providers, and regulatory instruments, the market could be opened to foreign pension managers with established records. The major American or European pension funds and brokerages, for example, might be invited to establish contributory schemes for citizens who wish to save for old age. Although this approach could provide a useful complement to state-run schemes, it is difficult to see how globalization could provide a replacement, especially when it comes to providing the minimum benefit.

Reforming Unemployment Compensation

Around the world, some 150 million people are unemployed. Of these, at most 30 million receive unemployment insurance. An additional 750 million to 900 million are in jobs that lack unemployment benefits altogether. Although this reflects the fact that labor markets in developing countries remain largely rural or informal, the need for unemployment protection has become more compelling in recent years, as global financial shocks have made all workers more vulnerable to economic dislocation.

Traditionally, social safety nets for the unemployed were provided by families and extended kinship networks. This was particularly true in the rural, agricultural context. Industrialization and urbanization have cast the long-term viability of that model into doubt. Further, as economies open themselves to market forces, they may become more prone to suffer repeated shocks, which these informal networks are poorly suited to meet.

Unemployment insurance was introduced in most industrial countries in the first half of the twentieth century and by many governments during the Great Depression of the 1930s. The purpose of this insurance was to enable households to maintain consumption levels during periods of joblessness. Given the covariance problem, or the fact that an increase in unemployment was often economywide as a consequence of low or negative growth rates, private insurers have generally been unwilling to offer such social insurance, and almost everywhere the state has played the leading role as provider. Recent years have seen a vigorous debate within industrial countries over the merits of unemployment insurance, especially when replacement rates are high and the payment duration is long.

It has been argued that (overly) generous unemployment benefits have encouraged idle workers, especially in continental Europe, to withhold their services from the labor force. Around the world, calls have been heard for more labor market "flexibility," meaning lower benefits and minimum wages and greater incentives for labor mobility, both geographically and across economic sectors. Labor flexibility has also been a theme in the emerging market context, where it has often been held that markets are made rigid owing to the role of the state as an employer and the scarcity of skilled workers.

As we have seen in previous chapters, few emerging market economies have well-developed social insurance programs for the unemployed, much less active labor market policies. It may be argued that one price these economies have paid for the lack of social insurance is greater labor market rigidity and regulation of the job market than otherwise would be the case. Székely and Fuentes, for example, state that Latin America "is a region with very inflexible labor markets." Tzannatos and Kaur remind us that over-employment in the public sphere in the Middle East and North Africa (MENA) region is an important form of social policy.

Most countries in Latin America and East Asia have relied mainly on private sector employers to meet their obligations to laid-off workers, with lump sum severance payments providing the main compensation scheme. More recently, a number of policy experiments to cope with unemployment have been launched, largely in association with ongoing economic reforms. Several countries in Latin America have begun to develop individual severance savings accounts, placing more of the burden on the individual and away from the employer in meeting the exigencies of joblessness. Yet another innovative scheme, highlighted by Székely and Fuentes, is the Bolivian government's Social Emergency Fund, which makes small-scale loans available for projects that generate employment. According to Tzannatos and Kaur, similar programs to help the unemployed become entrepreneurs have been launched throughout MENA. Public works programs have also been carried out, notably in Chile and Argentina. Overall, these various schemes get mixed reviews, given that they often have high administrative costs for the number of jobs generated.

Formal programs of unemployment compensation, in contrast, have received less attention—either from policymakers or from academics (a search of the website of the World Bank's Policy Research Division, for example, lists only five working papers related to this topic). Those programs that do exist on paper, as in the former Soviet Union, often provide so little income support that the jobless do not even bother to apply, as Barr tells us. Further, administrative red tape, such as residency requirements, can discourage potential applicants. In Latin America, Székely and Fuentes show that there are very few insurance schemes in place and those that do exist cover only a small percentage of the unemployed population.

Among students of labor markets, it is generally assumed that the nature of employment in emerging market economies—its informal and largely rural character—coupled with the costs of introducing social insurance, make such programs hardly worthy of serious consideration. Further, economists have hypothesized that unemployment insurance is less valuable the lower is the initial income level. But that hypothesis is based on a narrow view of what constitutes "utility." Recent research on economic crises in Latin America and in MENA, for example, has demonstrated a sharp drop in caloric consumption as individuals fall from near-poverty into poverty. That raises the question of what a "burdensome" decline in consumption really means.

The role of unemployment insurance in the process of economic reform has been little studied. Barr points out that such insurance can actually *encourage* the process of reform and restructuring. Job destruction in the state sector, for example, accompanied by unemployment insurance, makes workers with skills more readily available to foreign investors and the domestic private sector. In countries with weaker benefits, workers tend to remain with their existing employers for longer periods of time, prolonging the transition process. Unemployment insurance thus may enhance efficiency.

From a political economy perspective, unemployment insurance may play an important role in achieving a consensus among social partners as economic reforms are being undertaken, as Tzannatos and Kaur suggest with respect to MENA. Since workers with some skills are likely to suffer the greatest variability in incomes as a consequence of reform and market liberalization, they will seek programs that prevent them from falling into poverty. Incentives for flexibility are needed, but the provision of adequate unemployment insurance can, in fact, speed a transition process by providing a safety net underpinning labor market "flexibility." These points suggest the need to take a fresh look at unemployment compensation across the emerging market economies.

Concluding Remarks

A book like ours, which attempts to provide a snapshot of a rather large topic in several different corners of the globe, inevitably has something of an *Around the World in Eighty Days* feel to it. Yet we recall with some embarrassment that the hero of that story, Mr. Phileas Fogg, was noted, among other things, for his incredible, one might say obsessive, attention to detail. Constrained by the available data and adequate space, we can only claim to have given a partial view of our subject.

Still, some common themes have emerged from this discussion. The first among these is that social policy reform is now a topic of global interest, and it has risen high on the agenda of public officials in every nation and international organization. Although it may not be "at the heart of development strategy," as Székely and Fuentes call for, surely it has achieved a prominence in both economic research and policy analysis that promises active discussion, debate, and innovation in the years to come.

Second, this global interest suggests that social policy reform has not just domestic but also international sources. To be sure, some of these international sources more accurately reflect the convergence of distinctive national occurrences, like changing demographics and population aging. Still others are a product of the systemic pressures being generated by the neoliberal economic agenda. Although that policy ideology still provides governments with considerable "room to maneuver," it also presents them with certain common challenges, including decreasing tariff revenues, lower taxes on mobile capital, increasing economic volatility, rising levels of unemployment, and the need to make strategic investments that make their countries attractive sites for multinational enterprises.

Third, our case studies suggest that a set of common *ideas* about social policy have emerged, generated largely by international financial institutions but stimulated by national experiments and experiences as well, notably Chile's pension privatization. Those ideas include *privatization, decentralization* of service provision, and increased *targeting* of public programs. In nearly every region we have examined, these ideas reappear. Although there is still a legitimate debate about the degree of actual policy *convergence* that is occurring, if only because nations still have very different fiscal constraints, the way in which the debate over social policy reform has focused on certain key best practices is impressive, if somewhat disturbing. After all, as we have suggested, the extent to which each of these ideas can or should be exported to different countries is probably limited, and, as yet, there is no consensus with respect to the unique set of social policies that will improve national welfare.

At the same time, we do have some ideas about what constitutes *poor* social policy. If the objective of social assistance and insurance is to maximize an individual's life chances, no matter his or her background circumstances, it follows that policies that exclude particular groups of citizens for reasons of gender, race, religion, or ethnicity need to be rejected. Further, policies that encourage workers to move from the formal to informal sectors should be discouraged. Indeed, in this context we recall that one larger objective of social policy has traditionally been to promote social cohesion.

As international economic integration proceeds, states may need assistance in promoting social cohesion. Yet many people around the world seem to believe that globalization is doing just the opposite: undercutting the very fundamentals of national arrangements. Policymakers should not encourage that belief and must work hard to counteract it.

As we write these concluding remarks, the world has become an increasingly gloomy place in many respects. A global economic slowdown has swelled the number of people who are unemployed and in poverty, while the "war against terrorism" reminds us how far we remain from becoming an "international community." This disjunction between economic interdependence and political and cultural difference is provoking tension worldwide. If social policies can help to ease these tensions, they will prove to be a tremendous investment not just for those immediately concerned, but for the entire planet as well.

Index

Boldface numbers refer to figures and tables